T0317025

Ilex Foundation Series 2

STRĪ

Also in the Ilex Foundation Series

Dreaming across Boundaries:
The Interpretation of Dreams in Islamic Lands

STRĪ

WOMEN IN EPIC MAHĀBHĀRATA

Kevin McGRATH

Ilex Foundation
Boston, Massachusetts
and
Center for Hellenic Studies
Trustees for Harvard University
Washington, D. C.

Distributed by Harvard University Press
Cambridge, Massachusetts, and London, England

Strī: Women in Epic Mahābhārata
by Kevin McGrath

Kevin McGrath is an associate of the Sanskrit Department at Harvard University. His recent publications include *The Sanskrit Hero* (2004).

Published by Ilex Foundation, Boston, Massachusetts and the Center for Hellenic Studies, Trustees for Harvard University, Washington, D.C.

Distributed by Harvard University Press, Cambridge, Massachusetts and London, England

Volume editor: Christopher Dadian
Cover design: Joni Godlove
Printed in the United States of America by Edwards Brothers, Inc.

ISBN (paperback): 978-0-674-03198-2

Library of Congress Control Number: 2008942465

Contents

Acknowledgments

In this book I have attempted to follow in tracks set down by Edward Hopkins and amplified by Georges Dumézil and Stephanie Jamison, and to build upon some of their conclusions.

To my colleagues—past and present—in the Mahābhārata Seminar at Harvard, I am thoroughly grateful. This seminar is now in its fifteenth consecutive year, and I am profoundly indebted to its chair, Thomas Burke, for the great munificence of his scholarship and person.

I would also like to thank Ali Asani, Peter Banos, Homi Bhabha, Pradip Bhattacharya, Sugata Bose, Olga Davidson, Diana Eck, Rena Fonseca, Pramod Jethi, Jayasinhji Jhala, Leonard van der Kuijp, David Maybury-Lewis, Richard Meadow, Gregory Nagy, Susan Rosenfield, Prods Oktor Skjaervo, Stanley Tambiah, Calvert Watkins, and Michael Witzel, for their generosity, criticism, and many kindnesses. His Highness, the Maharao of Kacch, was most helpful with conversation and hospitality during time spent in the field. I am also grateful to the Das Family for a traveling fellowship which was given in the summer of two thousand and five. Lastly, this book has benefitted enormously from the editorship of Christopher Dadian and from the comments of an anonymous reader who helped with the final preparation of the text. My wife Leanna was for me the best of women throughout the production of this work.

I would like to dedicate this book to Stephanie Jamison, *ācāryasattamā*.

Cambridge, 2008

bhavitavyaṃ sadā rājñā garbhiṇīsahadharmiṇā

MBh. XII,56,44

I

INTRODUCTION

THIS BOOK IS A STUDY OF FEMININITY as it appears in epic Mahābhārata, focussing particularly on the roles of wife, daughter-in-law, and mother; on how these women speak and on the kinship groups which surround them. By feminine, I mean to portray those qualities which cohere about women in the poem, which are particular to them and which distinguish them as women.[1] This includes men who have been transformed into women and women who have been reincarnated as men.[2] The survey of this book builds upon a trajectory of analysis which Dumézil and Jamison have established, and which Hopkins originated in his *Appendix on the Status of Women*.[3] My overall method is that of performing an ethnography of text and describing a particular aspect of the Bronze Age world as it is represented by Mahābhārata.[4]

A description of the different kinds of marriage that are present in the poem is a central feature of this book, as well as the related topic of dowry.[5] Two particular types of marriage appear to receive the predilection of *kṣatriya* elites: the *svayaṃvara* and the *rākṣasa* forms of the rite. For a society where both polyandry and polygyny occur, the kinship patterns in ancient *kṣatriya* or heroic culture that surround courtship, weddings, and other affiliation are especially complex.[6] The

1. Femininity: *strītvam* or *strīsvabhāva*, although the latter term can refer particularly to menstruation.

2. Sometimes men even give birth to men, as with the birth of Māndhātar at III.126.25.

3. Dumézil 1979; Jamison 1994, 1996, 1997, 1999b; Hopkins 1888: 330ff.

4. By "Bronze Age" I understand the material culture manifest by Indo-European and idealized warrior literature, as in the Iliad or Mahābhārata. Certainly, these texts were still changing even into early Iron Age times, but the ethnos demonstrated by epic Mahābhārata is not one of a developed secondary urbanization, as is given in the Buddhist Jātakas: it is a hypothetical and idealized view of a past world. Much as the English poet Tennyson, in his *Idylls Of The King*, recreated a medieval past in order to represent the ideology of Victorian royalty, so the epic Mahābhārata poets formulated a conception of Bronze Age kingship, heroism, and kinship, and where coherent historicity is not significant. See below, note 53.

5. Jamison 1996: 253 notes that "the life of each individual Aryan male requires marriage as its centrepiece." Incest, abortion, and widowhood are minor related topics.

6. Arjuna reviews his kinship on the field of Kurukṣetra, prior to battle (VI.23.26–27; VI.23.34), where he includes the *ācārya*, 'teacher' in this formulation. The *guru* and the *sakhi* 'friend' are very much part of any kinship structure for *kṣatriyas*, regardless of the lack of affiliation or consanguinity.

kula 'clan' or 'family' is the nuclear model for kinship and supplies the situation upon which dharma is founded.[7] 'The dharmas of family are destroyed in the ruin of family,' says Arjuna, prior to the great battle: *kulakṣaye praṇaśyanti kuladharmāḥ* (VI.23.40). He adds,

> adharmābhibhavāt kṛṣṇa praduṣyanti kulastriyaḥ
> strīṣu duṣṭāsu vārṣṇeya jāyate varṇasaṃkaraḥ
>
> Due to the prevailing of adharma, Kṛṣṇa, the women in the family are spoiled.
> When women are spoiled there is born a confusion of caste.[8]
>
> VI.23.41

The implication here is that women are the focal unit of any kin group: they are the ones who form and sustain its primary patterns of dharma and the rules governing kinship.

It is telling that both Mahābhārata and the Rāmāyaṇa display offences committed against women: incidents that generate the narrative axis in both epics. Thus, the recumbent and moribund Bhīṣma, towards the end of his life, tells the young king Yudhiṣṭhira,

> na ... śakto nṛloke'smin rakṣitum nṛpa yoṣitaḥ
>
> O king, no one ... is able in this human world to protect women!
>
> XIII.43.26

There is such a power or force inherent to epic femininity that men—*kṣatriyas*—are unable to control that latent energy.[9] So, whenever the deities feel threatened by the extraordinary vigor generated by the austerities of an ascetic male they send down a beautiful woman in order to destabilize the focus of so much *tapas* 'heat'.[10] There is intrinsic to

7. 'Clan' concerns more the term *gotra*, especially as it relates to lineage; whereas *kula*, refers more to 'nominal extended family'. The former word has sacerdotal connotations and is not often used in the epic; I have sometimes translated *kula* as 'clan'. Perhaps the term *gotra* receives greater application among brahmins than it does among *kṣatriyas*.

8. I follow the convention here of giving a proper name in place of an epithet to avoid confusion for those readers not fully cognizant with the text. Thus, *vārṣṇeya* 'man of the Vṛṣṇis' is Kṛṣṇa. In a culture where there exists such a profusion of epithets—including patronyms and metronyms and other kinship terms used to avoid invoking a proper name—the only alternative for the analyst is to append a glossary or to footnote each title. See Scharf, in Rukmani 2005: 53, on this problem of translation.

9. Mankekar 1999: 114, on the situation of the feminine in contemporary twentieth-century India, remarks that since "respectability, sexual modesty, and family honor were predicated on the conduct of women, women's behavior was monitored especially intently."

10. Such as Tilottamā, at I.203.

feminine perfection an especial quality which neutralizes the spiritual tension and force generated by the restraints of male renunciation.

The feminine in ancient India possessed a highly charged potential that could appear as either positive or negative. This duality is key to archetypal feminine identity in the poem: a benevolent association with prosperity has the obverse valence of a malign and destructive potence.[11] These two contrasting forces are founded in the feminine—considered in a universal or cosmic sense—as *śakti* 'power, ability, energy' and *prakṛti* 'nature, the material world, undifferentiated matter'.[12]

One should recall that both Draupadī and Sītā are respectively born from a sacrificial fire and from the earth and possess no human mother: in terms of their generation they are natural forces. Hence perhaps, they were not to be successfully protected.

By way of prologue, allow me to briefly run through eight summary points: portraiture, terms, the nature of lineage, value and wealth, dharma, *kṣatriyas* and *varṇa*, the idea of epic, and myth and methodology.

Women are never truly given any realistic physical character in epic, individual likenesses are not in question. What few descriptions of women that exist in the poem are stereotypical and formulaic, as with two of the girls that Bhīṣma abducts:

> te cāpi bṛhatī śyāme nīlakuñcitamūrdhaje
> raktatuṅganakhopete pīnaśroṇipayodhare
>
> Both those tall swarthy women, hair curled and dark,
> [are] endowed with strong red nails, possessing full breasts and hips.
>
> I.96.14

Likewise, when queen Sudeṣṇā first sees Draupadī in Book Four, she praises her beauty. This speech is somewhat formal and *cliché*, insofar as it is a verbal portrait of a type. In fact, the speech is similar to how kings address women when they first see them and fall in love, the form is the same. I give the lines here in full, for they represent an ideal of feminine

11. Wadley 1988: 24–25 discusses a possible historical distinction here, relating the positive aspects of femininity to the Aryan tradition and the dangerous aspects of the feminine to the Dravidian tradition. "The earliest available Dravidian literature (specially, Tamil literature) refers frequently to dangerous female power, a theme not found until later in the Sanskrit literature of the Aryans."

12. In terms of onomasia, *śakti* is also a 'spear, lance', which certain of the greatest heroes possess: a weapon whose use is generally ultimate. Also, *śakti* can be read as 'the female organ' (Monier-Williams). Thus both the erotic and thanatic adhere to this term.

kṣatriya beauty, something which Draupadī characterizes completely in the poem.[13] In the epic, she represents the acme of woman's beauty.

> gūḍhagulphā saṃhatorus trigambhīrā ṣaḍunnatā
> raktā pañcasu rakteṣu haṃsagadgadabhāṣiṇī
> sukeśī sustanī śyāmā pīnaśroṇipayodharā
> tena tenaiva saṃpannā kāśmīrīva turaṃgamā
> svarālapakṣmanayanā bimboṣṭhī tanumadhyamā
> kambugrīvā gūḍhasirā pūrṇacandranibhānanā
>
> One who possesses concealed ankles, whose thighs are firm; one
> possessing the three deep spots, who has the six prominent parts of
> the body;[14]
> red in the five rednesses, whose speech stammers as a goose;
> with fine hair and dark nipples, with full breasts and buttocks;
> endowed in that manner like a horse of Kaśmir;
> slim-waisted, with curved eyelashes, red-lipped;
> whose face resembles a full moon, with three lines on the neck;
> whose tendons are concealed ...[15]
>
> IV.8.10–12

This is all very formulaic and conventional, and an audience receives nothing especial nor particular that would characterize Draupadī more

13. Yudhiṣṭhira speaks a similar, but not so detailed praise of Draupadī at II.58.32. Jayadratha, at III.248.10ff., and Duḥśanta, at I.65.10, adhere to the same formulation, although not so extensively as Sudeṣṇā.

14. Similarly, Haryaśva, describing the beauty of his daughter, says of her, *unnateṣu unnatā ṣaṭsu sukṣmā sukṣmeṣu saptasu / gambhīrā triṣu gambhīreṣv iyaṃ raktā ca pañcasu* 'she is prominent in six prominent spots, fine in the seven fine spots, deep in the three deep spots, and red in the five red spots' (V.114.2). The three deep spots refer to her speech, her intelligence, and to her navel; the prominent points are her nose, eyes, two ears, nails, breasts, and neck. The five rednesses relate to the soles of her feet and palms of her hands, to the corners of her eyes, to lips, tongue, and to her nails. Nīlakaṇtha supplies a gloss for these five spots, the *śabdabuddhinābhi*; for the six points, *nāsikākṣidvayaśrotranakhastanakṛkāṭaka*; and then for the 'five rednesses' (*pañcaraktāni*), the *pādapāṇitalanetrāntoṣṭhajihvānakha*.

15. Concerning the performance of such lines as these, let me say that I think of the Mahābhārata as being a literature that exists as part of song culture, that is, the poem is sung and not spoken: sung, in the sense of sonority, rather than of melody. A comparison would be to contemporary western opera. Recitations of the Mahābhārata nowadays, in villages and temples, are usually sonorous and sometimes with the accompaniment of a small harmonium. I like to think of the stanzas in non-*śloka* form—excluding the few and rare prose sections—as almost choral, as stanzas that are supposed to stand apart either as commentary or emphasis. J. D. Smith 1991: 8 describes a performance of the epic of Pābūjī in contemporary Rajasthan: "The singing of Pābūji's epic may constitute a religious liturgy, but it is a fairly formal and cheerful event ... He sings with his wife (*bhopī*) to the accompaniment of a spike-fiddle ... in between songs he declaims the narrative in a vigorous chant; during some songs he will dance, the bells around his ankles jingling and his red robe swirling."

"realistically" or individually. Epic is not an art of portraiture, and its characters receive little in the way of visual detailing that is not simply typical.

As far as terminology goes, there is a vast range of words which concern the feminine in Mahābhārata. *Kanyā, vadhū, bhāryā, patnī, sapatnī, nārī, strī, jāmi, vidhavā*, these are just some of the nomenclature that denote aspects of womanhood, each word possessing a more or less specific reference.[16] In a kinship system where both polyandry and polygyny exist, the taxonomy is necessarily precise, although, in an epic scheme of language, synonymity in the use of terms often poses problems of interpretation.[17] There are more words available in Sanskrit for the varying distinctions of femininity than there are for what pertains to the male or to manhood: femininity in linguistic terms demonstrates greater lexical richness, precision or degree.[18]

Kanyā refers to a 'girl' or 'virgin'.[19] *Bhāryā* and *patnī* refer to the status of 'wife'. *Sapatnī* is 'co-wife'. With *strī* and *nārī* there is a problem

16. I am grateful to Thomas Burke for his comments on these terms.

17. See Buck 1949: 2.22 on the lexeme woman: "many of the words for 'woman' were also the usual words for 'wife', and some became restricted to the latter use ... Words for 'woman' carry an emotional value which is liable to wide fluctuation, either at the same period, according to circumstances, or as between different periods, social classes, or languages. They may suggest the nobility of woman or her frailties. They may move up or down the social scale." The profusion of synonyms in the epic is due to the nature of its poetic production: the amalgamation of diffused pre-literate texts—which incorporate various dialect terms—into one large comprehensive and *synthetic* poem. Macdonell & Keith 1912, under the lemma *pati*, have: "the word *strī* includes all the 'womenfolk', daughters and slaves, as well as wife."

18. Macdonell & Keith 1912, under the term *strī*, have: "*Strī* is the ordinary word in poetry and prose for 'woman', without special reference to her as a wife or as a maiden. *Nārī* has the same sense, but disappears in later prose, while *Gnā* refers only to the wives of the gods, and *Yoṣit*, with its cognate words, denotes the young woman as ripe for marriage. In the Rigveda *Strī* stands opposed to *Pumāṃs*, 'man', and once to *Vṛṣan*, 'male person'; not until the Atharvaveda does it mean 'wife' as opposed to *Pati*, 'husband', and even in the Sūtras it is sharply opposed to *Jāyā*."

19. From √*kan* 'to enjoy': so Sūrya informs Kuntī at III.291.13. P. Lāl, in Bhattacharya 2005, in the Publisher's Note, remarks that "There are sixteen kinds of unmarried girls in the Sanskrit lexicon: 1. *nagnikā* (nude): a girl below the age of five; 2. *vāsū* (clothed): a girl of five; 3. *gaurī* (white): a girl of six; *vatsā* (calf): a girl of seven; *kanyā* (shining): a girl of eight; *lagnikā* (clinging): a girl of nine. These are undoubtedly 'virgins', since it was desireable that a girl get married between the ages of *nagnikā* and *lagnikā*. 7. *bālikā* (with downy hair): a girl of ten; *rajasvalā* (red-appearing): a girl of eleven at the onset of menstruation; 9. *rohiṇī* (red): a girl of twelve; *kumarī*: a 'girl' of thirteen; 11. *yuvatī* (juvenile): a girl of fourteen; 12. *duhitṛ* (who milks cows): a 'daughter', a girl of fifteen; 13. *yoṣaṇā* (young): a girl of sixteen; *kiśorī* (foal): an 'adolescent' girl of seventeen; *taruṇī* (forested): a girl of eighteen; *prauḍha* (mature): a girl of nineteen."

of distinction, perhaps akin to the distinction between 'woman' and 'lady', in that one is an unmarked term and the other is not: *strī* is the general term, referring to women at large.[20] The opposite to *strī* is usually *puruṣa* 'man', and that of *nārī* is *nara* or *nṛ*. *Vadhū* is 'young wife', one who is carried, a 'spouse'. *Jāmi* denotes a female relative, particularly the daughters-in-law, and is a term used often by the head of a family. *Vidhavā* denotes 'widow'.

Concerning the specificity of terms, the dying Bhīṣma supplies an exact catalogue for the stations in a woman's life. He begins,

> mātā dehāraṇi puṃsāṃ
>
> The mother is the kindling-stick of men.
>
> XII.258.24

He says, as a carrier of a child in her *kukṣi* 'belly' a woman is a *dhātrī* 'mother, bearer, or nurse'; because of *janana* 'birth' she is called *jananī* 'mother'; for causing his limbs to thrive, she is known as *ambā*; on account of bearing a hero she is known as *vīrasū*.

On the other hand there exists the phenomenon of synonymity, as in the Sabhā *parvan*, where a story about the dalliance of the deity Agni is related. In the town of Māhiṣmatī, *babhūvur anabhigrāhyā yoṣitaś chandataḥ* 'the women [or wives] were not to be grasped at will' (II.28.23). Then, after Agni had offered them a favor, *nāryo hi yatheṣṭaṃ pracaranti* 'women go as they wish': they became *aprativāraṇā* 'not to be prohibited' (II.28.24).[21] The situation at Māhiṣmatī is obviously unusual, for the name of the town itself bears the connotation of queen, the 'town possessing a queen'. Also, it is significant that in this short tale three terms are used to express femininity or womanhood: *yoṣitas*, *strīyas*, and *nāryas*. The tale collapses any distinction of the words so that they become less exclusive or marked and lose their particular kinship-oriented status.

20. I say *perhaps* here, for after doing many a word search and checking the usage of these two terms in hundreds of cases, I cannot prove such a distinction: the *perhaps* refers to my a priori sense of the two words. Mayrhofer for the lexeme *strī* has: "Das Etymon von ar. **strī*- bleibt hypothetisch. Zur Deutung **sŭ-trī́-*, gebaren (:*sū́te*)." Grassman has, "Weib [aus **sūtrī* von *sū*]." The word thus signifies a capacity for parturition, rather than any kind of affiliation or other status. When the old king instructs his minister Vidura to bring the women, he says—using three words to denote the feminine—*kṣipram ānaya gāndhārīṃ sarvāś ca bharatastriyaḥ / vadhūṃ kuntīm upādāya yāś cānyās tatra yoṣitaḥ* 'Quickly, lead Gāndhārī and all the Bharata women here, and bring Kuntī the spouse and whatever other young women [are] there' (XI.9.3).

21. The actual gift of the favor is expressed as *agnir varaṃ prādāt strīṇām* 'fire gave a favor to the women'.

Certainly, in an epic of this magnitude and given the centuries which went into its accumulation and aggregation, the phenomenon of synonymy repeatedly occurs: where various peculiar terms lose their marked or specific qualities and become simply general in signification.[22] Nevertheless, I would aver that the nouns which constellate about epic femininity often demonstrate a meticulous reference.[23] This either-or situation of the text is a problem, however, particularly as it relates to translation.

As the Mahābhārata was originally *kṣatriya* poetry or song, these terms refer of course, to *kṣatriya* women.[24] Yet such words for the stages of femininity are frequently also applicable to other ranks of twice-born women, especially brahmins, and often refer to womanhood in general, regardless of *varṇa*.[25]

Turning now to physiology in the Mahābhārata, at the level of the primary heroes and heroines, it is unusual for a husband to inseminate a wife and for a child to be born of that conjunction. The first tale of conception in the poem, about the brahmin Bhṛgu and his wife Pulomā, concerns such a pattern of reproduction. For here, the son Cyavana is born of the mother, but the insemination is not performed by Bhṛgu but by a *rākṣasa* Puloman (I.6.1ff.). Similarly, in ancient times, when Rāma Jāmadagnya had slaughtered all male *kṣatriyas*, the remaining women—presumably widows and daughters—turned to brahmins in

22. This partially illustrates what Lord 1995: 23, refers to as the "multiform" nature of the text.

23. One must assume that the women present in the drama of the Mahābhārata are *actually* feminine, for often—as with Draupadī, who has no human parent, or with Kuntī, who frequently participates in sexual intercourse with a deity, or Ambā, who is transexual—these women are not truly human, although they appear to be. From another point of view, these epic women with their brilliant intellects and their passion for violence, are originally present in what must have been a predominantly male audience, although one cannot assert this as more than a guess. In this case, this *femininity* is very much a view or construction of male ears and eyes, and possibly unreal. Similarly, epic itself, as a loom of poetry, casts figures onto an audial screen who actually in no way refer to *real* manners, history, or things; for epic is a palimpsest of literary forms and tropes. These are problems that the present study lays aside, however: my work lies in sifting through the Critically Edited text and presenting women as they appear within the poem. See Hiltebeitel 2005 on this presumption of textuality.

24. See McGrath 2004, Chapter One, on the question of *kṣatriya* literature. Yamazaki 2005: 63: "Epics sing the exploits of the kṣatriyas during this time [c.1000–600 BCE.] of kingship formation ..."

25. For instance, brahmin 'wives acquire the worlds attained by the husband' (*bhāryāḥ patikṛtāñ lokān āpnuvanti*; XIV.20.4). This is not true for *kṣatriya* women, and a reader must not conflate the two varṇas. By 'twice-born', I understand an Aryan born into one of the three upper castes, especially a Brahmin, who is *re*-born through investiture with a sacred thread. The *ekaja* are the *śudras* and outcastes.

order to reproduce. The sons born to these unions were *kṣatriyas*: *varṇa* followed in the matriline (I.58.4ff.).[26]

Sexual reproduction in the epic—as opposed to reproduction where there exists no human mother—typically occurs through the union of a woman and a male other than her husband: there is a lateral or oblique genealogical shift. This uncommon convention is a practice basic to any understanding of the feminine within the poem.[27] The displacement of eldest sons—in terms of generation—is a profound motif throughout the poem, therefore, and is a corollary to this lateral shift in descent; beginning with Bhīṣma, and continuing through Pāṇḍu and Yudhiṣṭhira, and concluding with—after a fashion—Karṇa.

The line which descends from Bharata, through Kuru, comes down through the male side, ultimately descending to Bhīṣma and ceasing in him due to his vow of celibacy. His is the only male line that connects with Bharata, for after this generation, the descent occurs via the feminine side of the family and the matriline predominates. Thus, in the Āraṇyaka *parvan*, when Kṛṣṇa takes his leave of the Pāṇḍavas, he takes with him on his chariot his nephew Abhimanyu (III.23.44). Similarly, in the next lines, the brother of Draupadī makes his departure—upon his chariot—taking with him his nephews, the sons of Draupadī. Then, Dhṛṣṭaketu, king of the Cedis, takes his leave along with his sister. All these formal departures underline well the importance of the brother-sister connection and that of the diagonal relation between a mother's brother and her sons. Such kinship paradigms are typical of matrilineal family structures.[28]

After Bhīṣma makes his vow of celibacy the male lineage is diverted, and the wife always becomes impregnated by a man—or deity, in the case of Kuntī and Mādrī—other than her husband.[29] Initially this is through the convention of *niyoga* 'the levirate', where a deceased or incapacitated man's role in reproduction is superceded by his brother.

> patyabhāve yathā strī hi devaraṃ kurute patim.

26. Inheritance is twofold: that of *varṇa* and that of *kula*. How these descend—either through the patriline or via the matriline—varies. Caste and lineage are conceptually distinct but this is not always practically obvious.

27. What actually happens at and beyond conception—according to Mahābhārata genetics—is that *pūrvam eveha kalale vasate kiṃcid antaram* 'at first it dwells a while in the unformed embryo', then *pañcame'atīte māse māṃsaṃ prakalpayet* 'when the fifth month is gone, it would produce flesh'; and finally, *sarvāṅgsaṃpūrṇo garbho māse prajāyate* 'in a [further] month it would generate a foetus complete with all limbs' (XI.4.2–3).

28. See Ostor et al. 1982, passim; Lévi-Strauss 1963.

29. What occurs is that 'semen, combined with blood, is gone to the receptacle of the womb of women' (*śukram śoṇitasaṃsṛṣṭaṃ striyā garbāśayaṃ gatam*; XIV.18.5). The admixture of blood and semen is requisite, prior to actual conception, in Mahābhārata genetics.

> So a woman in the decease of her husband makes her brother-in-law husband.[30]
>
> XII.73.12

For the Pāṇḍavas, it is only with the procreating by Arjuna, through his wife's co-wife, Subhadrā, that the line becomes a male line once again, descending to the primary audience of the poem, King Janemejaya. Strife occurs for the family during this period of matrilineal predominance. For the Kauravas, the male line returns with the offspring of Dhṛtarāṣṭra.

The war, leading to the great battle at Kurukṣetra, takes place during this phase when matrilineal descent has been the norm on Pāṇḍu's side of the clan: a contention where cousins are rivaling each other to the death. The conflict between rival factions of cousins could thus be interpreted as a contest between those sons of a matriline, the Pāṇḍavas, and those sons of a patriline, the Kauravas. The internecine struggle which destroys everything occurs between these two differing kinship systems.[31]

Marriage typologies in the epic are identical for both of these systems. In effect marriage is multiform, being by purchase, by agreement between parents or guardians, by elopement, and by capture or mutual consent. There is also the rite of the *svayaṃvara*, where a potential wife selects her own spouse on the basis of male contest. There thus exists a full gamut of practice concerning marriage procedures, few of which are uniform, however.

In a pre-monetary society, economic value consists in and is generated by the multiplicity of exchanges which take place and which then accumulate to form wealth. Where there is no market—in a modern sense—for there exists a system of exchange relations, there is also no play of supply and demand as movements of wealth assume relational forms, different from an economy where money exists.[32] "It has become

30. This injunction is asserted by Manu at IX.59.

31. This would perhaps indicate that the original or "core" epic, the hypothetical *ur*-text, concerned two differing social systems, rather than two rival sides of one clan or family. This is mere surmise, however.

32. Certainly there are references to *niṣkas*, as at VII.16.26. Monier-Williams defines the term as, "a golden ornament for the neck or breast ... later a particular coin varying in value at different times." The use of punch-marked coinage did not become current until "about the sixth century B.C.," Pal 1986: 81. Property or capital, moveable and immoveable, of intrinsic value or exchange value in this pre-monetary situation, is described by Arjuna in 'a city ... full ... with jewels and with wealth, with cattle and also with grain' (*ratnair dhanaiś ca paśubhiḥ sasyaiś cāpi / nagaraṃ ... pratipūrṇaṃ*; XIII.2.14). At II.67.18, Śakuni refers to *kośo hiraṇyam* 'a golden treasury', presumably a storeroom.

common practice to apply the term 'the *jajmānī* system' to the system corresponding to the prestations and counter-prestations by which the castes as a whole are bound together in the village ... To a large extent it is a question of natural as opposed to monetary economy."[33] This is not a system of barter, but of the hierarchical and reciprocal exchange of substances and services where "hereditary personal relationships express the division of labour."[34] These hereditary relations include marriage patterns.

In the Mahābhārata, quantities of wealth are usually described insofar as they relate to sacrifices, marriage, and occasionally gambling.[35] A single gambling scene—in which a woman is offered as a highly valuable stake—is the key motor of narrative for the whole poem.[36] When King Virāṭa determines that he and Yudhiṣṭhira shall play at dice, he proclaims his potential stakes:

> striyo gāvo hiraṇyaṃ ca yac cānyad vasu kiṃcana
>
> Women, cattle, gold, and whatever other valuables ...[37]
>
> IV.63.32

In the most crucial dicing scene, *matériel* is portrayed as:

> ... dhanaṃ gṛhya ratnāni vividhāni ca
> maṇimuktāpravālaṃ ca suvarṇaṃ rajataṃ tathā

33. Dumont 1970: 97. See also Wiser 1936; Mayer 1993. What is being described is a complementary and hierarchical relation between the categories of *jajmān* 'patron' and *prajā* 'client'. Naturally, one cannot retroject such an economy back two or three millennia into a hypothetical bronze and literary age, but the model does possess a certain hermeneutic utility. Dumont describes "family ceremonies which are remunerative occasions ... especially marriages." Ibid.: 100. Fuller, in Parry & Bloch 1989: 33–63, critiques the *jajmānī* system of Wiser.

34. Dumont 1970: 98.

35. The most important sacrifice being the *rājasūya* sacrifice of Yudhiṣṭhira, the wealth being described by Duryodhana at II.45.18ff.

36. In one of his early stakes in the gambling scene, 'a hundred thousand slave girls, juvenile and beautiful' (*sataṃ dāsīsahasrāṇi taruṇyo ... prabhadrikāḥ*), are put up by Yudhiṣṭhira (II.54.12). They are well adorned with jewelry and competent in song and dance and constitute a form of material wealth. When this stake is lost, Yudhiṣṭhira then puts up a thousand male slaves. Karṇa, in the *sabhā* pronounces that *dāsaḥ śiṣyaś ca asvatantrā nārī*, 'a slave, a student, and a subject woman', are *adhanā*, 'without wealth' (II.63.1): yet by affiliation these figures remain in the system.

37. **peku* is the IE term for 'livestock'. Benveniste 1969: I.47 explains, "le sens de «richesse», lorsqu'il apparaît pour ce terme ou tel de ces dérivés ... est dès lors tenu pour secondaire et on explique qu'il résulte d'une extension sémantique du terme qui désignait au départ la richesse par excellence, le bétail." The Vedic *paśu* "englobe même l'homme désigné comme *paśu* bipède," ibid.: 48.

goratnāny aśvaratnāni ratharatnāni kuñjarān
kharoṣṭramahiṣāṃś caiva yac ca kiṃcid ajāvikam

... and having taken the various jewels,
many gems and pearls and coral as well as silver and gold,
elephants, excellent chariots, horses and cows,
and water buffalo and camels and also some sheep and goats ...

I.105.16–18

All this constitutes the matter of wealth, and yet without any calibration of standard its value remained constantly unfixed: for in a pre-monetary economy there is no overarching signifier controlling exchange, and money, as a performative sign, does not exist.

The exogamous movement of women in this society—daughters or sisters—is the primary source of kinship structure: this is the engine, as it were, of the nuclear family or clan group, marriage being the exchange which maintains the social system at large. The valence that adheres to women in these transactions is—I would submit—a principal register of how wealth is calculated and how value—something which is not natural but social in generation—is produced within a culture. Women are the initial *tokens* of exchange, and as primary items of exchange, women are the principal measures of value, in that the transmission of wealth accompanies women as they shift between discrete households.

As women are in effect moved between different clans, it is thus necessary to examine the nature of exchange itself in a pre-monetary society where no centrally minted currency exists and where dealing occurs in kind or in forms of service. Quantities of wealth—in these transactions—often receive description in the poem on the occasion of weddings: where gifts are offered between two parties and wealth is distributed to guests.[38]

Thus the role of the feminine in the creation of value in pre-monetary society is a crucial determinant: hence these great and pyrrhic conflicts which are so central and concern the status of women. Before the establishment of any fixed calibration for wealth—specie—there existed this registration where one woman is exchanged for so much substance at a marriage rite. A single woman thus acts as an abstract

38. The other primary instance for descriptions of wealth in the poem occurs when an important sacrifice takes place and much substance is given to brahmins. The giving away of wealth by kings, just as the acquisition of wealth by kings—through warfare and raiding—is a major generator in the flow or circulation of *objects* in late Bronze Age society. "The rules of kinship and marriage serve to ensure the circulation of women between groups, just as economic rules serve to ensure the circulation of goods and services, and linguistic rules the circulation of messages." Lévi-Strauss 1963: 83.

standard—much like a "gold standard"—against which pre-monetary or pre-*specie* wealth is valued. Here, the question of whether this transaction concerns bride price or dowry does not come into play, for the function is everything: women plus substance supply the template of all that is deemed commensurate in society and marks the unsaid conception of unit wealth.[39]

Thereafter, the patterns of movement through the social orders which wealth incurs are pendant upon this registration. Woman are the initial signifiers for any connotation of value; like the *zero* cipher, they are mobile and there exists no other such primary quantification of valence which *simultaneously* maintains the social system itself. Even in the sacrifices wealth is unspecifically offered and does not undergo such registration, for the exchange is heavenly and not earthly; although in effect, brahmins stand in and secure the substance.

As an aspect of this point of view, for a single stake, Yudhiṣṭhira puts up his wife Draupadī, thus giving her a material worth. Similarly, Sukanyā, who is one day bathing *vivṛtām* 'naked', and seen by the two Aśvins, tells the deities that she is *vittaṃ bhāryāṃ ca cyavanasya* 'married and the wife of Cyavana' (III.123.4). The term *vitta* can also refer to material property, wealth or power.[40] Sustaining this connection, Vidura says in Book Five, 'one should protect a wife with wealth' (*dārān rakṣed dhanair*; V.37.17).[41]

Women are inherently and intrinsically highly potent figures therefore, and it is no wonder that the two "charter" myths of Indian culture—the epics Mahābhārata and Rāmāyaṇa—concern the movement of specific women among kin groups.

39. Bride price is what the groom's family offers, dowry is what the bride's family gives, to be used by the groom-husband in usufruct. "These institutions have no intrinsic property other than that of establishing the necessary conditions for the existence of the social system to which they belong; their presence—in itself devoid of significance—enables the social system to exist as a whole." Lévi-Strauss 1963: 159. He refers to this as "zero value," or "*mana*," in the sense of the nought cipher, 0; what Lacanians have referred to as "the *phallos*," the empty sign whose transaction generates all other signs.

40. The word *vittam*, in the neuter, means 'property, substance', yet *vittā*, the feminine, denotes a 'married woman'. There is little in the Mahābhārata concerning women and the inheritance of property, particularly dowry. Manu, IX.192ff., does deal with this question; at IX.131, the problem of *yautuka* 'portion', as it concerns the wife and her legacy, is briefly commented upon.

41. Jamison 1996: 256, on the woman's "role in creating the *horizontal*, synchronic bonds of Aryan society is ... critical: she is the ultimate exchange token." Dumont 1983: 103 writes, "The transmission of property is regulated in fact in two ways: a part of it is inherited by the sons, while another part is disposed of under the form of gifts (and ceremonial expenses), mainly as affinal gifts to the daughters, households and children."

All the above concern the physical aspects of *strī* dharma, that is, how a society is organized prescriptively as it relates to the feminine. The obverse of dharma is *karma*, roughly to be translated as 'action' and its specific applications. If dharma is a prescription of state, then *karma* can be said to consist in the correlating actions: the two words or concepts are inseparable. Dharma concerns value, that which is right.

The language of male heroes in the Mahābhārata entails the use of certain speech acts—like formulaic avowal and boasting—as well as a great range of formally abusive and insulting rhetoric. Women however, in their speech within the epic, are often a source of law and social convention: they are the figures who give judgmental utterance to dharma, a term that is often translated as 'rule' or 'decorum'.[42] It is the women who are the speakers of what *should* be done by the *kṣatriyas*.[43] They are *knowers* of dharma—that which is valued as appropriate—and in speech proclaim what *karma* is right at certain moments in the narrative. They are the vocal interpreters of what is worthwhile. I shall examine not only *what* these authoritative women say, but also *how* it is, in terms of poetics, that they use such words in an act of persuasion.

Although women do not possess any property, being *adhanā* 'without wealth' (I.77.21),[44] it is women in the poem who are typically the repository and voice of *kṣatriya* tradition. They are the SPEAKERS of what *should* be done at instants of crisis and they are the knowers of *kṣattradharma* who encourage or denigrate the heroes. Often, this ability is dramatized in an extreme, as with Sāvitrī: a woman clever enough to outwit an opponent with speech, in this case the ultimate of opponents, Death. The speech of a woman like Sāvitrī is capable of *effecting* actions, such is her profound understanding of the working of what constitutes value, or dharma.

Draupadī is a steady and highly critical voice in this respect. She is the one to raise the legal question as to the propriety of Yudhiṣṭhira's gambling in the *sabhā* 'assembly hall'. Kuntī offers a model of good kingship at a moment in the Udyoga *parvan* when kingship at Hāstinapura is undergoing a major quandary. Ambā, through her extraordinary zealotry, is able to punish a wrongdoing in what is a typical form of *kṣatriya* courtship procedure.

42. Yudhiṣṭhira gives a definition of what is *dharmya* 'legitimate, customary, just' when he says, on being interrogated by his father in the guise of a *yakṣa*: *dākṣyam ekapadaṃ dharmyam* 'cleverness—in a word—is just' (III.297.41).

43. The name of the first of the ten wives of Dharma is *kīrti* 'fame' (I.60.13). Curiously, Dharma himself was born from the right nipple of Brahmā, who is thus ambisexual (I.60.30).

44. Along with slaves and sons.

Draupadī is arguably the most dynamic and generative feminine figure in the epic, just as Karṇa is the most forceful and potent hero. In many vernacular traditions and retellings of the poem there is a passionate and romantic charge existing between this couple, but one which is neither fulfilled nor realised.[45] Much of the focus of this study is directed towards Draupadī as a SPEAKER of what *should* be happening or should be done. She is the most important *kṣatriya* woman in the epic and other women heroes present aspects of what she primarily demonstrates in extremis.

Thus in the pre-literate warrior society portrayed by the Mahābhārata—and this is situated at the end of the mythical *dvāpara yuga*—it is the women who often perform the function of being the living repositories of law and prescription. That is, they operate as one of the chief and most immediate media for the verbal maintenance of value in that culture: women are intrinsically allied with a fundamental social reticulation of dharma, via their speech acts.

At one point, early on in the Sabhā *parvan*, when Yudhiṣṭhira is asking Kṛṣṇa about the *rājasūya* 'rite of royal consecration', Kṛṣṇa says to him:

> kṛto'yam kulasaṃkalpaḥ kṣatriyair vasudhādipa
> nideśavāgbhis ...
>
> This determination of clan, O lord of the earth, is accomplished by *kṣatriya*s through statement and direction ...
>
> II.13.3

This "determination" does not only apply to the heroes, the men, but also to the authoritative speech of certain high ranking *kṣatriya* women in scenes of either distress or terrible predicament.

Yet certainly, there is without doubt a strain of anxiety or fear expressed as contempt for the feminine in the poem, typically from those older men who are in the position of counseling others. Vidura, in his long-winded soliloquy stuffed with maxims says, for instance,

> kautūhalamalā sādhvī vipravāsamalāḥ striyaḥ
>
> For a virtuous woman, curiosity is impure; for women—staying away from home is impurity.
>
> V.39.64

This is not the complete story however, as we shall see. Vidura also says that 'one who dislikes women', *vanitāsu dveṣṭā*, is guilty of one of the

45. See McGrath 2004 on this unrequited romantic theme that runs between the two.

seven 'dharmas of cruelty', *nṛśaṃsadharmāḥ* (V.43.11). Women in the epic are vigorous, authoritative, and often set the trajectory in which the narrative runs. This is not only in a household or marital setting, but politically and logistically. Their speech concerning what is *right* and what is dharma often creates the tone for much of the poem.

By epic Mahābhārata I would denote those parts of the poem which principally concern *kṣatriya* life: with emphasis on the *bhārata* itself, without the *upākhyānas* 'subordinate episodes' (I.1.56 and 61).[46] This would be to exclude such parts of the poem which deal with genealogy, narratives of ritually edifying nature, and also law texts such as the Śānti *parvan.*[47] Much of the four battle books—Books Seven to Nine—contain very little speech that is given by women and little that concerns women: the world of the battle books is one of men, and particularly of men as they relate to sons. Epic poetry was "prestigeous," and in its various transmissions carried with it the ideology of its patrons, the "ruling caste" or warrior aristocracy.[48]

The poem opens with an exchange between a *sūta* 'poet, charioteer'

46. This is the time between the *dvāpara yuga* and the *kāli yuga*, and a very different eon or epoch from that depicted in the Rāmāyaṇa. See III.148.10–39 for an epic depiction of time. The four *varṇas* are already present in the first eon, the *kṛta yuga* (III.148.21). Mārkaṇḍeya describes the closure of time at III.186.16ff. Daniel Ingalls 1995: 1, on the epic quality of the Mahābhārata, commented that the poem "has been called an epic, but the term is misleading. It contains an epic." Yamazaki 2005: 63–130 offers a compendious overview of what constitutes *kṣatriya* life. By *bhārata* I understand those elements of the poem which directly concern the narratives of the Pāṇḍavas and of the Kauravas.

47. Scharfe 1989: 109: "It is striking how in the epics, where events are dominated by Viṣṇu and his *avatāra-s*, the kings and their priests are devoted exclusively to Vedic rituals. This is, however, quite fitting since the events of the epics are supposed to take place in the *dvāpara*-age, when Vedic rituals (*yajña*) prevail according to Manu I 86." Ingalls 1995: 5, commenting on Sukthankar's view of the Bhārgavas, notes, "one must realize that these Bhārgavas did not transform an adventure of war into a didactic tale. They merely emphasized and expanded a didactic element that lay implicit in the oldest form of the tale that we can imagine." On the preliterate poet, Ingalls (ibid.: 7) summarized the conclusions of Parry and Lord, "He memorizes the plot, the names and epithets of the characters, and he saturates his mind with a large number of formulas and *clichés*. He then extemporizes when called upon to perform."

48. In terms of kinship, the primary relation between men can be construed as threefold in degree: 'Let father approach son, sister's son his maternal uncle, brother to brother' (*pitā putraṃ mātulaṃ bhāgineyo / bhrātā caiva bhrātaraṃ praitu*; VI.116.49). When, in Book Seven, Yudhiṣthira is asking Abhimanyu to penetrate the enemy formation, it is so that his 'fathers and maternal uncles' will be proud of him (VII.34.16). There exist only a few passing references to women in the battle books, usually in the form of simile: 'like an intoxicated woman' (VI.73.57, VI.96.18); 'like a frightened woman' (VII.144.31); 'like a parting on the head of a woman' (VII.156.9); and there are the laments for Abhimanyu.

and some *ṛṣayaḥ* 'seers': that is, between a *kṣatriya* and brahmins, bard and priests.[49] This tension between the two *varṇas* runs throughout the poem like a wire.[50] *Kṣatriyas* live by very different cultural rules from brahmins and the analyst must take precaution in drawing conclusions from data that is not specifically related to the *varṇa* under discussion.[51] For instance, a typical male *kṣatriya* convention is described by Kṛṣṇa, when he and Arjuna and Bhīma enter the household of Jarāsaṃdha with violent intent.

> kāryavanto gṛhān etya śatruto na arhaṇāṃ vayam
> pratigṛhṇīma tad viddhi etan naḥ śāśvataṃ vratam
>
> Intent—having entered a house of an enemy—we do not accept as an honorific gift:
> know that that is our perpetual vow.
>
> II.19.50

They had not entered the building by the door: entry by the doorway is reserved for friendly houses. For a *kṣatriya* to enter the house of an enemy, the public threshold is not to be crossed, for warriors only come with a prospect of violence in hand. Such a convention is of little concern for other *varṇas*. There exist many other such social, caste-oriented practices, codes that communicate certain expressions, particularly as they relate to conflict.

Book Eleven, the Strī *parvan*, concerns *kṣatriya* women participating in a cultural practice specific to that *varṇa*: they perform rituals of formal lamentation, an activity that is avoided by brahmin women due to the pollution involved. When the demon Hiḍimbā speaks to Kuntī, who has just become her de facto mother-in-law, in Book One, she says,

49. A *sūta* is not fully *kṣatriya* in terms of birth, but for the purposes of social life such poets in the epic are always closely and intimately allied with a king or hero.

50. One should recall that the Iliad opens with a dispute between a priest and a king, concerning the proper compensation that should be exchanged for a woman. Much of the rest of that poem hinges upon a sequence of questions relating to worth, *poinḗ* and *ápoina*, and ultimately finds resolution in Achilles' personal preoccupation with the value of a human life: what should life be exchanged for? The image of proto-litigation on the Shield in XVIII.497ff. concerns blood price: how much is a human life worth? See Nagy 1997a.

51. For instance, *kṣattraṃ yāti tathā svargaṃ bhuvi nigrahapālanaiḥ* 'So the *kṣatriya varṇa* goes to heaven by protection and coercion on earth' (III.149.52). The sign of the kṣatriya is bloodshed, the sign of the brahmin is the text; and, *na hi yācanti rājāna eṣa dharmaḥ sanātanaḥ* 'For kings do not implore, that is the perpetual law' (III.152.9). Concerning brahmins and the sacrifice, in order to perform this rite a sacrificer—a brahmin—must be married: this is an essential condition. See Olivelle 1993: 37–41, where he considers this "intimate and unbreakable union between husband and wife in the sacrifice." "Procreation, just like sacrifice, is a religious duty [for brahmins] that presupposes marriage." Ibid.: 42.

jānāsi yad duḥkham iha strīṇām anaṅgajam 'you are aware of the sorrow of women here, which is born of love' (I.143.5). This sorrow concerns the consequences of *kṣatriya* life, a life which is founded upon men's coercion of men.

This view of epic, therefore, poses a particular model, insofar as we are specifically limiting analysis to what is essentially *kṣatriya* or heroic literature.[52] Yet brahmin women exist extensively in this poetry as do a few women of other castes. What applies to *kṣatriya* woman, however, does not necessarily nor always apply to women of other ranks; yet conversely, when a brahmin wife says,

> etad hi paramaṃ nāryāḥ kāryaṃ loke sanātanam
> prāṇān api parityajya yad bhartṛhitam ācaret
>
> For this is the highest duty of a woman in the world, eternally:
> she must proceed for the good of a husband, even having disregarded life.
>
> I.146.4

Such is applicable to all stations of twice-born women; this is a fundamental claim of *strī* dharma. The speaker goes on to say that this form of conduct will be *yaśaskaram* 'conducive of glory'. Again, concerning all the *varṇas*,

> yajñais tapobhir niyamair dānaiś ca vividhais tathā
> viśiṣyate striyā bhartur nityam priyahite sthitiḥ
>
> A woman upright in devotion to her husband is better than
> various charities, pieties, austerities, and sacrifices.
>
> I.146.24

She also says that, *avadhyāḥ striya ity āhur dharmajñā*, 'the knowers of law say that women are not to be killed' (I.146.29); and, wives are 'friends' (*sakhā*; I.147.11).

The reader must thus always ascertain whether matters relating to

52. There is the slight problem of confusion here, as when Karṇa describes himself as, *brahmakṣatrāntare ... jātam* 'born between brahmin and *kṣatriya*' (XII.3.26), although Karṇa is ostensibly the best of the *kṣatriyas*. This confusion also occurs with figures like Droṇa or Rāma Jāmadagnya, brahmins who live like *kṣatriyas*, or Bhīṣma, who lives in many ways like a brahmin. Concerning a contemporary *kṣatriya* tradition in Himalayan Garhwal, Sax 2002: 93 writes that the "*pāṇḍav līlā* does not simply 'express' the dominance of the Rajputs but actively reproduces it through the medium of embodied performance." These "local Rajputs ... claim descent from the Pandavas themselves," ibid.: 94. The *pāṇḍav līlā* "is a public, ritual performance that, by obliging the participation of all members of society, helps to reproduce the very system of dominance that it simultaneously represents." Ibid.: 119.

the feminine in the Mahābhārata concern particular castes or a more general body.

Certainly, to speak of Bronze Age women as they appear in the Mahābhārata is to draw upon data which is distinctly artificial and denotes no extant culture.[53] The social world of epic is simulated and it is a fabrication of poetry that can in no way be said to signify any actual society.[54] Even in terms of time the epic world is a poetic view that is retrojected into a hypothetical past of heroes and warrior elites, deities and sometimes demons. In many other ancient cultures—Greece or the Hittites for instance—there are sufficient material objects retrieved through archaeological research to allow a further supporting reconstruction of cultural life. This study however is solely derived from textual analyses of the *un-natural*, composite and synthetic world of epic Mahābhārata, qua poetry.

Even though epic poetry is a literary and retrospective formulation and mirrors no point in time nor any historical society, one can discern—within the text—various distinct patterns of complex kinship structure which project paradigms of possible *kṣatriya* femininity and collective organization. The constitution—even if hypothetical or mythical—of these paradigms can be isolated, described, and sometimes analyzed.

What strikes a modern reader of the poem is that women are—and Draupadī is especially—figures of extraordinary complexity and authority, and yet due to their having no access to weaponry they become the focus of conflict, as opposed to being the agents of conflict. Through the organizations of kinship and within patterns of dialogue, *kṣatriya* women in archaic Indian poetry behave as agents of great dramatic force. For the male hero, the agonistic world is constituted by combat, whereas for women, ordeals are more bound by a need to create and maintain kinship and obversely, to lament its passing.[55]

Presumably the performance of the epic occurred before a male audience of *kṣatriyas*, this is an assumption: epic poetry is ideally a male medium.[56] Perhaps during more classical times and certainly in

53. The early Iron Age is typically dated as commencing in the tenth century BCE. Allchin 1995.

54. "Without the bronze, without the weapons there would have been no Bronze Age warrior idea." Renfrew 2001: 137.

55. "Wars are fought over the honor of women, which in turn is conflated with and subsumed by the honor of the patriarchal clan. The humiliation of women is avenged by men who interpret it as an assault on their masculinity." Mankekar *1999*: 217.

56. Flueckiger 1996: 140–141, commenting on a contemporary tradition in Uttar Predesh notes that "a male, martial epic ... has been appropriated to promote a particular *kśatriya*

medieval times—when the poem had been written down and was being recited—the audience might have then contained women.[57]

Yet during the weapons trial where the Pāṇḍavas display their skill at arms, women are present in the audience (I.126.27). These are *kṣatriya* women. During the battle books the women of King Dhṛtarāṣṭra are present beside him as the poet Saṃjaya sings of events occurring on the distant field: they are immediate to his inspired vision.[58] When Dhṛtarāṣṭra faints at the horror of what Saṃjaya describes,

> patitaṃ cainam ājñāya samantād bhāratastriyaḥ
> parivavrur mahārājam aspṛśaṃś caiva pāṇibhiḥ
>
> Having observed him fallen, from all sides the Bhārata women
> surrounded the great king and touched him with their hands.
>
> VII.9.3

Thus, the women of the court are the primary audience—within the poem—of the core element of the poem.[59]

Yaroslav Vassilkov, in an article on pilgrimage in the Mahābhārata, argues convincingly for the importance of priestly and non-*kṣatriya* recitation of the poem at various *tīrthas* 'ritual bathing sites'.[60] "In the MBh *tīrthayātrās* one can recognize unmistakably the voice of ancient *tīrtha purohits*, predecessors of the modern *paṇḍās*."[61] Such pilgrimage sites would not be limited to men, in fact, pilgrimage is one ritual activity in which women and men usually conduct themselves without exclusion of the other.

There is also the question of myth, as a genre which can be

---

image of the Ahir caste." She then comments on "the characterization 'male' because women are not part of its primary audience and may listen to its performance only when it is held in a setting that allows them to 'overhear' from behind a curtain or wall."

57. There is mention of a *strīrājyādhipati* 'king of the kingdom of women' at XII.4.7, but this is all that an audience hears concerning this unusual polity. It is mentioned at one other point only (III.48.22). In her study of the songs of heroic narrative in contemporary Rajasthan, Harlan has shown how both men and women celebrate a hero in their singing, and yet they do so differently. The male performers will emphasize their pride of lineage and martial vigor leading to an heroic death; women however, will sing of a hero's beauty and attractiveness and his potential as a bridegroom. Women as poets, singers, in the contemporary subcontinent, have a different view of heroism than men. Harlan 2000: 237–249.

58. "By *speech* I mean everyday or unmarked language, and by song I mean special or marked language that is set off from *speech* on the formal level of phonology, morphology, syntax, or any combination of these three." Nagy 1990: 30. I am in full accord with such sentiments.

59. Apart from Janamejaya, who is there listening to his poet, Vaiśaṃpāyana, in the outer frame. He exists in the epic only as the principal and hypothetical patron of the work.

60. Vassilkov, in Brockington 2002: 133–156.

61. Ibid.: 141.

discerned apart from the flow of epic narration.[62] How does the idea of the goddess enter into epic narrative, if at all, and can the reader distinguish between the archaic and the classical here?[63] The goddess Kālī, or Durgā, does appear in the poem at X.8.64, where Aśvatthāman during his night rampage is likened to her in horror. Given in the appendices to the poem, there are two occasions where heroes sing a hymn in praise of Devī, performed at the onset of battle.[64] Bhīṣma is the only hero who has a *devī* 'goddess' as a parent, and one who actually appears in the epic and addresses him (V.179.22).[65] The Pāṇḍavas and their brother Karṇa are the only heroes to possess male progenitors who are divine: they are therefore set apart from other heroes as mythic.

Does the epic dramatize on an heroic level stories from myth: can one make such an inference? Draupadī is at one point said to be deemed telluric and an incarnation of Śrī, and an analyst such as Parpola would propose that the figure of Sāvitrī is connected with a pre-Aryan divinity.[66] J. D. Smith in his study of the epic of Pābūjī writes of how his poet-informer, Parbū, considered the events of Mahābhārata: "In the story of the *Mahābhārata* (as interpreted by Parbū), it was Draupadī, incarnation of the Goddess, who secured the right outcome, the battle between the Kauravas and the Pāṇḍavas; yet the central god there is Kṛṣṇa, not Draupadī."[67]

Apart from this question concerning the status and presence of myth in the epic, always, when working with literature that originates from an oral tradition of prehistory, there are questions as to priority:

62. Hiltebeitel 1988: 264–265, on the subject of contemporary Draupadī cult worship, writes, "To the Pāṇḍavas she is thus goddess-and-wife (*devī*), whereas to others—not only her sons but the elders themselves and by implication the rest of the world—she is revealed as the universal mother, identified with the elements earth and fire ... Draupadī's mistreatment within the kula can cause failure of rains, even the end of the world." "The *līlās* are ways of worshipping Kālī, and Draupadī is regarded as Kālī's *avatāra*." Hiltebeitel, in Sax 1995: 207.

63. There are also *yakṣī*, *gandharvī*, and *apsarā*, and *rākṣasī* in the epic, who are entirely feminine and non-mortal/human. None of these are subject of worship however. The earth is also divine and feminine—and not merely gramatically, as with *devī pṛthivī* (V.29.10).

64. CE IV App. I.4 (D); VI App. I.1.

65. Kṛṣṇa, the hero-deity whose presence in the version of the poem that we now possess runs through the text like a current: at his theophany in Book Five, he reveals no feminine aspect to his godhead at all, he is *thoroughly* male. The same is true in his Gītā theophany. There is little about the cosmic Kṛṣṇa that partakes of the feminine, divine or mortal; unless one argues that his intelligent manipulation of mortal heroes is feminine—for Kṛṣṇa rarely uses physical force. I am grateful to Thomas Burke for this observation.

66. Parpola 1998. Dumézil 1968: I.9, comments on Draupadī's polyandric marriage: "un événement fortuit a transmis à Draupadī le caractère essentiel de la déesse trivalente."

67. J. D. Smith 1991: 97. "Parbū's explanation of these happenings is that whenever evil comes to oppress the earth, the Goddess takes human form to destroy it by precipitating armed conflict."

do certain episodes or characters originate from archaic or classical periods, or, do they occur with reference to physical locality? These are not problems that I try to answer in this study. I accept the critically edited text as a given unity and try to avoid the problem of distinguishing between what is archaic and what is classical.[68] It is obvious to any reader how different the Sanskrit is in the various *parvans* of the epic, grammatically, syntactically, in vocabulary, and in stylistic form.[69] The critically edited text of Poona is a unified work in terms of narrative, but certainly not in terms of formal composition.

For this project the text is central and my method a posteriori. This work examines—through a close reading of speeches in Mahābhārata—not only the explicit and substantial content of speech, but also the metaphors and metonyms that women deploy both socially and privately; it analyzes the underlying systems of reference to which these tropes refer.[70] Essentially, these speeches issue from members of the three great clans who are allied by virtue of kinship ties: the Kauravas, the Vṛṣṇis, and the Pāñcālas. Their alliances are formed by marriage contracts.

For instance, it is said that *dharmasya brāhmaṇā yoniḥ* 'law possesses a brahminical womb' (XII.91.19). Why such a feminine object as a womb should be used metaphorically in the place of brahmins—and the phrase is never used in this way for *kṣatriyas*—is remarkable. What would be the counterpoint metaphorically, and how would such a trope function? An audience also hears that,

> svargayonir jayo rājan svargayonir mahad yaśaḥ
>
> O king, victory is the womb of heaven, great glory is the womb of heaven!
>
> II.20.16

68. Fitzgerald 2003 presents an excellent overview of this approach; Hiltebeitel, 2004, reformulates the proposition, and again in Koskikallio 2005: 81–111.

69. To make an analogy, sometimes it is as if the styles of Milton, Wordsworth, Byron, and some Shakespeare and Jonson, had been compiled and displayed within the narrative of the poem; for the *parvans* and sometimes the *adhyāyas* differ so much in style and vocabulary and the *kind* of sentences vary greatly. Also, different parts of the epic represent very different kinds of perceived cosmos.

70 *Explication de texte*. Through such a method of reading, one can pinpoint separate details in the text that can be connected up to reveal basic structures. Via the evidence of the isolated repetition of cases, one can demonstrate—by inference—typical conditions or practice. For example, the repetition of metaphors or metonyms can illustrate referential systems which are hypostatic to the functioning of the poem. One metaphor might possess within its imagery many other metonyms which are attached to that primary figure, thus creating a fabric of reference.

Here, victory and martial glory are feminized as creative and generative, and are the objects or aims of service for good *kṣatriyas*. In likewise form, when the prototype of Death is created out of the body of Brahmā, she is referred to as a 'woman' *nārī* (XII.249.15).[71] Death appears in a woman's attire, in black with red eyes.

My method is thoroughly textual and inductive, a method utilized in the book, *The Sanskrit Hero*.[72] In that work I described the cultural organization of male *kṣatriyas* and examined the value system therein from both a social and poetic point of view. This present study extends that research to the feminine characters of the poem and, in part, offers a descriptive ethnography of some of the relevant social elements borne by the text.

In that book I founded my explorations upon the work of two other scholars: Gregory Nagy and Calvert Watkins.[73] The performative and preliterate model of epic poetry established by Nagy, carrying on the earlier ideas of Parry and Lord, is one of the primary assumptions underlying this present work.[74] The model of Indo-European poetics that Watkins has proposed—the cognate relationship which exists between the Sanskrit and other epics such as Homeric poetry—is similarly an assumption fundamental to this present study.[75] I firmly assume that "institutions materialise in specific and recurring ways that allow one to infer their cultural and historical formation and transmission in time and space."[76]

71. Śrī, the deity of fortune and benevolence—perhaps the opposite to Death—is always depicted as feminine.

72. McGrath 2004.

73. Nagy 1996, Watkins 1995; see also Witzel, in Koskikallio 2005: 21–80.

74. Hiltebeitel 2001 has treated the Mahābhārata not as a text sprung from preliterate traditions, but from a literal formulation. Curiously, at VII.74.7, the audience does hear of arrows that are *nāmāṅkitāḥ* 'marked with a name'; similarly at VII.113.5. To make a modern analogy, concerning how a text is composed from several "versions" by an editor, Mankekar *1999*: 171–180 writes of how the cinema "text" of *Rāmāyaṇa* was organized by Ramanand Sagar in the 1980's. "Several analysts contend that [he] 'homogenized' the *Ramayana* tradition by imposing a hegemonic north Indian, upper-caste narrative on its captive audience ... the serial's narrative was collated from several versions: the *Ranganath Ramayana* in Telegu, Eknath's *Bhavarth Ramayana* in Marathi, the *Kritivas Ramayana* in Bengali, and Malayalam, Urdu, and Kannada versions."

75. Bryant 2001, has compiled an exhaustive summary of "out of India" views and their development: views which are contrary to this Indo-European interpretation.

76. Kristiansen and Larsson 2005: 11. On the development of the Greek epic corpus: "On archaeological grounds their origin is safely anchored in Mycenaean times, possibly even the shaft grave period. Over time additions and slight changes were made to make them comprehensible to contemporary audiences. They are thus the result of an acculturated heroic heritage maintained by bards at the royal courts in exile." Ibid.: 229n18.

Unlike most of the other epics in the world today which are *frozen*, insofar as their textual corpus has become fixed and has remained unchanged for centuries if not millennia, the Mahābhārata in contemporary India exists *not* simply as a permanent, critically edited object of literature. It also functions as a scripture, supplying a ritual and mythical ground for modern Hindu religion—particularly in north India—and it is thoroughly multiform in its living non-written manifestations.[77] For instance, there are Mahābhārata films, on the big screen and television.[78] There are also annual village festival drama cycles, puppet theaters, and there exist comic books and customary oral narratives, as well as rural bards who still sing—in non-melodic recitative—performative renditions of the poem.[79]

For the analyst, this social and literary situation offers great scope for research. I have attempted to adduce contemporary supporting evidence, where appropriate, as a parallel to the Sanskrit text; this is supplied in my footnotes. Such current and vital epic phenomena impart enormous milieu or perspective to textual studies—a state which does not exist for the Homeric corpus.[80] This living background to the critically edited text is an especially fruitful field for inquiry; particularly given the conditions of communal conflict today and the

77. Nagy 2004, Ch. 2 passim has written of how—in the evolution of the Iliad—the multiformity of the text typically diminishes with time until the poem becomes fixed. On the contrary, the ongoing vitality of the Mahābhārata in modern society, sustains if not develops its multiform nature.

78. The television serial of the Mahābhārata—despite the fact that its script writer "Rahi Masoom Raza, a Moslem and a renowned leftist intellectual" (Mankekar 1999: 235)—was often seen as if it "represented the Hindu past," ibid.: 162. More seriously, the televised serial of Rāmāyaṇa, first screened in 1987, "was condemned by many media critics and secularists as a 'communal' text that had enabled the consolidation of Hindu nationalism." Ibid.: 165.

79. See Meyer and Deuel 1998 for the text of a twentieth-century dramatic folk rendering of the Mahābhārata, which is danced and sung by a chorus. Sax 1995: 138–139, makes the notable comment concerning a contemporary Mahābhārata dramatic cycle in the villages of the Garhwal, that the "*pāṇḍav līlā* is fundamentally a *Kṣatriya* tradition." In his later study, Sax 2002: 63, the author comments that "the heroes of *Mahābhārata* were portrayed not as great kings and princes but simple folk with lice in their hair, as ancestors with whom the villagers felt an experiential and physical bond." This kind of exclusiveness is certainly not the case with television or cinema representations of the epic, where, "the Mahabharat advertised itself as a tale of a lineage called Bharat ... it proclaimed itself the story of the Indian nation." Mankekar 1999: 249. Flueckiger 1996: 164, on contemporary performance traditions comments, "The style is composed of short, almost staccato couplets of nearly repetitious lines. Each couplet advances the story line, and little room exists for elaboration of scene or emotion or for commentary on motivation."

80. Sax 2002 offers a good example of this approach; also, Hiltebeitel 1988, 1991, on Draupadī cults in south India today.

presence of Moslem interpretations or performance of parts of the poetic tradition.[81]

Purnima Mankekar—working in modern cinema—has described how contemporary Indian woman draw upon the feminine characters of Mahābhārata, using them as crucial exemplars for feminist thought in the subcontinent.[82] These feminine figures include women who have reincarnated as men and men who have been changed into women.

These are some of the approaches taken in this examination of women in Mahābhārata. Draupadī supplies the central image of femininity in the poem, but I shall draw upon other characters in order to give dimension to her presence and force. This book is a survey of these various feminine personae as they appear during the major and minor narratives of the Mahābhārata.

Most of the material on kinship and marriage is drawn from the first five books of the epic. The four battle books supply little material that concerns the feminine, apart from a few similes and the women's laments sung for the fallen Abhimanyu in Book Seven. The Śānti and Anuśāsana *parvan*s and the final five books offer references to women that are either injunctive or a part of micro-narratives. The Strī *parvan* is unique and its subsection, the Vilāpa *parvan*, is rich in poetry that speaks solely for women in epic Mahābhārata.

Chapter Two deals with kinship patterns and the forms of marriage which occur in the epic. Chapter Three examines certain women heroes of importance, of whom Draupadī is preeminent; in Chapter

81. Hiltebeitel 1989: 347 writes of cult practices in contemporary south India, concerning a tomb "of Muhammad Khan. One is told that he was a Muslim devotee of Draupadī who died here." It is often the case that the sharp distinctions between Moslem and Hindu in the subcontinent today are due more to recent systems of census and enumeration, rather than to any actual practice of worship where such separations are frequently blurred if not fused.

82. That is, the Mahābhārata as it was screened on television in India, between September, 1988 and July, 1990, when "it was watched by more than 200 million viewers." Mankekar 1999: 224. Flueckiger 1996: 24–25 comments on the women's tradition of singing *paṇḍvānī*, the "Mahabharata performance genre": "When I asked what the difference was between *paṇḍvānī* and the recently televised serial production of the Mahabharata, one Chhatisgarhi villager answered that the latter was shastric (textual), where *paṇḍvānī* is 'sung from our hearts.'" On page 159, Flueckiger quotes, "The TV is for everyone; there are many written Mahabharatas. This [*paṇḍvānī*] stands alone. Those who read from paper, they know the TV Mahabharata." She observes (page 163) that, "There are a limited number of episodes of the 'unending' Mahabharata narrative current in *paṇḍvānī* performance, although many more episodes of the narrative may be part of the oral tradition, that is, known to the audience members through other performance genres as well as the televised serialization of the Mahabharata."

Four, her narrative is studied at length. The subject of Chapter Five is the part that women play in the epic as speakers and critics of dharma, and as the figures who perform laments for their deceased menfolk, the heroes. Chapter Six brings closure to the study and looks at two key metaphors, landscape and rivers. It also touches specifically upon aspects of feminine sexuality manifest in the poem and offers a brief depiction of some of the roles that Mahābhārata women heroes perform in contemporary Indian society, both in cult and in legend.

Heroic religion in India—classical, medieval, and modern—has received much of its contemporary substance from the Mahābhārata: heroes define meaning and their speeches and ACTIONS are representative of human values. The feminine heroes discussed in this book continue to inhabit and influence culture today throughout the subcontinent.[83]

Even though, in a pre-monetary society, reciprocity rather than judgment is what balances and maintains the social dynamic, men and women in the world portrayed by epic Mahābhārata are *not* equal. They live and function in two discrete social systems, systems that are intimately connected and thoroughly merged. Such an intertwining asymmetry is moderated by a formal deployment of kinship terms that avoid an historical setting and are engaged on a completely synchronic level: this supplies a curious fusion and enlargement to the culture.[84] Men and women are also very different in how they speak and in the effects of their language.[85]

I have used the Critical Edition of the text as produced by Bhandarkar Oriental Institute of Poona, and have supplemented that with the online text made available by J. D. Smith of Cambridge University, which is invaluable for making word searches.[86] I have complemented this

83. By "heroic religion" I understand a system of ritual where heroes—such as Arjuna, Kṛṣṇa, and Draupadī—receive worship as supernatural beings who can possibly affect the course of a worshipper's life.

84. See below, Ch. II.2, on this question of kinship terminology.

85. See below, Ch. V concerning the imbrication of dharma and women's speech.

86. There exists an underlying and irresolveable question concerning the text: namely, how far different parts of the Mahābhārata draw from different poetic traditions which may have created or presented different versions of the story; and to what extent these traditions were able to comprehend the continuity and amplitude of the epic as a whole? Similarly, how far did the final editors exert themselves to make the story internally consistent? As part of this original formation, the repetition of certain micro-narratives throughout the course of the poem—sometimes with slight variation, sometimes with a slight change of perspective or narrative voice—serves to bind the whole text together, in the same way that symphony or opera themes are reiterated—sometimes with variance—in order to unify the integrity and process of music. Sukthankar, in his *Prolegomena* to the Critical Edition of the Ādi *parvan* of 1933, page cii, wrote, "the Mahābhārata is the whole of the Epic tradition, the entire Critical Apparatus. Its separation into the constituted text and the critical notes is only a

process by making great use of Sörensen's wonderful *Index to the Names in the Mahābhārata*, and Mani's *Purāṇic Encyclopaedia.*[87] The commentary of Nīlakaṇṭha, which usually accompanies the Vulgate edition of the poem, is a rich source of brahminical gloss, particularly as it relates to technical terms and phrases in the interpretation of heroic culture.

---

static representation of a constantly changing epic text." On the nature of the Critical Edition, Ingalls 1995: 3 commented, "What we have in the Critical Edition is a written Mahābhārata of roughly 200 to 300 A.D. The general principle of constituting the text was to regard those passages where North and South agreed as genuine. Especially convincing was an agreement between the geographical extremes, between examples written in Śāradā Kashmiri and in Malayalam scripts." Deshpande, in Rukmani 2005: 7, observes: "while the critical edition cites relatively few textual variants for the *Bhagavadgītā*, that is not the case for the rest of the *Mahābhārata*. One can safely say that the text of the *Bhagavadgītā* attained a reasonably stable form due to its scriptural status relatively early, while the rest of the *Mahābhārata* continued its diverse regional transmission for many more centuries. As Cynthia Talbot showed in her essay ... the marriage of Arjuna to Subhadrā, a cross-cousin marriage, is much celebrated in the southern versions, while it is a problem to be dealt with for the northern version. This difference obviously needs to be related to the fact that cross-cousin marriage is the preferred form of marriage in the Dravidian south, while it is not acceptable to the northern regions."

87. Sörensen 1904; Mani 1993.

II

KINSHIP AND MARRIAGE

A KING, IN ORDER TO RULE, MUST POSSESS A WIFE, for kings do not exist without queens, this is not possible.[1] Marriage is a crucial rite if a kingdom or clan is to survive well and flourish.[2] It is only after their marriage with Draupadī that the Pāṇḍavas become *prāptarājyāḥ* 'possessing sovereignty' in the kingdom of Indraprastha (I.200.5). Women in the Mahābhārata actively participate in the business of rule and its discourse, just as they often dominate the procedure in which a spouse is acquired.

As Claude Lévi-Strauss has written, "Like phonemes, kinship terms are elements of meaning; like phonemes, they acquire meaning only if they are integrated into systems ... Although they belong to another order of reality, kinship phenomena are of the same type as linguistic phenomena."[3] It is the paradigms and syntax of kinship which supply meaning to a social system, and in this chapter I extrapolate from the epic and present distinct procedures of marital formation, as paradigms, and indicate how they influence the narrative, as syntax. Let us initially look at certain practical and emotional conditions.

1. West 2007: 415–419. In Ramāyaṇa, Rāma observes an extremely rigid and strict monogamy, which is unlike the patterns of marriage shown in Mahābhārata. In the Śānti *parvan*, Bhīṣma actually says to Yudhiṣṭhira, whom he is instructing in the lore of kingship, *bhavitavyaṃ sadā rajñā garbhiṇīsahadharmiṇā* 'a king should be possessed of the same qualities as a pregnant woman' (XII.56.44).

2. If kingship was good—and kingship implies a correspondent queenship—then, *nikāmavarṣī parjanyaḥ sphīto janapado'bhavat* 'the community was prosperous, rains fell abundantly' (II.30.2). "Teutonic heroic society knows of no ... seclusion of women. The queen is generally present beside her lord in courtly scenes; and she moves about freely among the assembled warriors." Sidhanta 1929: 160–161. Sidhanta, a scholar of Indo-European "heroic" society, compared the Indian epics with cognate European epic poetry. Macdonell and Keith 1912, in their Index, under the lemma *pati*, have: "The marriage was frequently arranged through an intermediary, the 'wooer' (*vara*), presumably after those concerned had come to an agreement."

3. Lévi-Strauss 1963: 34. The method of ethnography—including the ethnography of text—is that of *description*: it portrays the patterns, identifies the ideas, and delineates the generation of values which are at work in a social order.

When Yudhiṣṭhira is finally consecrated as king, Draupadī is seated at his side during the conduct of the rite (XII.40.14). When Pāṇḍu marries—and this is the second time, having taken a co-wife whom he had purchased—only then is he 'desiring to conquer the earth' (*jigīṣamāṇo vasudhām*; I.105.7).[4]

Similarly, when Kṛṣṇa meets up with the Pāṇḍavas in the forest in Book Three, their wives are present and participate in the immediate protocols:

> tathaiva satyabhāmāpi draupadīṃ pariṣasvaje
> pāṇḍavānāṃ prīyāṃ bhāryāṃ kṛṣṇasya mahiṣī priyā
>
> Then Satyabhāmā, beloved queen of Kṛṣṇa,
> embraced Draupadī, the beloved wife of the Pāṇḍavas.
>
> III.180.11

Rank is crucial in this culture—note the distinction made here between wife and queen—and marriage is usually horizontally equal or 'conformable' (*sadṛśī, anurūpā*), in terms of *varṇa*.[5] In terms of lineage—or spiritual life after death—without a child, *na dvāraṃ ... svarge*, there is 'no door in heaven' (I.111.11). The wife and co-wife are thus crucial for the complete or maximum well-being of a king even on the level of supernature; for as Yudhiṣṭhira says, *bhāryā daivakṛtaḥ sakhā* 'a wife is a friend made by destiny' (III.297.51).[6]

4. A bride is 'given' (*donnée*) and 'led' (*emmenée*) home; Benveniste 1969: I.239–240. As we shall see, however, this is often merely nominal. The terms of nomenclature for kinship divide along the margin between the agnatic and the affiliated, between consanguinity and marriage: these are two different systems of social organization. *Jñāti* denotes the agnatic relation, *saṃbandhin* the affiliated. Benveniste notes the frequent lack of symmetry between masculine and feminine terms, as in the case of 'brother' and 'sister': I.215, "Il est possible aussi que Skr. **strī* (< **srī*) «femme» soit une féminisation secondaire de l'ancien **sor* ... La position de la soeur se définirait donc par le rapport à une fraction sociale, le *swe* ... où se maintiennent les membres masculins." I.239, "dans la conjugalité, la situation de l'homme et celle de la femme n'avaient rien de commun." In this case, there is certainly a parallelism.

5. When Bhīṣma finds a wife for Vidura at I.106.12, she is *pāraśavī* 'of mixed caste', just like Vidura. A woman is *anulomā* 'hypergamous' when she is of a lower caste than the man with whom she marries; she is *pratilomā* 'hypogamous' when she marries down. Vidura, in his injunctions for the good or correct life, says that 'one makes marriage with equals' (*samair vivāhaṃ kurute*; V.33.98). Keith 1925: 373, notes: "The later texts prescribe that the maiden must be of the same caste and land, but not of the same Gotra as the father or a *sapiṇḍā* on the mother's side."

6. Concerning nomenclature within the Indo-European family, see Buck 1949: 2.31ff.: "The wife became one with her husband's family, and it was the relations between her and her husband's family that were important. The relations between the husband and his wife's relatives were remoter; and special terms for the 'wife's father', etc. arose only later, either by extension of the inherited group or otherwise."

Not only are marriages crucial for internal reasons within a family, but also externally: there are key dynastic marriages, which are wholly political and maintain the force of royal families. Marriage is therefore a time of evaluation, when the prospective bride and groom are considered in terms of worth: they are being weighed with the economics of amicability or alliance. In the Sabhā *parvan* for instance, when Duryodhana is listing the wealth that the Pāṇḍavas receive from their tributary allies—and these are enormous quantities of moveable goods of extraordinary value (II.47.1ff.)—he closes his account by saying that there are two clans who do not offer such payments: these are the Vṛṣṇis and the Pāñcālas. The former pay no tax 'on account of friendship' (*sakhyena*), whilst the latter give nothing 'on account of marriage' (*vaivāhikena*; II.48.42). The marriage is, of course, the polyandrous union of Draupadī with the five brothers.

Yet women and marriage are also areas of possible instability and hazard for men, and there are strict formalities that outline these zones in *kṣatriya* culture; the absence of such constraints can cause disorder. For example, Yudhiṣṭhira, whilst in conversation with the sage Mārkaṇḍeya during the forest sojourn, tells him that,

> strīṇāṃ dharmāt sughorād hi nānyaṃ paśyāmi duṣkaram
>
> For I see nothing more difficult than the very terrible dharma of women.
>
> III.196.8

For Yudhiṣṭhira, all dharma is difficult and problematic, but in this particular instance the *dharmarāja* is referring particularly to pregnancy and childbirth and to difficulties that parents make for women: *duṣkaraṃ bata kurvanti pitaro mātaraś ca vai* 'alas for sure, mothers and fathers make difficulties'. These difficulties, by inference, concern marriage.[7] From a male point of view, women are complicated and at times potentially destabilizing, due to their physiology. Yudhiṣṭhira then says however,

> nāryaḥ kālena saṃbhūya kim adbhutataraṃ tataḥ
>
> Then—what is more wonderful—having been born in the course of time from a woman!
>
> III.196.9

7. Vyāsa says, in the Śānti *parvan: hy ṛtunā śuddhaṃ cāturmāsyaṃ vidhīyate / striyas tena viśudhyanti* 'for women, it is ordained, are cleansed on account of menstruation four months after birth' (XII.36.26).

On the other hand, Vidura, whilst he counsels the old king one night during a period immediately prior to the outbreak of war, comments at random on the subject of marriage. He speaks of *ete'nuyānty anilaṃ pāśahastāḥ* 'those ones—noose in hand—follow the wind': those ones being men who should be avoided as potentially dangerous and volatile for they are destabilized by the force of womanhood. They are:

> vadhvā hāsaṃ śvaśuro yaś ca manyate
> vadhvā vasann uta yo mānakāmaḥ...
> striyaṃ ca yaḥ parivadate'tivelam
>
> A father-in-law who wishes mirth with a young wife;
> one who, living with a young wife, desires the excitement of jealousy...
> one who slanders a woman excessively.
>
> V.37.5

Similarly, the sage Kaṇva, in the *sabhā* of Dhṛtarāṣṭra, in an effort to convince the court to adopt a policy of peace rather than war, tells a story of Mātali, the charioteer of Indra. When the time came for him to marry off his daughter, Guṇakeśī, he and his wife considered the *pradāna* 'the giving away in marriage' and became anxious. Guṇakeśī was exceptionally beautiful, and no one in all the worlds pleased the father sufficiently for him to offer the girl. Thus she becomes a perilous liability.

> mātuḥ kulaṃ pitṛkulaṃ yatra caiva pradīyate
> kulatrayaṃ saṃśayitaṃ kurute kanyakā satām
>
> A virgin makes suspicious three families:
> the family of the mother, the family of the father, and that where she is given.
>
> V.95.16

Mātali sets off towards the subterranean world of snakes in order to discover a suitor who is decent enough for his daughter, so that stability can be maintained and this danger superceded.

Concerning the actual physical situation of wedded women, one cannot ascribe a situation of *pardā*, the 'curtain' or 'women's seclusion', to archaic times in India, for there is no firm evidence indicating this practice. There is frequent mention in the epic of the *antaḥpura* 'inner quarters', or as Monier-Williams has it, 'gynaeceum, the women's quarter'; what has been called the *zenana* since Persian times. Whether the term refers to an area of the palace that is solely restricted to women and eunuchs, or whether these apartments are merely the inner quarters or courtyards of the building itself is unclear.

When Saṃjaya returns from his embassy to Yudhiṣṭhira in the Udyoga *parvan*, he enters the *antaḥpura* in order to speak with the old king (V.32.2). The king is seated upon a *siṃhāsana* 'lion-chair', by implication a throne: *prājñaśūrāryaguptam* 'guarded by wise Aryan heroes' (V.32.6). Thus there are men present in that area of the palace.

Likewise, Vidura tells the audience that,

> pitur antaḥpuraṃ dadyān matur dadyān mahānasam
>
> One should present the inner quarters to the father, one should present the kitchen to the mother.
>
> V.38.12

The gynaeceum is not a situation for repression and subjection, as in modern and western popular imagination; the audience hears, for example of how,

> punar antaḥpuragataḥ strīṇāṃ madhye vṛkodaraḥ
> yodhyate sma virāṭena siṃhair mattair mahābalaiḥ
>
> Bhīma was made to fight again in the center of the inner quarters, with powerful and maddened lions.
>
> IV.12.28

Although the court of king Virāṭa does manifest aspects of decadence, nevertheless life in the *zenana* or interior of the palace does not appear to be one of meekness, gentility, and a restricted femininity.

The *śuddhānta* 'sacred interior' is probably a more precise description of the quarter in the palace where a king would find privacy with wives or concubines; as where Saṃjaya describes to Dhṛtarāṣṭra how, *prayato'haṃ kṛtāñjaliḥ śuddāntaṃ prāviśaṃ* 'prudently, hands folded, I entered the sacred interior'.

Let us review the words used within a system of kinship and then scrutinize certain procedures by which kinship is established.

1. Terms

Terms of address where kinship is concerned are never historically exacting: they concern consanguinity, affinity, and descent. Bhīṣma is usually referred to by the epithet *pitāmaha* 'paternal grandfather', although he has no biological offspring; he is simply the most senior member—in terms of generation—of the clan. At one point he says to Arjuna—as Arjuna reports this—*nāhaṃ tātas tava pitus tāto'smi* 'I am not your father, I am your father's father', equating the two terms *pitā* and *tāta* (VI.103.88).

Correspondingly, Dhṛtarāṣṭra can be addressed as 'father' by someone like Yudhiṣṭhira, his nephew; and co-wives address the sons of their husband by other wives as 'son'. "The sons of a living king ... are often also called *rājan* 'king'."[8] Draupadī similarly refers to Bhīṣma as 'father-in-law' (V.80.30), and Dhṛtarāṣṭra, speaking with Yudhiṣṭhira, refers to the latter's 'two mothers' *mātarau* (XV.44.18).

Yudhiṣṭhira, when he is instructing the emissary Saṃjaya to pass on formal greetings to the members of Dhṛtarāṣṭa's court, begins first with the *vṛddhāḥ striyo* 'senior women', *yā jñāyante ... mātaras* 'who are known as mothers'. He then requests that Saṃjaya address 'our wives'.

> yā no bhāryāḥ saṃjaya vettha tatra
>
> Saṃjaya, you know our wives there.
>
> V.30.32

He requests that the emissary enquire as to their activities and how they behave with their parents-in-law. He then refers to their 'agreeable husbands' (*patayo'nukūlās*), implying that the husbands are not the Pāṇḍavas.

This is intriguing, and Yudhiṣṭhira is supposedly using the term *bhāryāḥ* to refer to married women who are part of the immediate family, that is, the wives of Draupadī's sons; for he immediately enquires as to his *snuṣāḥ* 'daughters-in-law' (V.30.34). He also asks Saṃjaya to ask after the well-being of the *veśastriyaḥ* 'the concubines', which would seem to indicate a certain prior familiarity.

Earlier, when Yudhiṣṭhira had been answering the riddles posed by his divine father, Dharma in the guise of a *yakṣa*, he had referred to Kuntī and Mādrī thus:

> yathā kuntī tathā mādrī viśeṣo nāsti me tayoḥ
>
> As with Kuntī, so with Mādrī: of the two there is no distinction for me.
>
> III.297.73

Again, in nominal terms, family is much more extensive than if it was merely described historically and in terms of derivation, for the generational relation is everything. It is also noteworthy that wives and

8. Scharfe 1989: 32.

daughter-in-laws are so closely linked—in speech—with concubines, reinforcing this structural form.

There is also a scale of affection displayed in these words of Yudhiṣṭhira's: he commences with the senior women, then the 'wives' and daughters-in-law, next come the girls, the *kanyās*, and then concubines, concluding with the servant-girls, *dāsīputrā* (V.30.37).[9]

When Yudhiṣṭhira and the old king are exchanging formal greetings and enquiring after the well-being of their respective retinues, Yudhiṣṭhira refers to Kuntī, first as *jananī* 'mother', but then in the next sentence as *mātā jyeṣṭhā* 'elder mother', implying an extended family nomenclature where kinship is not simply immediate but syntagmatic (XV.33.12).

Kinship—from the point of view of verbal address—is therefore a matter of synchronic relations and does not refer to situations particularly historical.[10] Thus Saṃjaya, in speaking to the old king Dhṛtarāṣṭra, speaks of his 'grandsons', Lakṣman and Abhimanyu—the sons of Duryodhana and of Arjuna respectively—when technically the latter is really a great-nephew (VII.45.14). Bhīṣma, in the same way, when addressing the paramour of his father, Satyavatī, addresses her saying, *adhiroha ratham mātar* 'mount the chariot, mother!' (I.94.91)[11] When he abducts the three girls from Kāśi, he treats them *snuṣā iva... bhaginya iva...yathā duhitaras* 'like daughters-in-law, like sisters, as if daughters', when he has in fact wooed or won them for his half brother (I.96.44).

Sons are vital to *kṣatriyas*, and given the complexity of kinship in the Mahābhārata the nature of son-ship is equally complicated. Certainly, it would seem that the relation between a father and a son is more important than any other kin relation: 'nothing greater than a son is known' (*na sutād vidyate param*; III.10.5); 'a wife has the fruits of [sexual] delight and of sons' (*ratiputraphalā dārā*; V.39.51).[12] 'The body is made twofold' (*aṅgaṃ dvidhā kṛtam*) by the birth of a son, says an aerial voice at the end of the Śakuntalā episode (I.69.31).

Dhṛtarāṣṭra, refers to the Pāṇḍavas as his 'sons' (*putrāḥ*) even though they are in fact nephews, but he does distinguish his true son,

9. The terms *dāsa* and *dāsī* are sometimes translated as 'slave', although the words actually refer to a client system of kinship and do not denote a chattel or property relation.

10. Benveniste 1969: I.213–214, makes a similar observation for the IE term for 'brother', "**bhrāter* dénotait une fraternité qui n'était pas nécessairement consanguine."

11. Demanding that she 'mount the chariot', from √*ruh*, has resonances with the formulas used during the *rākṣasa* marriage rite, when a girl is abducted.

12. Conversely, the 'absence of sexual union is the decrepitude of women' (*asaṃbhogo jarā strīṇām*; V.39.63).

Duryodhana in this respect as *mama dehāt prasūtaḥ* 'born from my body' (III.5.18).[13] Again, one observes that within these central marriage systems terms of address are not limited to genealogical relations but are used in a constitutional sense and polyandry and polygyny only compound such usage.

When Draupadī has collapsed during the *vanavāsa* 'forest residence', due to exhaustion and meagre living, Bhīma summons his son by another marriage, Ghaṭotkaca, and instructs him to carry *tava mātā* 'your mother' on his shoulders (III.145.4–5). This is despite the fact that Ghaṭotkaca is not only unrelated biologically to Draupadī but he is also not human, being a *rākṣasa*.

Bhīma, on meeting the ape-deity Hanūmān in Book Three, describes himself and his lineage as:

> kauravaḥ somavaṃśīyaḥ kuntyā garbheṇa dhāritaḥ
> pāṇḍavo vāyutanayo bhīmasena iti śrutaḥ
>
> Of the Kuru clan, belonging to the Lunar line, borne by the womb of Kuntī,
> of Paṇḍu, a son of Vāyu: Bhīma, I am known.
>
> III.147.3

The clan, the larger lineage, the mother, the husband of the mother, the father, and then himself: this is how Bhīma catalogues his genealogy, apparently on a scale where the mother is more significant than her husband and her mate. Paradigm is once again more important than actual genetic derivation: it is structure, not history that counts.

Karṇa, in his strangely unseasonal or disconnected conversation with Kṛṣṇa, when he speaks of kinship says that 'I was rightfully born a son of Pāṇḍu', even though his progenitor was actually the Sun: (*jātaḥ pāṇḍoḥ putro'smi dharmataḥ*; V.139.4). This again signifies that paternity derives its nature from a proximate system rather than anything directly lineal and genetic: which is a very different view of what constitutes fatherhood in contemporary Anglo-American society.[14] As Karṇa was not formally adopted by Pāṇḍu, as his half brothers were,

13. "It is English and other European languages that insist on a distinction between sons and nephews, brothers and cousins. Sanskrit and modern Indian languages treat *bratṛ*, *putra*, etc., as more general terms, which may be used in a broader and in a narrower sense." Thomas Burke, personal communication.

14. Where divorce procedures can often turn upon direct historical or biological generation. 'Divorce' in the Mahābhārata does not really appear to figure much: it is not a legal concept although 'repudiation' does occur. 'We are abandoned by our husbands' (*vayaṃ ... parityaktā bhartṛbhir*, perhaps approaches this procedure; III.219.3).

he is technically not the eldest Pāṇḍava and precluded from titular inheritance. Karṇa was adopted by a low-caste figure, and hence that is his position in life: a son remains at whatever rank he was socially incorporated.

For Karṇa was given to his foster mother *sauhṛdāt* 'because of affection' by his foster father who had discovered him floating on a river. She gave him milk 'because of love', *snehāt* (V.1139.5–6). So Karṇa, in his person, demonstrates three patterns of simultaneous kinship: biological, legal, and emotional.

It was for his foster mother that he would offer the *piṇḍa* 'ancestral offering', not to Kuntī. Also, it was his foster father who had the 'birth rites' (*jātakarma*) performed for him, and on Karṇa's coming of age, it was his foster father who found him 'wives' (*bhāryās*). With them, he had sons and grandsons, with whom his 'heart' (*hṛdayam*) had 'bonds of love' (*kāmabandhanam*; V.139.7–11).

After the same fashion, when Śaṃtanu had found a pair of twins in the forest—they had been conceived by an emission of semen and were, without a human mother, born from a reed—he had taken them *kṛpayā* 'with compassion', and,

> tataḥ saṃvardhayāmāsa saṃskārais cāpi ayojayat
>
> Then he reared the boys and also undertook their ceremonial rites.
>
> I.120.17

Karṇa—in his one exchange with Kṛṣṇa—states that his *āvāhās* and his *vivāhās*, 'giving in marriage', 'taking in marriage', were always performed according to the rank which he received from his foster father: with *sūtas*,'charioteer' families who are his foster rank (V.139.14).

2. Wooing and Marriage

For the young Janamejaya, for whom the Bhārata song was first performed, when it is time for him to marry, his ministers set off—as proxies—to accomplish the wooing.[15]

> ... tasya nṛpasya mantriṇāḥ
> suvarṇavarmāṇam upetya kāśipaṃ
> vapuṣṭamārthaṃ varayāṃ pracakrumuḥ

15. Bhīṣma, 'with the aged *kṣatriyas*' (*vṛddhaiḥ kṣatriyaiḥ*), similarly wooed on behalf of his father Śaṃtanu, going to the father of Satyavatī, the *dāśarāja* 'king of fishermen', and asks for her hand (I.94.67). He is described as *nāthaḥ paryāptaḥ ... kanyāyāś ... dānāya caiṣvaraḥ* 'an appropriate master ... husband for the gift of the girl' (I.94.81).

> The ministers of that king having approached Suvarṇavarman king of the Kāśis, they wooed for the sake of Vapuṣṭamā [the daughter].[16]
>
> I.40.8

The king of Kāśi—modern Benares—then 'gave Vapuṣṭamā' (*dadau vapuṣṭamām*), 'having made correct enquiries' (*parīkṣya dharmataḥ*).[17] It is remarkable that Janamejaya is marrying into the Kāśi clan, just as his ancestors had five generations previously: the pattern of exogamy continues through time.[18] On that prior occasion the wooing had been performed differently, by Bhīṣma, who used violence rather than speech to secure three brides by abduction.[19] Implicit in this system of wife-giving and wife-receiving is the function of hierarchy: rank is sustained.

After the same fashion, when Arjuna takes as a wife for his son Abhimanyu, the daughter of the Matsya *rāja*, Arjuna's grandmother, Satyavatī, had a brother who had been king of the Matsyas (I.57.51ff.) Again, one notes that the pattern of exogamy is maintained across generations. This is what Dumont refers to as "the repetition of intermarriage."[20]

Likewise, Mādrī, the co-wife of Kuntī, was purchased with great wealth: for the sake of his step-nephew, *vivāhaṃ kārayāmāsa bhīṣmaḥ pāṇḍor* 'Bhīṣma accomplished the marriage of Pāṇḍu (I.105.5–6). Again, the business of marriage is performed by a wooer, and in this case the wealth exchanged, the 'price', is arranged on that point. On this occasion the wealth represents bride price rather than dowry.[21]

Bhīṣma also secures a wife for Vidura—who is like a nephew to him—and 'having selected her he made the marriage' (*varayitvā tām, vivāhaṃ kārayāmāsa*; I.106.13). Once again, it is Bhīṣma who does the

16. The verb 'to woo' 2.√*vṛ*, is also the verb used for 'to choose', as when a girl 'chooses' in a *svayaṃvara*. It is the same verb that is employed when someone grants a favor, and also when someone chooses a favor.

17. At III.132.7, the expression used is not *dadau*, but *prādāt* 'to give in marriage' or 'to bestow': √*dā*, is typically the verb employed for a father's bestowal of a daughter upon a groom.

18. This demonstrates Dumont's point (1983: vii): "affinity is transmitted from generation to generation, is thus permanent or durable, and so has *equal status* with consanguinity, or a value equal to it." Concerning the distinction between the affinal and the consanguine, he writes that, such societies "make a simple, straightforward, symmetrical distinction between them, where we maintain a hierarchical distinction". "We" being the West.

19. See below, section 4.

20. Dumont 1983: viii.

21. In contrast, Gāndhārī brought a dowry when she married Dhṛtarāṣṭra (I.103.14). Marriage with a co-wife, it seems, requires different arrangements in terms of material transaction. This is also apparent when Arjuna takes a co-wife: see below.

wooing and arranging and then accomplishes the weddings for the clan. He, as the most ancient male of the clan, organizes the marital alliances of the younger scions.[22]

In the mythical days of old—before marriage was actually instituted—women were *anāvṛtāḥ* 'uncovered' and *kāmacāravihāriṇyaḥ svatantrās* 'roaming and indulging their desires, self-willed' (I.113.4).[23] Then, however, such random and transient conjugation was dharmic, as it was among animals. In epic times, however, when a woman is 'seasonal' she is not to be avoided. Nevertheless,

> śeṣeṣv anyeṣu kāleṣu svātantryaṃ strī kila arhati
>
> In the remaining other times, a woman may indeed have claim to her own will.
>
> I.113.26

The marital situations depicted by Mahābhārata confront the unique instance of polyandry that obtains between Draupadī and her five husbands without seeming to offer recognition: it is present but none emulate the situation. Apart from karmically, the epic does not explain this structure; one might hypothesize, but there is no data that can even illuminate the origin and rationale of this phenomenon.[24]

On the periphery of formal marital union, in terms of how sexual reproduction occurs in the Mahābhārata, a woman's spouse does not usually impregnate her and beget her child—ideally a son. Another male, divine or mortal, generally performs this function. It is as if lineage descends only nominally via the patriline and genetically through another branch. Neither Pāṇḍu nor Dhṛtarāṣṭra are conceived by their nominal father, nor does Pāṇḍu beget his own offspring: they owe their birth to an external genetic incursion.

Referring to a similar pattern, Bhīṣma, in his discourse to Satyavatī,

22. He is what Dumézil described as "le marieur" (1979: passim). Another instance of wooing occurs when *ṛṣi* Vasiṣṭha intercedes for Tapitī on behalf of the *gandharva* king Saṃvarana at I.162.14ff.

23. Much as Bachofen describes in 1948: II.238ff.

24. See below, Ch. VI.2. I.157.5ff. and I.189.1ff. supply the karmic explanation, given in terms of rebirth. To be thoroughly a priori, recherché, and non-inferential, one could say that, as the king during the *aśvamedha* was supposed to possess three wives in order that the ritual could be completed, so too Draupadī possesses three senior husbands, equivalent to: the *mahiṣī*, the 'chief wife', who would be the monogamous Yudhiṣṭhira; the *parivṛktā*, the 'avoided wife', who would be Bhīma; and the *vāvātā*, the 'favorite', Arjuna. This is merely an interesting notion. Nakula and Sahadeva do not figure much as spouses, apart from nominally.

who is demanding that he serve as procreator upon his brother's widows, tells of how, when all male *kṣatriyas* had been slaughtered, their widows turned to brahmin men in order to reproduce. For Bhīṣma, this circumstance where an appropriate man is not available is an instance of *āpad-dharma* 'crisis dharma' (I.97.26). He suggests to Satyavatī that his half brother Vyāsa beget sons upon the two widows of the deceased king, in order to sustain the lineage of the family.[25] The maternal brother, rather than the paternal brother is thus the progenitor.[26]

Wedded, the loyalty of a married woman is to her husband, not to her brothers: for culture displaces nature.[27] Once married, a woman has allegiance firstly to her affines.

> patisneho'tibalavān na tathā bhrātṛsauhṛdam
>
> The love of a wife is very powerful: not so the affection for a brother.[28]
>
> I.139.15

Yet Bhīṣma does make the definitive injunction that,

> yasyās tu na bhaved bhrātā pitā vā ... nopayaccheta tāṃ
>
> Of whom there would be no brother nor father ... one should not marry her.
>
> XIII.44.14

Such a woman, he says, is a *putrikā dharmiṇī*, that is, a virtuous 'daughter appointed to raise male issue to be adopted by a father who has no sons'.[29] In this case she does possess a male parent, but lacks a male sibling: her child of marriage is to be adopted by her father as his own son, in order that the obsequies might be performed correctly, for that father.

25. Sons are more important than daughters insofar as kingship—as a function—excludes the priority of women. 'In kingless states, there is no rain nor deities' (*arājakeṣu rāṣṭreṣu na asti vṛṣṭir na devatāḥ*; I.99.40).

26. Vyāsa's maternal grandmother is a fish, an unusual ancestor for the Kurus (I.57.49). Perhaps it is thus appropriate that Duryodhana, at the conclusion of his life retires to the depths of a lake (IX.29.54).

27. "Women's faithlessness to a husband ... will be like the wrong done in killing a foetus' (*vyuccarantyāḥ patiṃ nāryāḥ ... bhrūṇahatyākṛtaṃ pāpaṃ bhaviṣyati*; I.113.17).

28. Hiḍimbā, a *rākṣasī* 'demon', who speaks these words, chooses her own husband—that is, Bhīma—out of desire and without advice or constraint. He later weds Draupadī.

29. Olivelle 1993: 45 quotes from the Aitareya Brāhmana VII.13: "A wife is called a 'wife' [*jāyā*], / Because in her he is born again." "He" being the man, husband. This can also apply to the sonless father, with the birth of a grandson; what in classical Greece was considered the *epikleros* pattern of descent.

In his peroration upon the protocols of marriage, Bhīṣma does declare, however, that the cultural force for marriage should not become unconditional.

> na hy akāmena saṃvādaṃ manur evaṃ praśaṃsati
> ayaśasyam adharmyaṃ ca yan mṛṣā dharmakopanam
>
> Thus Manu does not urge an agreement without love:
> dishonored, unjust, and which is vain, irritating to dharma.
>
> XIII.44.22

He adds that woman should not live with a man whom she dislikes.[30] To conclude, even the tedious Vidura says that, *na kāmena striyaṃ jayet*, 'one should not win a women [only] with desire' (V.39.66).

The work of Dumézil and Jamison have delineated many of the patterns and forms of *vivāha* 'marriage' process in the Mahābhārata.[31] In the epic there are marriages that are arranged, those where capture of the bride is necessary and formal; and there is matrimony where a bride is the prize of competition. The first two of these form part of the scheme which Manu describes as the eight legally recognizable arrangements for sexual union. They formally relate to *varṇa* and are supplied in III.20–34 of the *dharmaśāstra.*[32] These categories of marital union are not strictly observed within the Mahābhārata and when marriages occur it is not always obvious what the paradigm is: *śāstra* and epic do not always coincide in their observance, and sometimes what is actually being observed is somewhat blurred.

As marriage is typically patrilocal, it is possible to say that *patayo bāndhavāḥ strīṇām* 'husbands are the kin of women' (V.34.36), implying that, for women, once they are married, primary kinship derives from the husband. The antithesis would not hold true for men.

30. The audience hears elsewhere, *na rocet ... patiḥ kumāryā iva ṣaṣṭivarṣaḥ* 'a husband of sixty years does not please a young woman (II.57.15). This proverb is repeated at III.6.15. Manu, III.8, prescribes that 'one should not marry a hairless girl' (*na udvahet ... kanyām ... alomikām*), the hair in this case being indicative of puberty.

31. Dumézil: 1979; Jamison: 1996,: 207ff. The term for marriage, *vivāha*, literally denotes a 'leading away' of a bride from her father's house. Jamison 2002: 70ff., examines how the usual operation of marriage can be reversed, where it is the queen who *gives away* a bride, a reversal of the usual *kanyā-dāna* 'gift of a maiden'.

32. Jamison 1996: 250 comments: "Texts concerning the types of marriage in ancient India thus show a thorough-going preoccupation with the type of *exchange* each involves, and the difficult cases of abduction (Rākṣasa) and mutual agreement (Gāndharva) test but do not pass beyond the limits of this exchange system."

The eight patterns are typified nominally as, the *brāhma* rite, the *daiva*, the *ārṣa*, the *prājāpatya*, the *āsura*, the *gāndharva*, the *rākṣasa*, and the *paiśaca* rite. Duḥṣanta, at I.67.8ff., adumbrates this system during the Śakuntalā wooing.[33] He says that the first four types are appropriate for a brahmin, the first six types for a *kṣatriya*, and the *rākṣasa* form is suitable for kings. Kaṇva, Śakuntalā's ascetic father, says that the *gāndharva* rite is best for *kṣatriyas*:

> kṣatriyasya hi gāndharvo vivāhaḥ śreṣṭha ucyate
>
> For the *gāndharva* marriage is considered the best for the *kṣatriya*.
>
> I.67.26

This, he adds, is 'without mantras' and 'secret' (*nirmantro rahasi*).

The first four forms of marriage occur when a father gives away his daughter: according to his choice, according to the rank of the groom, according to what he receives in exchange,[34] and according to—what seems to usually be—mutual acceptance rather than arrangement. The second four classes of marriage, according to Manu, occur when a groom offers a bride price, when the couple desire each other, by abduction, and by the rape of a sleeping, stupid, or intoxicated woman.

Manu considers that 'poets' (*kavi*) view only the seventh form of marriage, the *rākṣasa*, distinctly a *kṣatriya* form.[35] In Book One of the epic, Bhīṣma at *adhyāya* ninety-six, introduces the notion of *svayaṃvara*, where the intended bride is supposed to choose her spouse, although in fact the opposite is more common, where the bride is usually won by contest.[36] Manu ignores this form of union.

In the Anuśāsana *parvan*, Bhīṣma lists the conventionally accepted forms of marriage: here they are fivefold, unlike the eight which Manu describes. The first, the *brāhmaṇa* form, takes place when the father selects a groom who is *guṇavate vare* 'distinguished in quality'. The

33. "The most famous Gāndharva marriage in Indian literature." Jamison 1996: 249.

34. For example, when Śaṃtanu desires Satyavatī, he approaches her father and makes his request for the girl, and the father then binds him to a covenant that their child shall inherit Śaṃtanu's royal title (I.94.46–51). This would appear to be an *ārṣa* form of union.

35. Dumézil 1996: 35ff. offers a general overview of other legal texts and how they describe the eight acceptable varieties of marriage. Baudhāyana I.20.1–16; Nārada XII.38–44; Gotama IV.6–15; Viṣnu XXIV.17–28; Āpastamba 2.5.11.17–20, and 12.1–3; Vasiṣṭha I.28–35. Macdonell and Keith 1912, under the lexemes *pati*, *patnī*, examine the various dimensions of matrimony from a Vedic point of view.

36. Draupadī is definitely won by the successful contestant at the ceremony. Damayantī, on the other hand, actually selects her spouse. The term *svayaṃvara* covers both of these processes. See below.

second form of marriage is similar, but here the father offers a dowry: this is the marriage dharma, says Bhīṣma, 'of cultivated *kṣatriyas*' (*śiṣṭānāṃ kṣatriyāṇāṃ*; XIII.44.4). The acceptance of the *śulka* 'dowry or price' does not constitute marriage however, it is only the actual rite that confers this state. Bhīṣma is definite on this.

> na hy eva bhāryā kretavyā na vikreyā kathaṃcana
>
> A wife is never to be purchased nor to be sold.
>
> XIII.44.45

For marriage can only be 'established in the seventh step', that is, at the conclusion of the rite itself: *niṣṭā syāt saptame pade* (XIII.44.52).[37] Without this ceremony as sufficient condition, there is no marriage. *Kṣatriyas* are allowed two wives, brahmins three, he adds (XIII.44.10).[38]

The third, the *gāndharva* form of marriage, in this account, occurs when a father—contrary to his own wishes—gives a daughter to a man, when both man and woman are mutually desiring of each other. This is not an elopement, as in Manu. The *āsura* rite takes place when the groom secures the bride after offering a bride price. The final form of marriage, the *rākṣasa* rite, occurs when the girl is forcibly captured and removed, against the wishes of her kin and sometimes with violence done against her kin: *hatvā chitvā śīrṣāṇi* 'having struck and cut their heads'.

The question typically asked of a woman when she is encountered alone is, *kasya tvam asi* '*whose* are you'?[39] This formula is employed for both *gāndharva* and *rākṣasa* rites.

3. *The* svayaṃvara

The *svayaṃvara* is an Indo-European institution which occurs, for instance, when Penelope holds a contest in Scroll xxi of the Odyssey to

37. The seven steps refer to the seven paces that a couple make together about the fire towards the end of the marriage ritual. Seven steps shared together are traditionally also the fundamental ground for friendship.

38. In Vedic times "the king regularly has four wives attributed to him, the Mahiṣī, the Parivṛktī, the Vāvātā, and the Pālāgalī". Macdonell and Keith 1912, under the lemma *pati*. These names refer to, respectively, "the chief wife, the first one ... the neglected ... the favourite ... and the daughter of the last of the court officials." At II.16.16 in the epic, the audience hears of king Bṛhadratha: *sute yamaje ... upayeme* 'he married twin daughters', which is *hapax legomenon* in the poem. The girls were *rūpadraviṇasaṃmate* 'esteemed for wealth and beauty'.

39. At III.123.4. Hiḍimbā employs such language, usually addressed by a man: *kutas tvam asi ... kaś cāsi* (I.139.19).

determine whom she will select as a husband.[40] The father of Sītā, similarly, organizes such a competition in Rāmayāṇa.[41]

It is a *kṣatriya* institution, and when at Draupadī's *svayaṃvara* Arjuna, disguised as a Brahmin, succeeds, the assembled *kṣatriyas* raise an outcry: *svayaṃvaraḥ kṣatriyāṇām iti*, they say, 'the bride-choice is for *kṣatriyas*' (I.180.1ff.) What they do then is to attack Draupadī's father, the king and host, for allowing such an outrage to occur: something which is contrary to their dharma (I.180.11).

Before looking at the formal rite itself, let us briefly regard a few instances where it can be seen that women are the agents of non-ritual choice. In Book One there is an instance of what could be construed as an inchoate form of a non-ritual *svayaṃvara*: where there is no contesting by a band of suitors and the woman is literally deciding whom she wants as her man, simply on the basis of her own individual choice. In I.76.16, when Devayānī makes an outright proposal of marriage to Yayāti, she offers a prototype of this model of marriage, where a woman selects a husband. Earlier, she simply said to Kaca, her previously selected man:

> gṛhāṇa pāṇiṃ vidhivan mama mantrapuraskṛtam
>
> Take my hand with incantation, according to scriptural rule.
>
> I.72.5

To Yayāti she says, *bhartā ca me bhava* 'and be my husband!'. This is after only a couple of minutes of acquaintance with the man. He rejects her offer because she is the daughter of a brahmin and he is a *kṣatriya* and her father has not offered her to him: he will not accept her hand if she is *adattāṃ ca pitrā* 'not given by the father' (I.76.25). She insists that she has chosen him, and five *ślokas* later having gone to inform her father about her decision, the brahmin accepts his daughter's determination of husband and proclaims to Yayāti that the girl is *mayā dattām* 'given by me'. The only reference to the rite of marriage itself, is that Yayāti *kṛtvā pradakṣiṇam* 'he circumambulated [her] worshipfully' (I.76.35).[42]

40. In the cognate Greek epic corpus, athletic competition between young men is most typically associated with funeral games, as in Scroll XXIII of the Iliad. There are, however, agonistic events described in Scroll viii of the Odyssey which are related neither to death nor to marriage; as at I.124ff. in the Mahābhārata, where young men compete with weapons. Vernant 1974: Ch. III. passim, discusses the many various kinds of Greek *svayaṃvara*.

41. Rāmāyaṇa I.66.

42. Later, within his own household, he takes her to the *antaḥpura* (I.77.1). Macdonell and Keith 1912, under the lemma *pati*, concerning the wedding ceremony in Vedic times, have: "The ceremony commenced at the bride's house, to which the bridegroom with his friends and relations repaired ... A cow or cows were slain for the entertainment of the guests. The bridegroom having caused the bride to mount a stone, formally grasped her hand, and led

Later in the same story Śarmiṣṭhā, a high-born servant to Devayānī, informs Yayāti that she too has chosen him—not so much as husband—but as an impregnator: *me'si patir vṛtaḥ* 'you are my chosen master' (I.77.19). She discourses with him, trying to convince him about the propriety of her demand and informing him as to the dharma of the situation. He submits to her desire on three separate occasions, as:

> ṛtum vai yācamānāyā na dadāti pumān vṛtaḥ
> bhrūṇahā iti ucyate ...
>
> A chosen man [who] does not give an imploring woman her season is called an embryo-killer.
>
> I.78.32

Śarmiṣṭhā defends her action, when Devayānī questions her, by saying, 'for by dharma the husband of the friend becomes the husband' (*sakhībhartā hi dharmeṇa bhartā bhavati*; I.78.20). Śakuntalā, similarly, in describing her 'marriage' with Duḥṣanta, tells her father, *mayā patir vṛto yo'sau* 'that husband who was chosen by me' (I.69.31).

An earlier—both in the narrative and in the depiction of the form itself—pattern of the *svayaṃvara* occurs when Gaṅgā, who had assumed human form in order to bear the incarnation of the Vasus on earth, goes to King Pratīpa in order to become impregnated. She openly and without ado demands his compliance, *tvām ahaṃ kāmaye rājan* 'I desire you, king' (I.92.5). He refuses her and she then sits upon his thigh, but it is his right thigh, the place of children and daughters-in-law; the left thigh is the place of the *kāminī* 'the lover' (I.92.10). As Gaṅgā had not accomplished the correct protocol her desire was thus not to be perfectly fulfilled. She was thus only able to return later and couple with Pratīpa's son and so resume the place of daughter-in-law.[43]

Likewise, Śivā, when she seeks to seduce Agni, exhibits no hesitation or suppression of desire either, saying,

> maithunāyeha saṃprāptā kāmaṃ prāptaṃ drutaṃ cara
>
> I am arrived here for lovemaking. Without delay, perform the present love!
>
> III.214.6

---

her round the household fire. This act constituted the marriage, the husband hence being called 'he who takes by the hand' (*hasta-grābha*)."

43. In the Sukanyā micro-narrative in Book Three, Sukanyā is repeatedly asked by the Aśvins to 'choose' one of them (*varayasva*; III.123.7), *vṛṇīṣva* (18); and then, *vavre*, 'she chose' (19). Although this is not an instance of a *svayaṃvara*, the burden of the decision falls upon the woman and there exists a minor degree of choice.

This basic action of choice—concerning mating—whereby a woman selects a husband, is not only a *kṣatriya* practice, for when Pāṇḍu is in the forest in Book One, living a life of austerity, he tells the tale of a particularly ardent young woman.[44] She stood, *puṣpeṇa … snatā niśi … catuṣpathe* 'with a flower, bathed, in the night at a crossroad', and there, *varayitvā dvijam siddham* 'having chosen a perfected brahmin' she lived with him and produced three sons (I.111.34).[45]

The *rākṣasī* Hiḍimbā similarly falls in love with Bhīma in the forest and announces her love for him: *nānyaṃ bhartāram icchāmi* 'I choose no other husband', *bhajasva mām* 'choose me', *bhartā bhava mama* 'be my husband', she pleads enthusiastically (I.139.23–25). She instructs him to, 'mount my hip' (*āruhemāṃ mama śroṇīm*), so that she can protect him from her voracious demon-brother and they can fly away (I.140.5). As we have seen, mounting one's darling upon the hip is something that men usually do to certain classes of women and children. The coy offer does work, however, and Bhīma's heart is immediately captivated. He replies with many flattering endearments as he describes the power of his own anatomy and strength (I.140.7–10). Hiḍimbā later informs Kuntī that, *vṛto mayā bhartā tava putro* 'your son is chosen by me as husband' (I.142.9).

Nevertheless, before the *kautukamaṅgala* 'marriage thread'[46] is tied upon Bhīma, Hiḍimbā formally requests of Kuntī, in the presence of Yudhiṣṭhira, that she be permitted to marry her chosen spouse: an interesting reversal of the norm where a groom requests the hand of a bride from his prospective in-laws (I.143.9). This is the first marital union to occur among the Pāṇḍava sons.

The actual *svayaṃvara* rite takes two basic forms: the first, where the bride—like Damayantī—simply chooses her future spouse; the second, where the bride—like Draupadī—selects the victor from among suitors who have competed for her.[47] Damayantī selects Nala as her husband

44. In response to this tale, Kuntī tells Pāṇḍu the story of a devoted wife who had no sons, who became impregnated 'by the corpse' (*śavena*) of her deceased husband, such was her strength of fidelity (I.113.15–33).

45. At the *svayaṃvara* of the daughter of Yayāti, the father travels to a hermitage with the girl and two of her brothers in a chariot: there, he holds the rite. She declines all the *varās* 'suitors' and chooses the forest as her spouse, where she lived like a 'deer' (*mṛgacāriṇī*; V.118.5–8).

46. Literally, 'the garland of ceremony' (I.143.17).

47. Benveniste 1969: I.239, would assert that a woman does not marry, but is married: "elle entre dans la «condition d'épouse», recevant ainsi une fonction plutôt qu'accomplissant un acte." Marriage is "non un acte, mais une destination," ibid: 243.

according to unconstrained volition (III.54.25), which is not the case when Draupadī is won by Arjuna after a trial of weapons.[48]

Bhīṣma, in answer to Yudhiṣṭhira's questioning about 'the root of all dharma' (*mūlaṃ sarvadharmāṇām*), speaks 'of begetting, of the household ... of the ancestors, the deities, and of guests' (*prajanasya gṛhasya ca ... pitṛdevātithīnāṃ ca*) and of the conditions in which a girl should select her own spouse. Concerning this latter situation,

> trīṇi varṣāṇy udīkṣeta kanyā ṛtumatī satī
> caturthe tv atha saṃprāpte svayaṃ bhartāram arjayet
>
> A girl, being fertile, should wait three years;
> but when the fourth is arrived, she should procure a husband herself.
>
> XIII.44.15

In this case, the situation is one where her father has failed to obtain a spouse for her. The only qualifying conditions here are that the groom must not marry a woman who is:

> asapiṇḍā ca yā mātur asagotrā ca yā pitur
>
> One who is not of the same clan as the father, and not of the same ancestral kin as the mother.[49]
>
> XIII.44.17

For, *taṃ dharmaṃ manur abravīt* 'Manu declared that dharma'. The possibility for incest is implicit in such cases where exogamy is so particularly constrained.

Although *svayaṃvara* is usually termed a "self-choice" of the bride, selection in fact usually occurs by virtue of a martial trial in which the victor is garlanded—the de facto "choice"—by the bride. There might perhaps exist a token of discretion, for, as Drupada advises his daughter:

> vidhyeta ya imaṃ lakṣyaṃ varayethāḥ śubhe'dya tam

48. I.179.15–23. In Rāmāyaṇa I.65, Sītā is given to Rāma after he has triumphed in martial accomplishment: this is the *vīryaśulka* 'having valor as a bride price'. "The vīrya is the fighting ... and serves as a substitute for a more material śulka, like cows or gold, to be expected in so many epic weddings ... In this way the fighting is brought within the orthodox system of gift and countergift, and the abduction made equivalent to other types of marriages." Jamison 1996: 225.

49. Monier-Williams defines *sapiṇḍa* as 'a kinsman connected by the offering ... to certain deceased ancestors ... the kinship is through six generations in an ascending and descending line ...' This applies on both the male and feminine side.

Whoever would pierce that mark, choose him now, O lovely one!

I.177.22

To begin, when Damayantī's father becomes aware that *svāṃ sutāṃ prāptayauvanām* 'his daughter had obtained adolescence', he determines to hold a *svayaṃvara* for her (III.51.7). He only assembles 'kings' (*mahīpālās*) for this rite. The deities or 'world guardians' (*lokapālās*) hear of the ceremony from the *ṛṣi* Nārada, and among them Indra, Agni, Varuṇa, and Yama decide to attend. This is a supernatural occasion, for deities do not usually take a direct interest in non-solemn human rites.

Nala, whom Damayantī is already completely in love with due to the fortuitous intercession of a wise goose, makes his way into the town and to her quarters where they meet. She tells him,

tvatkṛte hi mayā vīra rājānaḥ saṃnipatitāḥ

For it is on your account [that] kings are assembled by me, O hero!

III.53.3

Here the agonistic procedure of the *svayaṃvara* does not obtain and the ritual is engaged with an express purpose of drawing Nala into the palace, where the princess might select him as spouse. Even though the two have already exchanged hearts, as it were, Damayantī must nevertheless still proceed with the appearance of this ritual. There is no competition, unlike the other similar rites of which the audience has heard; and so this event actually does function as a "self-choice," although the selection has occurred prior to the ceremony. She says,

yadi ced bhajamānāṃ māṃ pratyākhyāsyasi mānada
viṣam agniṃ jalaṃ rajjum āsthāsye tava kāraṇāt

If you repudiate me who am devoted [to you], O honorable one,
I shall resort to rope, water, fire or poison, because of you.

III.53.4

This is not a choice among potential husbands, but a threat in order to provoke his decision. The possibility of suicide is invoked in order to intimidate or ensure.[50] Feminine determination is not to be deflected for it becomes wrathful, which is often the case with *kṣatriya* women in the poem.

She tells him, *tvāṃ ... varayiṣye* 'I shall choose you', even though all the deities will also be there, similarly seeking her hand. There is no

50. A not uncommon occurrence in the Mahābhārata, where someone—man or woman—will threaten death in order to achieve a point. Yudhiṣṭhira does this at XII.27.22, saying that he intends to enter *prāya* 'meditative suicide'.

question of any contest nor of her equivocation. This is literally a "self-choice."

On the appropriate day many royal and splendid suitors assemble in the *raṅga* 'arena' (III.54.3ff.) Damayantī appears, and her radiant beauty captures the hearts of them all as their names are announced. Five Nalas appear before her eyes, as the four deities have taken on this guise hoping to confuse Damayantī and be selected themselves. This is reminiscent of Draupadī's marriage to five husbands: for the tale is after all, being told to Yudhiṣṭhira as a parable or fable concerning his own person.

Damayantī chooses the real Nala, by virtue of a "truth act," a moral convention in ancient India.[51] In this, the performer states: if X is true, then may Y be true also, and such a statement has the power of moral suasion. The key terms are *yathā* 'if, as' and *tena satyena* 'by this truth' (III.54.18).[52] This makes Damayantī's *svayaṃvara* unique, for she displays neither dubiety nor hesitation in the selection of her mate: the ceremony simply confirms her prior choice. Her purity and desire compel the deities to reveal their identities, so that she might choose Nala: thus, *naiṣadhaṃ varayāmāsa... dharmeṇa* 'she chose Nala according to *dharma*' (III.54.25).[53] Feminine probity has great causal power, as is evidenced on other occasions in the epic; it is in fact one of the dynamic forces of the poem.

'She took the edge of his clothing', and 'threw a very beautiful garland on his shoulder' (*vastrānte jagrāha... skandhadeśe'sṛjac cāsya srajaṃ paramaśobhanāṃ*). A cry of *hā hā* issues from the assembled kings: how one exclaims in Sanskrit. Gods and *ṛṣis* all shout 'good, good' (*sādhu sādhu*). As gifts, the deities offer Nala divine 'favors' (*varān*): one of these being the production of twin children (III.54.28).

At the end of the proceedings Nala offers up a 'horse sacrifice', the

51. See Brown 1972. There is a performative action taking place, whereby speech has efficacy. The speech act is a similar act of illocution but lacks the *if-then* binary quality of the truth-act statement. Given the correct context, a pronouncement can cause change to occur socially. Promises, vows, commands, curses, etc., these are some of the kinds of speech act. Both truth acts and speech acts are performative and make something happen by virtue of the utterance. Austin 1975: 6: "The term 'performative' will be used in a variety of cognate ways and constructions, much as the term 'imperative' is. The name is derived, of course, from 'perform', the usual verb with the noun 'action': it indicates that the issuing of the utterance is the performing of an action."

52. The wife of Indra, Śacī, makes such a truth act at V.13.22 in the *Indravijayopākhyānam*. The import of this particular story is that the wife of Indra is instrumental in saving Indra from dereliction and defeat.

53. The language is similar when a man likes a woman and approaches her father for the hand of his daughter: [*tāṃ*] *varayāmāsa sa ca tasmai dadau nṛpaḥ* 'he chose [her] and that king gave [her] to him (III.116.2).

aśvamedha, as token of his joy and success (III.54.36). So concludes this most lavishly and lovingly described marriage ceremony, which Indian poets have long celebrated in their songs; in Indian culture even today, this tale is an epitome of unalloyed romance. It is a story where the feminine behaves as the dynamic partner.

Secondly, at Draupadī's rite, her father, Drupada had been inclined towards Arjuna even before the ritual actually occurred, knowing of the hero's prowess. He says, *dharmeṇa vindeta sutāṃ mama* 'may he rightly marry my daughter!' (I.185.19).[54]

Her *svayaṃvara*, the most prominent in the epic, is the centerpiece of a *devamahotsava* 'a divine and great festival', attended by many brahmins (I.175.11). Poets, dancers, wrestlers, eulogists, and conjurors are present at the *kautūlaha* 'the celebration', and great wealth is distributed by her sponsoring father in the form of cattle and food; it is a munificent and spectacular occasion (I.175.14–16). The place of contest itself, the 'festival enclosure' (*samājavāṭa*), is profusely decorated, luxuriously furnished with tents and carpets, perfumed and gay with flowers and sonorous with music. Within this opulent stadium the many guests congregate (I.176.16–25). Seers, brahmins, kings, as well as the town populace and many deities, all make their way to this great and public ceremony. Draupadī is described as a *kanyā* 'girl, virgin, or daughter'.[55]

In order to win the bride the champion had to string a 'massive bow, not to be strung' *dṛḍham dhanur anāyamyaṃ*, and successfully shoot at a difficult target (I.176.11). Only on the sixteenth day of the festivities does Draupadī actually appear: she is described as entering the 'concourse' (*raṅga*), carrying a *vīrakāṃsyam* 'a hero-cup', something that is made of gold (I.176.30). It is her brother Dhṛṣṭadyumna who speaks, opening the contest and offering his sister. He then announces the names and lineage of the contestants and advises his sister to select the victor.[56] It is at this moment that Kṛṣṇa first makes his entry into the poem (I.178.8).

At the sight of Draupadī the five disguised Pāṇḍavas are 'struck with arrows of love' (*kandarpabāṇābhihatā*; I.178.12). The metaphor of

54. See below, Ch. IV, where the life of Draupadī is specifically examined.

55. In the *Tharu Barka Naach* (ed. Meyer and Deuel 1998: 31ff.), the refrain to the stanzas of the Third Song is, "The one chosen by Princess Draupadi will be immortal forever." Her choice in the svayaṃvara confers such superhuman benison to the selected spouse. The *Barka Naach* is a contemporary Nepalese dramatic song cycle performed by the Tharu people.

56. When Bhīṣma attends the *svayaṃvara* at Kāśi, as the names of the kings are proclaimed, Bhīṣma makes his choice and seizes the girls: *vārayāmāsa tāḥ ... ratham āropya tāḥ* (I.96.6–7).

the arrow here nicely reverses the actual process of the trial. Arjuna of course triumphs and flowers rain from the sky: it is as if this moment is a miraculous cosmic event presaging great fertility. Draupadī goes up to him, *utsmayantī* 'smiling', and makes the required gesture of garlanding the winner and follows her new husband out of the arena as his 'wife'.

The assembled guests—splendid kings—are enraged, for Arjuna is disguised as a mendicant brahmin and no non-*kṣatriya* should enter the lists; they try to attack the five brothers. Arjuna and Bhīma easily repel them, the former using the bow that he had just strung and which had become his 'dowry' (*śulka*; I.181.4).

In the wedding procession—after the contest has been decided and after Draupadī has been taken and has spent a night with her new husbands—the priest of Drupada leads the way, followed by the Pāṇḍavas on their chariots, who are followed by Draupadī together with Kuntī (I.186.3). This is the *vivāha* proper, 'the wedding'. They walk to where Drupada has prepared a celebration feast, *janyārtham annam*, literally 'food for the groom'.

There is displayed a great quantity of material wealth—cattle, textiles, tools, furnishings, and also of weaponry: bows, chariots, horses, armor, spears—for these are *kṣatriyas*. In a pre-monetary society wealth exists only in the physical form of 'goods', *vasūni* or *dravyāṇi* (I.186.14), and this is presumably some of the bride's trousseau, and constitutes—in part—her dowry. After this procession arrives at the court, it is Kuntī who takes Draupadī and leads her into the *antaḥpura* of Draupadī's father, where she is greeted by the women: 'they saluted her' (*pratyarcayāṃcakrur*; I.186.9).

The escorting of the new bride into her own family's women's quarters by the bride's mother-in-law is an unusual moment, for Draupadī should be performing the introduction to the women of her father's family, and not her widowed mother-in-law. One would expect that Kuntī would be the figure to lead her new daughter-in-law into the *antaḥpura* of her own Pāṇḍava household and not into that of Draupadī's father.

The fact that Kuntī lacks any court or domicile at this moment in the narrative and that she accompanies her footloose and incognito sons in their peripatetic life is a key determinant in this reversal. What one can observe at this instant is an occasion where, following the *svayaṃvara*, the women of either side of the marriage endorse their relationship with the newly incorporated bride. Marriage establishes an attachment not merely between a man and woman but moreover cements the affinity between pertinent women.

The place or presence of the bride is focal to this exchange of wealth—she is the key token—and these goods are not only luxury or elite items and weaponry, but often simply accumulated chattels: as with cattle or rope or hides (I.186.5).[57] On a similar occasion, Pāṇḍu returns to his wife and palace from a campaign, bringing booty—wealth obtained by warfare or from tribute—and:

> bhīṣmāya satyavatyai ca mātre copajahāra saḥ
>
> He offered [it] to his mother, to Satyavatī, and to Bhīṣma.
>
> I.106.1

Here, the wealth arriving at the palace is thus initially given to the triumphant king's mother and grandmother and then to the most ancient patriarch of the clan, one who holds an ostensibly avuncular position: the superiors of the family.[58]

It is only at the wedding feast a day or so later and prior to the actual marriage rites with Draupadī that Yudhiṣṭhira announces the true identity of himself and brothers (I.187.8ff.). For when the *svayaṃvara* had been held and the son of King Drupada had acted as herald and announced the names of the competitors, the Pāṇḍavas, disguised as poor and itinerant brahmins, went unheralded. This moment at the feast counts as the formal instant of disclosure and recognition.[59]

The ritual is concluded by the customary ceremony of marriage in which the partners circumambulate the sacred fire led by a priest, the man having taken the woman's hand. The father-in-law, Drupada, instructs Arjuna: *vidhivat pāṇim gṛhṇātu* 'take her hand properly' (I.187.21). Yudhiṣṭhira immediately corrects him, informing the king that Draupadī shall become polyandrous:

> sarveṣāṃ dharmataḥ kṛṣṇā mahiṣī no bhaviṣyati
>
> Draupadī shall rightly become the queen of us all.
>
> I.187.22

57. At I.191.13ff. there is given a comprehensive list of the kinds of wealth that are being exchanged, or offered, in this case by Kṛṣṇa, including *suvarṇaṃ ... akṛtakam* 'unworked gold'.

58. Similarly, at the end of the poem, it is the elder women, Kuntī along with Gāndhārī, who 'stipulate the obligations' (*saṃdiṣṭāś cetikartavyam*) to Draupadī and other wives who are about to leave the two senior women in the forest and return back towards Hāstinapura (XV.44.50).

59. They ironically expose their *kṣatriya* and non-brahmin identity by ignoring the wealth of gifts offered and only show interest in the weapons which are presented: *utkramya sarvāṇi vasūni tatra / sāṃgrāmikāny avivíśur nṛvīrāḥ* (I.186.14).

The prospective father-in-law hesitates and suggests that Kuntī and his son Dhṛṣṭadyumna discuss the matter, *kathayantv itikartavyam* 'let them discuss what is to be done', he says (I.187.31). Again, it is Kuntī, the mother-in-law who actually sees to the arrangements.[60] King Drupada continues to cavil on the following day when Vyāsa appears. He says,

> na ca dharmo'py anekasthaś caritavyaḥ sanātanaḥ
>
> So eternal dharma founded on multiplicity [polyandry] is not to be conducted.
>
> I.188.8

Vyāsa convinces him of the rectitude of the situation, however, and the wedding proceeds, with many guests and much decorative festivity and further displays of wealth (I.190.7ff.).

After the ceremonies have concluded, 'the women of Drupada' (*nāryo drupadasya*) approach Kuntī and touch her feet with their heads (I.191.2). Again, one observes the importance of the mother-in-law. Draupadī, *kṣaumasaṃvītā kṛtakautumaṅgalā* 'wearing a marriage thread, dressed in linen', approaches to make her obeisance; and Kuntī *avadat premṇā* 'spoke with affection'.[61]

To conclude, the *svayaṃvara* is a *kṣatriya* practice for marital selection; it is generally a male rite of contest, but not always, as we have seen in the case of Damayantī. The actual ritual of marriage remains separate and is not specifically a *kṣatriya* affair. As with other forms of matrimony there exists a movement of wealth, which appears to be in the form of dowry and is presented at the nuptial rite.

This is an athletic contest among warriors, in which events from the battlefield—specifically archery or the stringing of a bow—are removed from the domain of death and bloodletting, and made simply agonistic and contentional.

4. Tke rākṣasa *Form of Marriage*

The Mānava *dharmaśāstra* describes this form of marriage rite as:

> hatvā chittvā ca bhittvā ca krośantīṃ rudatīṃ gṛhāt
> prasahya kanyāharaṇaṃ rākṣaso vidhir ucyate

60. When the war finally approaches, however, it is this father-in-law to whom the Pāṇḍavas turn and whom they appoint as their leader: the *senapati* 'commander' of the force (V.149.16). Then his authority is ultimate in the male domain of violence.

61. This *kautukamaṅgala* 'the ceremony with a marriage thread preceding marriage' is mentioned in the Mahābhārata, as at I.143.17, but is never actually described.

> The capture of a girl forcibly from a house, weeping and crying, having struck and cut and broken: this is known as the *rākṣasa* rite.
>
> III.33

In this traditionally *kṣatriya* form of marriage, a young woman is abducted and taken away on a chariot, her abductor performing certain formulaic verbal protocols in the process.[62] The cutting and striking refers to what the abductor does to the male kin of his captive bride. Like the *svayaṃvara*, this is also an Indo-European custom and Jamison has dealt succinctly with this kind of ceremony.[63] Helen, in the Greek tradition, could be said to have been "married" according to this practice, as too was Persephone.[64]

I would like to consider four variations upon the theme of this ritual, as it concerns Duryodhana, Arjuna, Jayadratha, and Bhīṣma.

A completely and clearly successful form of the *rākṣasa* rite occurs in Book Twelve, at a *svayaṃvara* in Rājapura in Kaliṅga, where Duryodhana, accompanied by his henchman Karṇa, was one of the kings seeking to obtain a spouse. When all the suitors had taken seats,

> viveśa raṅgaṃ sā kanyā dhātrīvarṣadharānvitā
>
> The girl entered the arena, accompanied by eunuchs and nurses.
>
> XII.4.10

Then, as the names of the kings were announced, the girl *atyakrāmat* 'neglected' Duryodhana, which displeased him, and *nāmarṣayata laṅganam* 'he did not tolerate the violation'.

62. There is the near phonetic coincidence of terms for 'victory', what all *kṣatriya*s desire, and 'wife': *jaya* and *jāyā*.

63. Jamison 1996: 218ff. This form of marriage is "a thoroughly rule-governed, inherently unruly act," (235): "Most ... codified types of marriage in ancient India involve the *gift* of the maiden by the father ... Since the *Kṣatriya's* ideology bars him from accepting gifts, he is thus theoretically prevented from participation not only in marriage but in society itself. Rule governed abduction is the uneasy solution."

64. See Leduc, in Pantel 1992: 239–294. Randhawa 1996: 64, describing a similar situation in modern western India today states that, "The main ways of winning a bride are by 'capture', elopement, exchange, service of the prospective groom in the girl's house (*beena* marriage), sometimes in lieu of bride price, and mutual consent. Marriage by capture has several aspects of historical significance; perhaps it arose out of a shortage of girls in the clan (infanticide?); or it could be that having a wife as a captured trophy reflected favourably on the tribal's machismo and valour. Now, however, the 'capture' is a ritual, more feigned than real, the form being gone through later, just for the fun of it, after everything has been negotiated. Etiquette requires that the bride put up a token resistance."

pratyaṣedhac ca tāṃ kanyām asatkṛtya narādhipān
ratham āropya tāṃ kanyām ājuhāva narādhipān

Having restrained that girl, he ignored the kings.
Having mounted the girl on the chariot he challenged the kings.

XII.4.12–13

The assembled kings then give vociferous pursuit. Karṇa drives the chariot as *sūta*, whilst they are assailed by various missiles. Their pursuers are soon overwhelmed and relinquish the girl, who is thus successfully married according to form. This is the classically correct pattern of the *rākṣasa* rite.

Arjuna during his ascetic year away from Draupadī and his brothers, having met and joined up with Kṛṣṇa, visits Mount Raivataka. There he spies the Kṛṣṇa's sister, Subhadrā, and is smitten with yearning for her.

dṛṣṭvaiva tām arjunasya kandarpaḥ samajāyata

Having observed her, love was born for Arjuna.

I.211.15

'Love' (*kandarpa*) can also be glossed as 'lust' or 'desire', for it is both sexual and emotional.

Arjuna asks Kṛṣṇa for her hand, and is told, *svayaṃvaraḥ kṣatriyāṇāṃ vivāhaḥ*, 'the *svayaṃvara* is the marriage for *kṣatriyas*'.[65] He says that he will speak to his father about her for Arjuna, but soon qualifies this by adding that 'forcible abduction ... is enjoined as the mode of marriage for heroes' (*prasahya haraṇaṃ ... praśasyate vivāhahetoḥ śūrāṇām*; I.211.21–22). 'Take her', he says, *hara*! This is a cross-cousin marriage, where a son marries his mother's brother's daughter, and is a form of union typical of many cultures where the matriline is to be sustained; in fact, in many such cultures this form of marriage is virtually compulsory.[66]

Before embarking on this abduction, Arjuna sends to Yudhiṣṭhira at Indraprastha in order to obtain his elder brother's consent: this marriage will acquire for Arjuna a wife who will technically be a co-

65. Kṛṣṇa had taken his own wife at a *svayaṃvara*, mentioned at VII.10.10, and also given in the Bhāgavata Purāṇa X.53–54. The other kings whom he had defeated in this rite were 'yoked to his nuptial chariot' like horses (*rathe vaivāhike yuktāḥ*), an unusual if not unique increment to the ritual (VII.10.11). In Harivaṃsa LXXXVII.41ff., the abduction is again described.

66. Ostor et al. 1982; Lévi-Strauss 1958, Ch. II passim. The actual term for 'cousin', *bhrātṛvya*, is unusual in the Mahābhārata. I am grateful to Susan Rosenfield for this observation.

wife to Draupadī. This is not a mere liaison that he is indulging in, but a formal union that has great political import for both clans involved, the Pāṇḍavas and the Vṛṣṇis. In this case, therefore, consensus on the part of the potential husband's male kin is necessarily sought prior to the abduction.

Arjuna sets off on a chariot well-equipped with weapons as if to go hunting. 'Having run up to her' (*abhidrutya*) 'he mounted her on his chariot' (*āropayad ratham*; I.212.7); he then proceeds to drive away.[67] Kṛṣṇa says to the outraged Vṛṣṇis, justifying Arjuna's action: *hṛtavān kanyām dharmeṇa pāṇḍavaḥ* 'Arjuna took the girl rightfully' (I.213.5).[68] Later, Arjuna formally holds a *vivāha* 'wedding' at her paternal household and not back with his own kin, which would indicate how formal the abduction had been (I.213.12).[69]

After Subhadrā has been accepted into the Pāṇḍava household—by Draupadī in particular—Kṛṣṇa and his brother visit Indraprastha with gifts: *dadau ... janyārthe dhanam uttamam* 'he gave great wealth for purposes of the groom', and 'the gift of kinship', (*jñātideyam*), presumably the dowry of Subhadrā (I.213.40).[70] Both male and feminine seem to receive gifts on this occasion; this is not simply a case of offering a bride price or dowry, but appears more like an official and mutual exchange of valued objects. It is 'a flood of jewels and wealth' (*mahādhanaratnaugho*) which binds the political allegiance: a 'great river' (*mahānadaḥ*), which entered 'the Pāṇḍu-ocean' (*pāṇḍusāgaram*; I.213.50–51).[71]

Even when there is no exchange of gifts there is usually some form of avowal or promise: something is always surrendered by one side or party to the union. Vyāsa, for example, when he makes love with the widows of his half brother, only does so after they have promised to accomplish something that he demands; there is a *vrata*, an 'avowal' (I.99.38). Desire in the Mahābhārata is rarely ever without an economy of sorts, either verbal or material.

67. 'He seized the wife' (*labdhavāṃs tatra ... bhāryām*; I.55.33).

68. Later in the poem, Arjuna himself says to Kṛṣṇa, 'you carried off your Bhoja queen having conquered Rukmin in battle' (*avākṣir mahiṣīṃ bhojyāṃ raṇe nirjitya rukmiṇam*; (III.13.28).

69. Sītā, in Hanūmān's account of her 'abduction' is *hṛtā* (III.147.30), as too is Devasenā, who is *hṛtā* when her abductor 'desires to take her' (*jihīrṣati*; III.213.16). 'Rape' is perhaps too strong a word to use in translation here, as a recognized formality is at play and the violence is conventional and *only* concerns the male kin of the potential bride.

70. This wealth—and it is all *moveable* wealth—consists of chariots and horses, cattle, mares, mules, women, gold, elephants with trappings, and gems (I.213.41ff.)

71. See below, Ch. VI.1, for this image of women and rivers.

Remarkably, it is not Arjuna who accepts this wealth, but Yudhiṣṭhira. It is questionable if this exchange constitutes an actual marriage gift rather than serving as the substance which secures what is in reality the most singularly crucial political alliance of the poem (I.213.52). Gifts, as we know, are given as a means of establishing reciprocity and equivalence: they formalize a conventional relationship.[72] Thus, when the Vṛṣṇis depart and return homeward, they leave taking with them 'beautiful jewels', given by the Pāṇḍavas (I.213.56).

Thus, first there was the stylized taking of a bride—an appropriate cousin—into a household, then an exchange of gifts, followed by the certainty of *saṃbandha* 'alliance'. The bride thus augments not only an existing kinship structure, but is the causal figure in generating a coalition of clans.[73]

It is significant that the paternal figure who conducts the various coming-of-age rituals for the son of this marriage—Abhimanyu—is not the genetic father but his *mātula* 'maternal uncle', Kṛṣṇa: *kṛṣṇaś ca cakre tasya kriyāḥ* 'Kṛṣṇa performed his rites' (I.213.64). Again, one observes the importance of a son's mother's brother exceeding that of his father.

During their time in the forest the Pāṇḍavas one day go hunting together, leaving Draupadī alone in the hermitage at Kāmyaka. Jayadratha, king of the Sindhus, happens to be driving past on his chariot and sees her. Being in a mood of *vivāhakāma* 'desiring marriage', he is instantly smitten with desire (III.248.6). The model of a transient king coming across a beautiful woman in a forest hermitage is not a usual one, the audience has heard this before, most notably and famously with Śakuntalā. It is a situation that recurs in the Rāmāyaṇa, with great effect.[74]

Jayadratha sends a messenger to enquire as to who she is. He does not use the usual formula of *kasya tvam* 'whose are you?', but merely

72. See Mauss 1950.

73. The great-grandson of this union is Janamejaya, the king to whom the Mahābhārata is ostensibly sung. Sidhanta 1929: 147, observes: "... even in the more martial parts [of the epic], kinship and ties of marriage seem to have played a prominent part ... in forming and cementing military alliances." He cites Drupada of Pāñcāla, Virāṭa of Matsya, and Kṛṣṇa of Dvāraka, as three crucial allies who also created marriage links with the Pāṇḍavas. Each of these three marriages is of a completely different form: the *svayaṃvara*, the—presumably—*brāmana*, and the *rākṣasa* respectively.

74. Jamison 1996: 226–232 examines this scene in the poem. "These verses are so-called 'irregular' Triṣṭubhs and, as such, belong to the oldest, *Kṣatriya* core of our surviving Mahābhārata, as convincingly argued by M. C. Smith."

says, *kā tvam* 'who are you?', implying her lack of affiliation (III.249.1).[75] He appropriately describes his companions with due protocol and only then enquires as to whose wife and daughter she is.

Draupadī, *avekṣya mandam* 'having idly perceived [him]', lets slips a branch that she is holding, and demurely draws in her outer garment. She says bashfully, *buddhyā abhijānāmi ... na mādṛśī tvām abhibhāṣṭum arhā* 'I know, in my mind ... I am not worthy to address you' (III.250.2).

There is a languid coyness about Draupadī's manner here, this queen who possesses such a ferocious and merciless temper. She is anxious about being alone and speaking with him as it offends her *svadharma* 'decorum'. Draupadī is also obliged to observe the dharma which she must perform for guests, her *atithisvadharma* (III.250.9). She must invite him and his retinue to her household and she has to offer hospitality to them: food and water to wash their feet.

Jayadratha says to his messenger,

> darśanād eva hi manas tayā me'pahṛtaṃ bhṛśam
>
> At the sight of her, my mind is greatly captivated.
>
> III.251.4

He then enquires if she is human or not, and goes over to meet her.[76] Then he says,

> ehi me ratham āroha sukham āpnuhi kevalam
>
> Come! Mount my chariot! Obtain utter bliss![77]
>
> III.251.14

He tells her to forget her husbands, and, *bhāryā me bhava*, 'become my wife!'

Draupadī, *kāṅkṣamāṇā bhartṝṇām ... vilobhayāmāsa paraṃ vākyair* 'expecting her husbands, perplexed the other with speech' (III.251.21).

75. This is the usual formulation of greeting given to a solitary woman who is a possible lover: 'what or who are you and whose?' See I.94.43. Strangely, Kuntī herself uses this 'male' form of address when she first greets Hiḍimbā in the forest (I.142.3). This blurring of male-feminine verbal demarcation is not uncommon in the Mahābbhārata, with a woman speaking in what is usually a male manner.

76. Odysseus at Scroll vi.149, speaks with a similar formulation when he first casts eyes on Nausikáa: *theós nú tis ẽ brotós essi* 'are you divine or mortal?'

77. Jamison 1996: 224, on the "crucial thematic element" of causing the woman to mount the chariot, comments: "when the maiden is made to mount the chariot, this act is done not merely to ensure a quick getaway, but also serves as the single ceremonial action standing for and telescoping the entire wedding ceremony as performed under less trying circumstances."

She then begins to insult him with her usual eloquent and abrasive tongue, calling him *mūḍha* 'idiot', *śvanarāḥ* 'dog-like', *matta* 'drunk'. This is not the model form of a *rākṣasa* marriage, for the dialogue is too extensive and Draupadī's threats too vivid; besides, she is already wed. She tells Jayadratha how her husbands, individually, will attack him if she is taken, and she details their prospective revenge, using the language of a poet describing battle. She also refers to herself in heroic language as *mahābalā* 'mighty', which is ironically quite accurate.

Then, as she is forcibly removed by Jayadratha and his men she becomes *bhītā* 'fearful', and cries, *mā mā spṛśata* 'do not touch me!' Jayadratha then seizes her upper garment, for token violence is a necessary condition for this kind of abduction (III.252.23). Draupadī pushes him away, and he falls 'like a tree with cut roots' (*śākhīva nikṛttamūlaḥ*), a formula typically employed when one hero fells another (III.252.23). She is dragged and mounted on the chariot.

Dhaumya, the *purohita* 'chaplain' or 'housepriest' to the Pāṇḍavas, approaches when called by Draupadī, and warns Jayadratha that this abduction is dharmically incorrect: for he should have beaten the family members of Draupadī—usually not husbands—before taking her onto his chariot. That is the 'dharma of a *kṣatriya*' (*dharmaṃ kṣatriyasya*) he says (III.252.25).[78] Jayadratha is soon to be pursued by Draupadī's menfolk, for they, having been informed of the situation by a *dhātreyikā* 'confidante' of their wife, are verbally impelled by her and set off in pursuit.

This scene is the most detailed and dramatized of all abductions: it is as if a camera has zoomed in on the moment, and what usually takes up a few lines in the poem becomes over a hundred lines.

There occurs a formulaic episode now, where Draupadī describes to her captor—with great force and precision—the names and qualities of those who are giving pursuit, closing with the phrase, *ete vai kathitāḥ pāṇḍuputrā* 'these indeed are called the sons of Paṇḍu'. Jamison has examined this declamation at length, likening it to how Helen explains to Priam and other elders upon the walls of Troy, whom the assembled heroes are upon the plain below.[79]

Once Draupadī has been saved by her husbands and her Sindhu captor defeated, she is ruthless and bloody in her insistence that Jayadratha be killed, ordering Bhīma and Arjuna to accomplish the death:

78. In the Rāmayāṇa episode in the Mahābhārata it is the bird Jaṭāyu who is the one to resist the abduction and who is defeated by the abductor, Rāvaṇa (III.263.1ff.)

79. Jamison 1994: *Draupadī On The Walls Of Troy*.

kartavyaṃ cet priyaṃ mahyaṃ vadhyaḥ sa puruṣādhamaḥ

If a favor is to be done for me, that vile man is to be killed!

III.255.45

Her wrath is as brutal and pitiless as it was after the dicing scene. Only when the subjected Jayadratha is brought to her and symbolically humiliated by having his head shaved does Draupadī relent and command that her attacker be freed.

Thus the abduction goes completely awry, with Jayadratha defeated and forced to accept symbolic servitude. There is no marriage accomplished, and the procedure—in the form of a *rākṣasa* marriage—becomes in fact the bungled molestation of an already married woman.

The account of Ambā's abduction is probably the most well known of all the *rākṣasa* marriages in the epic and it best represents the formalities of this pattern of union.[80] It too is an abduction that goes terribly wrong.

Bhīṣma, as regent to the consecrated *yuvarāja*, Vicitravīrya, wishing to conclude a 'marriage' (*dārakriyā*) for his half brother, carries off Ambā, Ambikā, and Ambālikā from Kāśi, according to this scheme.[81] For he had heard that these three daughters were about to have a *svayaṃvara* held for them. He does this in order to simultaneously supply Vicitravīrya with a wife and co-wives.[82]

When he abducts these three girls on his chariot in Book One, as part of his formal proclamation Bhīṣma publically states the eight forms of marriage, but with the difference that—unlike with the series given in Manu—the *svayaṃvara* is the eighth and the manner praised by *kṣatriyas*.[83] On this particular occasion, Bhīṣma has hijacked a *svayaṃvara* and transformed it into a *rākṣasa* form of matrimony: "the violent seizure or rape of a girl after the defeat or destruction of her relatives."[84]

80. Jamison 1996: 219ff. has dealt with this episode in detail.

81. This is, 'according to the wishes of Satyavatī', Vicitravīrya's mother, who is also Bhīṣma's stepmother: *satyavatyā mate sthitaḥ* (V.170.6). It is noteworthy that it is the mother who is ordaining these events.

82. Bhīṣma has, of course, although the elder brother, renounced his title to the kingdom and kingship. Vidura, at I.103.8 refers to Bhiṣma as 'a noble mother and father' (*bhavān pitā bhavān mātā*).

83. *Rājanyāḥ* is the word he uses, an old term for *kṣatriyas* (I.96.11). For Bhīṣma is certainly one of the more archaic of the epic heroes and he is the first hero to be mentioned in the poem who later participates at the Kurukṣetra battle.

84. Monier-Williams.

Bhīṣma declares that 'some find their own [marriage partner]' (*svayam anye ca vindate*), which is what Śakuntalā and Gaṅgā had done and which in Bhīṣma's ranking is the eighth form of espousal (I.96.10). He then comments that,

> pramathya tu hṛtām āhur jyāyasīṃ dharmavādinaḥ
>
> Expounders of the law say a woman taken forcibly is superior.
>
> I.96.11

Alone, he repels the kings who give pursuit and proceeded to take the three girls back to Hāstinapura. There, he recounts his exploit to his mother, Satyavatī, and to his half brother:

> imāḥ kāśipateḥ kanyā mayā nirjitya pārthivān
> vicitravīryasya kṛte vīryaśulkā upārjitāḥ
>
> Having beaten the princes, these girls of the king of the Kāśis
> whose bride price was bravery, were won by me for the sake of
> Vicitravīrya.
>
> V.171.2
>
> tato'haṃ tān nṛpān sarvān āhūya samare sthitān
> ratham āropayāṃś cakre kanyās tāḥ ...
>
> Then after challenging in battle all those kings [who] stood there,
> I mounted those girls on my chariot ...
>
> V.170.12

His mother, who is effectively ruling, insofar as she had been the one to instruct Bhīṣma to consecrate his half brother and then procure the brides, responds,

> tato mūrdhany upaghrāya paryaśrunayanā ...
> āha satyavatī hṛṣṭā diṣṭyā putra jitaṃ tvayā
>
> Then, Satyavatī, eyes full of tears, having sniffed his head,[85]
> said happily: Conquered by you! Bravo son!
>
> V.171.3

A problem arises, however, with one of the girls whom he has abducted: for she—Ambā—had already espoused herself, with her father's agreement and with the mutual accord of her chosen lover (I.96.48).[86] This

85. See Hopkins 1907 on the nature and function of the "sniff-kiss." Kissing with the lips is uncommon.

86. This would indicate that the svayaṃvara was a formality, if Ambā had the consent of her father, *kāmaś ca pituḥ*. The assembled kings at the court of Yudhiṣṭhira listen to a similar

particular girl, like Damayantī, had already undergone the determination if not the process of a *svayaṃvara*; any subsequent rite would be a secondary formality which would merely have confirmed and embellished a previously settled espousal.

The conflict engendered here for Ambā is ultimately the cause of Bhīṣma's death: for Ambā's prior decision effectively overrules the abduction and renders it illicit. For the abduction—the *rākṣasa* form of marriage—to be lawfully successful, a girl cannot have participated in a *svayaṃvara* nor in any of the other forms of marriage. So the crisis begins 'when the marriage approved by Satyavatī approached' *satyavatyās tv anumate vivāhe samupasthite*, and Ambā 'modestly' (*savrīḍā*) comes to Bhīṣma.[87] She says,

> mayā śālvapatiḥ pūrvaṃ manasā abhivṛto varaḥ
> tena cāsmi vṛtā pūrvaṃ rahasy avidite pituḥ
>
> The king of Śālva was previously chosen by me as husband,
> and I was previously, in secret, chosen by him, unknown to father.
>
> V.171.6

First, there was the intended *svayaṃvara*, then the abduction, and now, this confession of a previous and private betrothal, which is in fact prelude to a *gāndharva* form of marriage.[88] Thus the situation no longer permits of finality to any of these processes: too many conflicting vectors are simultaneously occluding any one resolution.

Ambā appeals to Bhīṣma because of his reputation for being one who is true to vows. She says of her suitor: *māṃ pratīkṣate* 'he awaits me' (V.171.9). Bhīṣma permits her to depart, thus abnegating the *rākṣasa* marriage. Unfortunately, however, her abduction has tainted her and the Śālva king spurns her: for she has become, *anyapūrvā* 'a woman previously betrothed', and he is no more a *bhāryārthī* 'one seeking a wife' (V.172.4). 'Go!', he tells her, *gaccha*.

This is the same crisis that Rāma was presented with after the return of Sītā. When the hypothetical purity of a woman, her ostensible chastity, was put into question, Rāma had become *parāmarśaviśaṅkitaḥ*

---

claim about the sister of Kṛṣṇa, who had been previously wooed and rejected by Śiśupāla. The import was that they should consider her dishonored by such an encounter, for there existed dubiety concerning her subsequent chastity (II.42.18–19).

87. For a further treatment of Ambā's heroic narrative, see below, Ch. III.6.

88. At I.96.48 the audience had heard that Ambā received the consent of her father when she and the Śālvarāja fell in love: *eṣa kāmaś ca me pituḥ*. Yet when she herself speaks in the *Ambopākhyāna*, she says that the affair was *rahasi* 'clandestine'. Whether this is the poet's nodding or her own equivocation is uncertain.

'suspicious of the touch of another' (III.275.10). This is not something physiological, but emotional, the fantasy smirching a possible reality.

The Śālvarāja says of Ambā,

> tvaṃ hi nirjitya bhīṣmeṇa nītā prītimatī tadā
>
> For you were won by Bhīṣma, then happily led.
>
> V.172.6

Although he and Ambā had verbally given their word to each other in private, the rite of the *rākṣasa* marriage holds sway, canceling out the *gāndharva* ritual which had been put into process but not completed: it is the completed *rākṣasa* custom that takes priority. He says,

> katham asmadvidho rājā parapūrvāṃ praveśayet
>
> How would a king like me bring into his house a woman who has had a former husband?
>
> V.172.7

Now the audience hears the voice of the abducted, for Ambā tells her previous suitor *maivaṃ vada mahīpāla* 'do not speak so, king!'

> nāsmi prītimatī nītā bhīṣmeṇa
>
> I was not led happily by Bhīṣma!
>
> V.172.9

Bhīṣma, of course, is one whose very name refers to the greatness of his vow of celibacy: his austerity is 'terrible'. It is not as if she was captured by some licentious *kṣatriya*—like Jayadratha—but by the man whose ethical conduct throughout the poem is even superior to that of Yudhiṣṭhira, the son of Dharma.

She was *balān nītāsmi rudatī* 'weeping, I was led by force', she says. 'Be devoted to me who am devoted', she implores, *bhajasva māṃ ... bhaktām* (V.172.9–10). She refers to the dharma of this moment:

> bhaktānāṃ hi parityāgo na dharmeṣu praśasyate
>
> For abandonment of those who are faithful is not extolled in the dharmas.
>
> V.172.10

'I speak the truth', she says, *satyaṃ bravīmi*, referring to her emotional situation, for she had never loved another. She pleads her condition with great pathos and simplicity, yet Śālva continues to reject her, 'as a snake its old skin' (*tvacaṃ jīrṇām ivoragaḥ*; V.172.17). The poets refer to his behavior critically: *nṛśaṃsaḥ … parityajata … karuṇaṃ paridevatīm* 'the cruel one abandoned the lamenting woman', saying, *gaccha gaccha* 'go, go!' He admits that,

> bibhemi bhīṣmāt … tvaṃ ca bhīṣmaparigrahaḥ
>
> Because of Bhīṣma I am frightened—you are Bhīṣma's wife![89]
>
> V.172.22

The two other sisters, however, are duly married, the indication given in the text being: *tayoḥ pāṇiṃ gṛhītvā* 'he took their hands'; he being Vicitravīrya, the half brother of Bhīṣma (I.97.53).

Thus concludes a *rākṣasa* marriage which has gone tragically awry and which ultimately becomes the cause of Bhīṣma's death. As usual, ritual precision must always be maintained or disorder ensues. As the audience shall hear, the sexual and devoted love which Bhīṣma had attempted to renounce in his life, with his terrific vow of celibacy, returned with vengeance to destroy him: when Ambā later appeared in male form on the battlefield at Kurukṣetra, causing his death.

In sum, the *svayaṃvara* ritual would appear to possess the seeds for a *rākṣasa* form of marriage, insofar as it offers the necessary conditions for the latter: the presence of male *kṣatriya* kin who could be assailed during the required pursuit. The nature of the *rākṣasa* rite follows a pattern of *vigraha* 'seizure' or 'war'. It merely precedes the actual marriage ceremony, however, where a material exchange of goods may or may not be incorporated. We observed this in the case of Arjuna and Subhadrā.[90] Both of these forms of marital rite are thoroughly precise and any ritual uncertainty clouds the issue. Both procedures involve the use of weaponry, and heroes must perforce struggle in order to gain a spouse.

5. *The* gāndharva *Form of Marriage*

In the Mānava *dharmaśāstra*, this form of marriage is described as:

89. Śālva had been thrashed by Bhīṣma in a *dvairatha* 'duel', when he had pursued Bhīṣma during the abduction. This is related later, at I.96.25–40.

90. 'Seizure' or 'war' (*vigraha*) is one if the six *guṇas* of royal policy or action given in Manu at VII.16: 'peace, war, march, halt, strategy, alliance' (*saṃdhiṃ ca vigrahaṃ caiva yānam āsanam eva ca / dvaidhībhāvaṃ saṃśrayaṃ ca* …).

icchayānyonyasaṃyogaḥ kanyāyāś ca varasya ca
gāndharvaḥ sa tu vijñeyo maithunyaḥ kāmasaṃbhavaḥ

The mutual union by inclination of a girl and a lover:
that is to be known as the *gāndharva* rite, arising from desire caused by lust.

III.32

Marriage that happens where both parties are willing and desirous occurs throughout the epic.[91] Often it is the case that a *kṣatriya* is with a woman who becomes fecund or seasonal and she, attracted by the virility of the hero, admonishes or incites him to fulfill her needs. The man will often attempt to spurn the woman, but usually she succeeds in joining with him, and on certain occasions a child or children are born.[92]

The generation of Vyāsa comes of such a union, where—according to the poets—a king and a fisher-girl mutually agree to make love (I.57.55ff.). Parāśara, the seer, and the desiring girl, who is *prītā strībhāvaguṇabhūṣitā* 'affectionate and ornamented with the qualities of femininity' together produce a son, Vyāsa.

Later, however, when the conjunction of Śaṃtanu and Satyavatī first occurs in the poem, it is said that Śaṃtanu, having fallen in love, approaches the father and the usual exchanges are made, in this case verbal assurances. A few *adhyāyas* after this, when Satyavatī describes her previous union with Parāśara in her own words, she says,

abhibhūya sa māṃ bālāṃ tejasā vaśam ānayat

He, overcoming me, subjected my youth by his power.

I.99.10

That is another story altogether, and is not quite according to the principle of mutual delight which marked the *gāndharva* rite that an audience had already heard about. Parāśara had merely assured her that she would lose her fishy odor and become forever fragrant, and that her chastity would be restored and her virginity uncompromised. Whereas she only surrendered to him out of fear, she says: she was *śāpabhītā* 'fearful of his curse', and *pitur bhītā* 'fearful of her father'. It is uncommon in the poem to have two such explicit points of view, particularly

91. Essentially the verbal form is: *upatiṣṭhasva mām ... tatheti*, 'come to me ... alright!' (III.1373–4). In this particular case, the word employed to describe the coition is, *majjayāmāsa* 'he inundated [her]'.

92. Thus Svāhā longed for the love of Agni, the deity, and took the form of Śivā, wife of Aṅgiras. They made love, and Skanda was born of that union (III.213.50–214.16).

when lovemaking is concerned. Some lines later, she is referred to solely by the epithet *kālī* 'the dark one' (I.99.21).

Arjuna, at I.206, whilst he is exiled for a year in the forest because he had intruded upon Yudhiṣṭhira and Draupadī when they were alone, is seduced by the daughter of the king of snakes, Ulūpī, who had pulled him into the river Ganges as he bathed. In her attempt to convince him to make love with her, she says:

> prāṇadānān mahābaho cara dharmam anuttamam
>
> Perform the best dharma, strong-armed one, through the gift of life!
>
> I.206.30

Much later in time, in the Bhīṣma *parvan*, the son of this *gāndharva* union, Irāvān, appears and introduces himself to Arjuna. The poets recount his generation, as to how his parents came together out of desire for each other:

> bhāryārthaṃ tāṃ ca jagrāha pārthaḥ kāmavaśānugām
>
> Arjuna took her—a servant to the will of love—as a wife.
>
> VI.86.8

This is the perfect paraphrase of such a union, where two partners join out of mutually shared—and primarily sexual—desire for each other.

In Book Three, we hear of another such combination, when Mārkaṇḍeya tells the tale of Parikṣit. This is an account of a king who whilst out hunting came across an unattended *kanyā* beside a lake.[93] He asks the usual question, 'whose are you?' (*kasyāsi*: III.190.12). She replies that she is a *kanyā*, meaning that she is unattached and nubile. He then tells her that he is *arthī*, that is, 'one who woos'. 'You can have me, she responds', adding that *udakaṃ me na darśayitavyam* 'water is not to be shown to me'.

The story proceeds according to *gāndharva* form, and—reminiscent of the wonder-tale genre—there are complications and she soon turns into a frog. The king, however, *suratagunanibaddhahṛdayaḥ*, his 'heart bound with the strands of their lovemaking', by submitting to her royal frog-father, secures her hand and her favors again. Here, the amity is again reciprocal and the love produces three sons (III.190.43). It is an odd tale of equal and initially unimpeded desire; and although she is actually an amphibian their respective ranks are the same and social order—always crucial in this society—is maintained.

93. This micro-narrative is unusual in the Mahābhārata for being one of the very few passages that is in prose. This Parikṣit is not the grandfather of King Janamejaya.

The *gāndharva* marriage characteristically possesses this manner of purity, charm, and equilibrium, and it is not too prevalent in the epic, yet its operation stands at the core of the poem. It is an idyllic form of romance typical of pastoral settings, where a pacific mood obtains and the contestation of court life is lacking. Vyāsa's birth presents its most exceptional case, for he becomes the omniscient, the magister behind the text, organizing its process; and Śakuntalā's love affair is the most paradigmatic of this pattern of union. Such joint love, without domination at play, produces offspring who, as love-children, accomplish unusual deeds in the poem.[94] Bharata—who gives his name to the epic—is the son produced from the union of Duḥṣanta and Śakuntalā. Karṇa, the preeminent hero of the Mahābhārata, was similarly born of *gāndharva* nuptials, as were his three co-uterine Pāṇḍava brothers.

6. Other Aspects of Marital Union

Let us now consider four instances where marital conjunction varies slightly from the three models which we have delineated above.

Firstly, at the city of Maṇalūra during his year's sojourn away from his brothers and Draupadī, Arjuna perceives a young woman by the name Citrāṅgadā, of whom he immediately becomes enamored. He approaches the king, her father, Citravāhana, and makes known his desire for her.

The king agrees to give him his daughter in return for a *śulka*, a 'bride price' (I.207.22).[95] According to Manu's marriage typology this would be:

> ekaṃ gomithunaṃ dve vā varād ādāya dharmataḥ
> kanyāpradānaṃ vidhivad ārṣo dharmaḥ socyate
>
> Having received correctly from the suitor one or two pairs of cattle:
> the gift of a girl, accordingly, is known as *ārṣa* dharma.
>
> III.29

This price is to be the son that she will bear, crucial for the king in

94. When Vyāsa sleeps with a *dāsī* 'servant' woman, there occurs in the epic a rare instance where sexual gratification is described. This is the occasion for the conception of Vidura, the wisest of counselors. The poet says: *kāmopabhogena tu sa tasyāṃ tuṣṭim agād ṛṣiḥ / tayā sahoṣito rātriṃ maharṣiḥ prīyamāṇayā* 'The sage obtained satisfaction in her, with pleasure and love. The great sage spent a night with her who was being delighted' (I.100.25).

95. *Śulka*, "orig. a price given to parents for the purchase of a bride, but in later times bestowed on the wife as her own property ... dowry," Monier-Williams. XIII.4.11 mentions this *śulka* as an offering that is given by a husband for a wife as bride price: *kiṃ prayacchāmi rājendra tubhyaṃ śulkam* 'O king, what bride price do I present to you?'

a patrilineal kinship system when he only possesses a daughter.[96] Citrāṅgadā has no brothers, for her father possesses no sons: thus her male offspring are essential for him if his line is to continue and if there are to be men who will offer the father the rightful obsequies after his death. So, curiously, the patriline is momentarily diverted through a daughter.

Arjuna agrees to this 'contract' (*samaya*) and the couple cohabit for three 'seasons' (*sāmāḥ*). No marriage rite is specified.[97] The child born of this conjunction is the future king Babhrūvāhana. He is destined to kill his father: an event which is related in the Aśvamedha *parvan*, where Arjuna perishes, only to be revived again by Ulūpī. This is a strange little micro-narrative within the body of the epic, and it is as if the poets have drawn the story from another tradition and compressed it into merely a few verses.

Secondly, due to her extraordinary *tejas* 'energy, power', Sāvitrī is unable to attract suitors, even though she performs many rituals in order to secure a husband. Her father is deeply troubled, for to have an unmarried daughter in the family is problematic. He tells her, *svayaṃ anviccha bhartāram* 'seek a husband yourself!' (III.277.32). In pursuit of a potential groom, she sets off: *sā haimaṃ ratham āsthaya sthaviraiḥ sacivair vrtā* 'she, having mounted a golden chariot, surrounded by venerable counselors' (III.277.39). It is notable that her father, anxious that she will not be approached and that there would be no suitors, does not consider a formal *svayaṃvara* as a means to secure a spouse for his daughter, and also that he allows her to go off on a quest of her own.

She herself does select her future husband, but is soon informed by the seer Nārada that Satyavat, her man, will die imminently. Sāvitrī remains undeterred, however, saying, *sakṛt kanyā pradīyate* 'only once is a girl given' (III.278.25). As we have observed on many occasions, the reality and irrevocability of *kṣatriya* speech is sacrosanct: there is no question of revoking her decision once the words have been proclaimed and made public. Speech, like time itself, cannot be regained once it has been given. She repeats, *sakṛd vṛto mayā bhartā na dvitīyam* 'a husband is chosen by me once, not twice', adding *pramāṇaṃ me manas* 'my will is authoritative'. The decision of Sāvitrī, like that of a king, is binding upon all parties, including herself. The audience observed the same

96. At III.115.11–12 this *śulka* is *ucitaṃ naḥ kule* 'a custom in our clan'.

97. In Book Five, when 'a king married a girl' (*rājā kanyāṃ pratigṛhītavān*), 'he gladdened her' (*reme sa tasyām*: V.115.7–8). This is the formal condition of their union, sex is often both the necessary and sufficient condition.

force of diction when Kuntī declared that all five brothers were to marry Draupadī.

Her father then goes to the forest and seeks out the father of the prospective husband, and offers his daughter. He says, *snuṣāṃ pratīcccha me kanyām* 'accept my daughter as daughter-in-law' (III.279.12). The father must still mediate the marriage, even though the daughter has been autonomous in her selection. He then, *dattvā ... kanyāṃ yathārhaṃ ca paricchadam* 'having given the daughter and suitable goods', departs, leaving the bride with the husband's family, where the couple live together (III.279.16). The goods, one infers, are the substance of dowry.

According to the *dharmaśāstra* of Manu, this would constitute the highest template of marriage, although her own primary selection of a groom happens prior to this function, and so blurs its precision of form.

> ācchādya cārcayitvā ca śrutiśīlavate svayam
> āhūya dānaṃ kanyāyā brāhmo dharmaḥ prakīrtitaḥ
>
> The gift of a girl—clothed and honored—having himself made the summons
> to a man skilled in sacred lore: this dharma is called the *brāhma*.
>
> III.27

Sāvitrī becomes the good daughter-in-law, performing dutifully and correctly in the new household.

> śvaśrūṃ śarīrasatkaraiḥ sarvair ācchādanādibhiḥ
> śvaśuraṃ devakāryaiś ca vācaḥ saṃyamanena ca [paryatoṣayat]
>
> She delighted her mother-in-law with care of the body, with all attention to clothing and such,
> and her father-in-law with attention to the deities and by restraining speech.
>
> III.279.20

Sāvitrī, as the audience will realize in her ensuing narrative, is one of the most sagacious and competent of women in the poem. For modern Indian women, she offers a feminist ideal, where desire and accomplishment match each other.

Thirdly, King Virāṭa, on realizing that Arjuna has saved his son and cattle from molestation and capture by the raiding Kauravas, publically determines that he intends to bestow his daughter Uttarā upon Arjuna in marriage, 'if that is approved by you', he adds (*yadi te matam*; IV.66.16). He is offering his daughter not only as a reward but—having learned that Arjuna was one of the Pāṇḍavas—to bind him in political alliance. To possess such a son-in-law would be palpably advantageous for the kingdom, and he even makes a token remittance of the whole polity to Yudhiṣṭhira (IV.66.26).

Arjuna accepts the hand of Uttarā not for himself, but for his son: she becomes his *snuṣā* 'daughter-in-law'. She is *dattā* 'given', and Arjuna is 'to receive' (*pratigrahītum*), and thus political union is completed, sealed with the exchange of a bride. Virāṭa is happy just to have Arjuna as a *saṃbandhī* 'kinsman by marriage' (IV.67.11). This marriage form, according to Manu's nomenclature, would appear to be of the *brāhma* type, as it applies to *kṣatriyas*.

Arjuna diplomatically explains why he will not marry Uttarā himself, for having lived privately with her in the *zenana* for a year he was *pitṛvat* 'like a father', and *ācāryavat* 'like a teacher'. He feels that she would be then considered 'suspect to the world' (*atiśaṅkā… lokasya*): that is, her modesty would be questioned (IV.67.4). This is an odd hint at the possibility of incest, unusual in the poem.

It is from this marriage that the line of the Pāṇḍavas proceeds, and the grandson of the couple is the patron of the original singing of the Mahābhārata. This conjunction, and the wedding of Draupadī and also the union of Śakuntalā, are the three most vital nuptial moments in the epic in terms of narrative source.

At the marriage itself, other allies of the Pāṇḍavas attend the ceremony, as well as Draupadī's brother and her sons, and Kṛṣṇa, the uncle of Abhimanyu, the groom (IV.67.16ff.). These make up the *janyās* 'companions of a bridegroom'.[98] The ritual is an occasion for a political demonstration of allegiance, particularly as it comes at the end of the thirteen years of exile when the Pāṇḍavas are returning to political life, and the moment marks a first congregation of the allies who will appear together on the battlefield at Kurukṣetra.

At the wedding there are drums and conches being sounded, and various kinds of poets sing verses; the royal women are all adorned and exquisite as they surround the bride, with Draupadī the most surpassing 'in beauty, glory, and fortune' (*rūpeṇā yaśasā śriyā*). The actual recipience or acceptance of the bride is not performed by the groom, but

> tāṃ pratyagṛhṇāt kaunteyaḥ sutasyārthe dhanaṃjayaḥ
>
> Arjuna, the son of Kuntī, accepted her for the sake of his son.
>
> IV.67.32

Then, Yudhiṣṭhira, the senior brother and potential king, 'accepted

98. At III.115.17 these *janyās* are *surās* 'deities'.

her as daughter-in-law' (*snuṣā tāṃ pratijagrāha*). Abhimanyu's role in this process is slight, as he is but an instrument in the formation of this military association. It is Yudhiṣṭhira who appears to oversee the nuptial ceremony, not Arjuna or Virāṭa.[99] He is the one who 'gave away wealth to brahmins when the wedding was accomplished' (*kṛte vivāhe ... brāhmaṇebhyo dadau vittam*; IV.67.36).

This is one of the most political marriages in the poem and the audience hears nothing about the actual couple themselves. The father of the groom, as the marriage is patrilocal, is the one to take charge of affairs. It is telling that at the beginning of the Udyoga *parvan*, the marriage celebrations immediately translate into a counsel of kings, prior to the onset of the initial stages of negotiation which precede war. It is here that the Pāṇḍava coalition first assembles, ostensibly on the occasion of marriage, and 'they make all the war plan' (*cakruḥ sāṃgrāmikaṃ sarvam*; V.5.12). Marriage and politics are inseparable for *kṣatriyas*.

Whilst still an unborn foetus, the child of this couple is killed by a missile of Aśvatthāman, *brahmāstreṇābhipīḍitaḥ* (XIV.65.9).[100] In the Aśvamedha *parvan*, when this dead foetus is delivered, Kṛṣṇa enters the women's area of the palace and is approached by Kuntī, his maternal aunt, and Draupadī and Subhadrā, all weeping. Kuntī plaintively asks that he 'restore to life' (*ujjīvaya*) the dead baby (XIV.65.16).

He then enters the *janmaveśma* 'lying-in apartment', which is described in detail as being furnished with appropriate white garlands of flowers and,

> apāṃ kumbhaiḥ supūrṇaiś ca vinyastaiḥ savatodiśam
> ghṛtena tindukālātaiḥ sarṣapaiś ca mahābhuja
> śastraiś ca vimalair nyastaiḥ pāvakaiś ca samantataḥ
> vṛddhābhiś cābhirāmābhiḥ paricārārtham ...
> dakṣaiś ca parito vīra bhiṣagbhiḥ kuśalais tathā
>
> With full pots of water placed on every side,
> with ghee, with torches of *tinduka*, with mustard, O great-armed one:
> and with spotless weapons laid down and with fires all about,
> with beautiful old women whose purpose was service ...
> everywhere, O hero, with expert and skilled physicians also.
>
> XIV.67.4–6

99. It is unclear as to who actually receives the girl, as the text only says, *pratigṛhya ca tāṃ pārthaḥ* 'the Pārtha received her' (IV.67.34). Yudhiṣṭhira is the one implied.

100. The incident occurred towards the end of the Sauptika *parvan* (X.15.32). This terrifically destructive weapon, at the injunction of Vyāsa and Nārada, is redirected towards the wombs of the Pāṇḍava women. It is Kṛṣṇa who then proclaims that the child of Uttarā shall survive and continue the line of Paṇḍu.

Kuntī and Draupadī and other principal Bhārata women are there with the mother of the stillborn, and when Uttarā speaks to Kṛṣṇa, she is *susaṃvītā* 'well-covered' (XIV. 67.10). The women are lamenting for the dead infant, crying and filling the palace with their voice. Uttarā threatens to use poison or to 'enter the fire', if 'permitted' (*anujñātā*), by Yudhiṣṭhira; as we have noted elsewhere, suicide is acceptable for *kṣatriya* women, under certain conditions

Then Kṛṣṇa, speaking a combined truth act, revives the babe and names him Parikṣit (XIV.68.18–23). This little narrative is the only instance in the poem where pregnancy and childbirth are featured so prominently and the scene possesses an unusual quality of charm.

Finally, as a rider to the above three vignettes, it is worth remarking upon a further small and unique illustration of femininity, when the mother of the great warrior-brahmin Rāma Jāmadagnya was killed by her son at the command of her irate husband. She had seen the king Citraratha, bathing with his wife, and 'desired' him (*spṛhayāmāsa*). This is unusual, for it is generally men who desire women in the epic, except where women desire men for reasons of insemination and procreation.[101]

She became *klinnāmbhasi* 'moist, lubricious' and was *vicetanā* 'senseless' whilst this happened, 'because of that transgression' (*vyabhicārāt ... tasmāt*; III.116.7–8). Her brahmin husband realized this immediately upon her return to the household and gave Rāma the order to kill her, to decapitate her with an axe.[102]

It is rare in the poem for such intimate details of feminine desire to be given, even if there is no actual coition occurring between man and woman; and the sexuality manifest on this relatively innocent occasion elicits a terrific response in terms of male jealousy and anger. As with Sītā in Rāmāyaṇa, the putative virtue of a woman is crucial for the self-esteem of a man, especially a king. Women—apart from the exceptional Draupadī—must remain true to one husband: for it is as if their emotional impurity might have physiological consequences. The converse, concerning men, does not hold, for male purity, in this sense, has no physiological effect: men—from such a corporeal point of view—cannot become contaminated by sexual admixture.

101. This would of course be at an appropriate instant for the woman. The term which denotes feminine ovulation is *ṛtukāla*, as at I.77.5; this being when the *garbha* 'foetus' is conceived.

102. This is the Rāma who destroyed all *kṣatriya* men repeatedly, twenty-one times. He is a unique figure in the epic and skirts about the main narrative as if drawn in by the poets from separate poetic tradition.

7. The Co-Wife

The co-wife is an important figure in *kṣatriya* housholds, and yet she never receives any particular focus as to her standing. When Arjuna and Kṛṣṇa go to Khāṇḍava in the forest, Arjuna takes his two wives with him. The two men, merrymaking in the woods, become *madotkaṭe* 'both excited by drink', and bestow costly clothes on the other women (I.214.22).[103] There appears to be an easy and fluid society among the women in the family, without the inhibitions that accompany monogamy. I would like to offer three exempla as to how such married women behave and are treated in the epic.

First of all, when Arjuna returns to Indraprastha with his new wife, a 'co-wife' (*sapatnī*), he goes to Draupadī. There is no mention of the two other liaisons which he had entered into during his year's exile in the forest, one of which had produced a son.[104] Draupadī rebukes him and tells him to return to his co-wife, Subhadrā, saying with an acerbic touch,

> subaddhasyāpi bhārasya pūrvabandhaḥ ślathāyate
>
> The previous binding of the well-bound burden loosens.
>
> I.213.15

Arjuna attempts to conciliate her by instructing Subhadrā to remove her decorative red *kuśa* grass garment—perhaps the sign of a newlywed—and to appear in the form of a cowgirl. She must modestly abase herself before meeting the other women in the household.

Entering the household, Subhadrā first greets her mother-in-law, who is also her aunt, and then proceeds towards Draupadī, saying *preṣyāham* 'I am a [your] handmaid' (I.213.19).[105] Draupadī replies by saying, *niḥsapatno'stu te patiḥ* 'let your husband be not claimed by another!' To this bitter double-entendre Subhadrā responds in the affirmative and the Pāṇḍavas and Kuntī are happy and feminine hierarchy is established (I.213.21). The *sapatnī* would thus appear to hold an inferior status.

103. Of all Draupadī's five husbands, it is only Arjuna who is not monogamous. Bhīma's liaison with Hiḍimbā is prior to his union with Draupadī and only lasts for one year (I.143.36); Yudhiṣṭhira is certainly monogamous; and the twins are apparently so, for there is something ephebic about these latter two men. There does exist a unique prose reference to Yudhiṣṭhira's co-wife Devikā, whom he won at a *svayaṃvara*, and to Bhīma's taking a co-wife from Kāśi, Baladharā; as well as Nakula taking a Cedi wife, Kareṇuvatī, and Sahadeva a Madrasī wife, Vijayā, who was also won at a *svayaṃvara*. They receive but a unique mention (I.90.83–87).

104. Allen 1996 has analyzed these unions.

105. She is actually her cousin by marriage.

In Book Fourteen, as Citrāṅgadā says to Ulūpī, her ex officio co-wife—for there was no cohabitation involved with Arjuna, only a temporary consorting of lovers—*nāparādho'sti ... narāṇāṃ bahur bhāryatā nārīṇāṃ tu bhavati* 'there is no offence of men possessing many wives, but there is of women' (XIV.7914). This of course, excludes the unique situation of Draupadī.

In this scene, Citrāṅgadā then threatens to enter *prāya* 'meditative suicide' unless Ulūpī uses her divine powers to restore their recently deceased joint husband, Arjuna, to life. Ulūpī accomplishes this and Arjuna is revived. When all has been explained, he then enters the city *bhāryābhyāṃ saha* 'with his two wives' (XIV.82.27). Citrāṅgadā and Ulūpī then meet up with the women of the palace at Hāstinapura, including Subhadrā, Draupadī, and Kuntī, who offer the new women gifts; and the two become part of the royal household (XIV.90.2–4).

Secondly, when Mādrī, the co-wife of Kuntī, desires to have sons also, she appeals to Pāṇḍu and requests that he approach Kuntī to arrange this. She makes her request *stambho hi me sapatnītvād* 'because of my co-wife suppression' (I.115.6).[106] There does appear to be a definite and formal gradation concerning this marital rank, yet Kuntī says of Mādrī,

> bibhemy asyāḥ paribhavān nārīṇāṃ gatir īdṛśī
>
> I fear her insult—such is the way of women!
>
> I.115.23

There is a tension there which would seem to be irreducible. When Kuntī finds Pāṇḍu and Mādrī lying together and the husband dead because he had desired to make love, she shouts angrily at her co-wife, blaming her for the death. 'I am the elder wife by dharma', she says (*ahaṃ jyeṣṭhā dharmapatnī*; I.116.23).[107] The two then argue as to whom the privilege of accompanying the dead husband onto the pyre should be accorded. Mādrī pleads more eloquently and so enters the fire: *sā gatā saha tenaiva patilokam* 'she went with him to the world of the husband' (I.117.29).[108]

106. Keith 1925: 373 observes in his discussion of marriage that, concerning the co-wife there exists "a rule by which each caste could have a wife of its own and one of each inferior caste." That is, marriage with a co-wife would constitute a *pratiloma* union, from the husband's point of view.

107. A *dharmapatnī* is also the wife who is entitled to participate in Vedic rituals.

108. The lengthy description of the obsequies at I.118.1ff. show that Mādrī does not ascend the pyre like the typical *satī*, but is already dead and lying beside her deceased husband (I.118.21). This is perhaps an occasion where the poets nod.

Thirdly, Dhṛtarāṣṭra, at the end of his life, after Yudhiṣṭhira had finally become sovereign, retires to the forest in the company of Gāndhārī and his sister-in-law, Kuntī. There, they all perish in a conflagration (XV.45.7ff.). Kuntī is not exactly a co-wife, but the ostensible paradigm of a king and two women is sustained at this point. She is referred to as *vadhū* 'a younger woman-relation'. Bṛhadratha, after his son Jarāsaṃdha had been consecrated as king, similarly retires from the throne and goes to the forest, accompanied by two wives (II.17.22).[109] It is as if two wives were a norm for ruling *kṣatriyas* and certainly the practice when *vanaprastha* was embarked upon.

The audience does not hear of Dhṛtarāṣṭra's actual co-wife by name, but only by titular reference when he refers to Duryodhana as *jyeṣṭo jyaiṣṭineyaḥ* 'the eldest, the son of a first wife' (II.50.1). Similarly, Yuyutsu, another son of his, second to Duryodhana by birth, is born to a woman who is not Gāndhārī.[110]

As a rider to the above instances, there is in Rāmāyaṇa an occasion when the co-wife is portrayed in a much darker light. Daśaratha, the father of the eponymous hero Rāma, has three wives: the third wife, Sumitrā, gave him two sons, whilst the other two wives each bore only one son. The rivalry between the first and second wives, Kausalyā, mother of Rāma, and Kaikeyī, mother of Bharata, is the primary germ which sets off the narrative of the epic: the second wife, Kaikeyī, ousting Rāma from his inheritance and from the succession. It is this rivalry between co-wives which generates the main axis of the poem and causes the death of the king.

Given all that we have observed in the preceding pages concerning marital form, I would conclude this section by submitting a definition of epic polygyny as 'a system or kind of relationship among similarly married women'. It is not simply an occasion for a man to enter into marital relations with more than a single woman.

In the foregoing paragraphs I have extrapolated from the poem all the elements of the epic which portray events where male-feminine kinship structures are presented. Frequently, the marriage paradigms are blurred, and the standard eightfold distinction is not always perfectly

109. There are other occasions when a king possesses more than two or three wives; as, for instance, Somaka at III.128.2. This is more within the realm of *myth*, rather than epic, however.

110. It is Yuyutsu who becomes regent to the child Parikṣit, the penultimate king of the poem, when Yudhiṣṭhira and his brothers finally take their leave of the kingdom and set off on their last journey towards death, in the Mahāprasthānika *parvan*. He was conceived at I.107.36, of a *karaṇa* 'outcaste'.

clear; epic usage—also in its grammar—is not always exact or "correct."

Kinship—as it functions—is, I believe, the engine which generates human consciousness, particularly in a pre-modern community. In what is now referred to as "traditional" society, the individual—as we think of agency in the West today—does not exist, and self exists primarily within a reticulation of threads woven by kinship.[111]

In the above catalogue of marriage typologies as they are given in the poem, femininity—in its lateral movements—is manifest as a key token in the creation of social order. Even in the *rākṣasa* and the typical *svayaṃvara* paradigms of matrimony, the feminine is the desired object, so that patrilocal family systems can be sustained.[112] I would submit that it is this movement which creates the primary substance or comprehension of value in epic culture: this movement of women is the primary, if sometimes invisible, transaction.[113] As a complement or obverse to this, the male—in this study a *kṣatriya*—lives according to warrior ideals which organize violent death: the death of members belonging to other clan groups. Ambā, as we shall see below, cleverly confounds this understanding of object and death, by virtue of her poetic ambi-sexuality.[114]

111. Analysts and critics who seize upon one or two concepts taken from a system of philosophical thought, such as twentieth-century psychoanalysis, and apply these terms to societies far removed in time and space—in this case Bronze Age north-western India—are open to accusations of reductiveness. The nature of human identity is polymorphous and multiple, and modern and Western notions of consciousness are not simply applicable to *all* cultures. Structures of *self*, even the sexual-self, vary enormously and one particular template cannot be laid upon all models. I would strongly aver that the aim of humanism seeks to understand what it is not, and not to impose systems of thought where those systems do not exist. To draw upon an etiology of hysteria formulated in the early European twentieth century, and to presume that the formation of an unconscious in the Bronze Age psyche can readily receive the application of such a concept, is to take an imperial stance: if there is no evidence of an oidipal dynamic then one cannot make rigorous inferences about an ego structure. I know from my own field work in the Kacch in this present century that one cannot make such intellectual leaps, for kinship patterns are so profoundly different from what obtains in the West, and certainly, anatomy is *not* destiny.

112. An audience hears little as to feminine desire except in the *gāndharava* rite. However, one recalls how much potence lies with the mother or mother-in-law, within that patrilocal setting of family.

113. With the term *value*, I understand: "conceptions of what is ultimately good, proper, or desirable in human life ... the degree to which objects are desired ... [and] meaningful difference." Graeber 2001: 1–2. He adds, "ambiguity really *is* the point," for any creation of worth concerns an initial making of distinctions.

114. These women are expected to desire a spouse, whereas these men are expected to desire death (of other men). This is the initial cartography of desire in epic Mahābhārata, establishing the syntax of narrative.

At the end of the Kali *yuga*, which is actually the end of the cycle of eons, Mārkaṇḍeya, a *ṛṣi*, says,

> na kanyāṃ yācate kaścin nāpi kanyā pradīyate
> svayaṃgrāhā bhaviṣyanti yugānte paryupasthite
>
> No girl is asked for, and also, no girl is given [in marriage];
> at the imminent end of the age each will be self-selecting.
>
> III.188.35

That is, marriage at this final time is no longer systematic but random, and this is a condition of *adharma*, unlaw.[115] Similarly,

> abhīkṣṇāṃ krūravādinyaḥ paruṣā ruditapriyāḥ
> bhartṝṇāṃ vacane caiva na sthāsyanti tadā striyaḥ
> sūdayiṣyanti ca patīn striyaḥ putrān apāśritāḥ
>
> Repeatedly speaking with anger, bitter, women whose affection is tearful
> will not be obedient to husbands.
> Inclined to [their] sons, women will kill husbands.
>
> III.188.77–78

According to this *kṣatriya* worldview, the sign for complete dissolution and annihilation of the worlds is the end of conventional marriage and procreative practices. As we have seen, in these practices women play a central role, physically, socially, and emotionally, especially in the *svayaṃvara* and in the *gāndharva* forms. When marital procedures collapse nothing of worth remains, for a world without values is one of chaos.

115. Life then will only last for sixteen years, girls will be pregnant at five or six, and men become fathers at seven or eight (III.188.48). The quality of marriage is a key marker for the nature of each *yuga*: marriage is a vital token or emblem for the status of time.

III

WOMEN HEROES

IN TERMS OF MAHĀBHĀRATA MYTH, an audience hears that the feminine marks the point of all origin, for when the various *dānavas* and *daityas* at the primal churning of the ocean crave the *amṛta* 'ambrosia', Viṣṇu transforms himself into a woman: *strīrūpam adbhutaṃ kṛtvā* 'having made the wonderful form of a woman'. Enamored of her, the Dānavas offer her the liquid, and so the deities—through this intercession of the feminine—secure the life-fluid for the good of the cosmos (I.16.39–40).

Karṇa, speaking to his father, the Sun, Sūrya, says that,

> kīrtir hi puruṣaṃ loke saṃjīvayati mātṛvat
>
> Fame gives life to a person, like a mother, here in the world.
>
> III.284.32

It is remarkable that the greatest of the Mahābhārata heroes looks upon *kīrti* 'fame' as something so profoundly feminine and maternal. In *kṣatriya* ideology, fame is a warrior's primary aim in life, what he seeks above all else on earth.

Likewise, in Book One, when Dhṛtarāṣṭra sings his long monody to Saṃjaya, summarizing the key events in the epic, he commences with Draupadī's *svayaṃvara*, 'Draupadī taken whilst all the kings watched' (*kṛṣṇāṃ hṛtāṃ paśyatāṃ sarvarājñām*); followed by Arjuna then abducting—as co-wife—Subhadrā (I.1.102–3). Dhṛtarāṣṭra concludes his plaintive précis of the epic by describing how Uttarā's womb was struck by the missile of Droṇa's son (I.1.156). For him, these events enclose the whole narrative of the poem: these are the signs that frame and they are denoted by the feminine and concern marriage and reproduction.[1]

The first woman to be named in the Mahābhārata is Gāndhārī, followed by Kuntī and then Mādrī (I.1.59 and 66). These are the three mothers who produce the sons whose conflict supplies the core

1. Each verse of this song commences with *yadā aśrauṣam* 'when I heard'. The distinction between what is *heard* in epic, and what is *seen*, is always significant.

narrative of the poem. During the final great conflict, the royal women are stationed close to the battlefield at Kurukṣetra and are not secluded in safety away from the field. When, after all the affairs of war are concluded and the Pāṇḍavas finally enter the city of Hāstinapura, they first greet the old king Dhṛtarāṣṭra, and then his queen Gāndhārī, who is accompanied by Kuntī; then they proceed to greet various ministers and sons (XIV.70.6). As we shall see, the senior women are thus never put aside during the crises of the poem but actively participate in the business and order of rule, and are not simply spectating. Women are always present and observant and are frequently commentators.

In this chapter I shall trace and survey some key aspects of femininity as this relates to women heroes, in general and in particular. On the one hand, women often appear to stand upon the margins of hostility, never actually participating yet always party to the scene. On the other hand, it is the alleged purity of women that often allows them to perform heroically. Let us make a sketch review of some specific incidents where women act on the periphery of martial action, even if only verbally; and similarly, of incidents where feminine sexual integrity is a referent. Then we can examine certain women heroes in particular.

For instance, when Abhimanyu has been killed, Kṛṣṇa, speaking to his sister Subhadrā and to Abhimanyu's widow, Subhadrā's daughter-in-law, addresses the former as *vīrasūr vīrapatnī… vīraśvaṣurabāndhavā* 'mother of a hero, wife of a hero, woman whose kin and father-in-law are heroes!' (VII.54.17). Women in the poem, although not agent in the way that male heroes are, participate in heroic culture in a manner that is intrinsic to their affiliation. The wrath of Draupadī functions as an engine within the epic as well as an emotion in itself; and in terms of language, this far exceeds the heroic anger of most of the male heroes.

The usual attitude towards epic women—concerning what constitutes *akṣayam… yaśaskaram,* that which 'conduces to imperishable glory'—praises the devotion of a wife to her husband, even to a point of death.[2] As we shall see, anger can draw *kṣatriya* women like Draupadī to much further emotional lengths than mere service to a husband; yet the femininity of Draupadī is unique, and no other woman is like her.

Thus Bhīṣma, during his long deathbed narration can declare,

> rūpayauvanasaubhāgyaṃ strīṇāṃ balam uttamam
>
> The greatest power of women is their fortune, youth, and beauty.
>
> XII.308.73

2. On the idea of 'imperishable fame', see Watkins 1995: 12ff.

This is far removed from strength of arm or physical prowess, which are the principal concerns in the world of heroic men. How women relate to women in the poem is very different from how men relate to men: these processes are parallel in operation but not symmetrical.[3] Women do not fight, fighting is not culturally part of their function in society, although Kṛṣṇa does give cursory mention to the women of Kuṣasthalī, a town where his clan once fled on being assailed by Jarāsaṃdha. He speaks of the women of that town: *striyo'pi yasyāṃ yudhyeyur* 'in which [place] even the women would fight' (II.13.51).[4] Only in terms of myth is combat thus not entirely a male task.

Another instance of when a woman presents herself in the field of male action occurs when, in the Aśvamedha *parvan*, Duḥśalā, the daughter of Dhṛtarāṣṭra and Gāndhārī, approaches Arjuna. He had just slain her son and she pleads for peace and for the life of her infant 'grandson' (*naptaram*); although he—a child of Arjuna—is in fact a cousin twice removed. The classification is in fact according to generational level. She actually comes to him on the battlefield, presenting the *svasrīyasyātmajaḥ śiśuḥ* 'the infant child of a sister's son'; thus putting herself in the place of Arjuna's sister, even though they are actually cousins and the child is her grandchild (XIV.77.25).

'Be peaceful', she says imploringly (*śamaṃ gaccha*), and 'be kind' (*prasādaṃ kuru*); 'do not be wrathful' (*mā manyuvaśam anvagāḥ*; XIV.77.37).

> duḥśalā cāpi tān yodhān nivārya mahato raṇāt
>
> Then Duḥśalā turned back the fighters from the great battle.
>
> XIV.77.42

It is remarkable to see a woman, a princess of the first rank, in command and successful. This is especially so when her husband, Jayadratha, had been the one enemy whom Arjuna had vowed to kill, with the threat that if he failed he would commit suicide; for Jayadratha had been instrumental in the slaying of Arjuna's own son, Abhimanyu. Duḥśalā

3. Sax 2002: 135 comments on how "South Asian Hindu women are caught in a double bind: the dominant ideology requires that they be chaste, submissive wives, even as it recognizes that their dangerous and polluting sexual powers are indispensable for the reproduction of households, lineages, castes and larger communities." This bivalence is not reflected in what it means to be male or masculine.

4. Praise, for a woman, is not connected with violence but with right conduct. Also, *praśaṃsanti bhāryāṃ gatayauvanām* 'they praise a wife whose youth has gone' (V.35.59). Harlan 2003: 89, commenting on the violent death of women upon the funeral pyre of their husband writes, "It is often said that *satis*' deaths make their families illustrious ... As the ballad *Sati Godavari* ... and the recent case of Roop Kanwar make explicit, a sati makes not only her husband's family (*sasural*), but also her natal family (*pihar*), resplendent."

thus demonstrates great courage in going out between the warriors and using her baby as an icon of peace. This is a unique instance in the poem of a woman taking an active role on the field of battle itself, and it is a role that only seeks the pacific.

When in the next *adhyāya*, Babhruvāhana, ruler of Maṇipūra, hears that the sacrificial horse has approached his kingdom, he goes out *vinayena* 'mildly', not seeking confrontation. He is rebuked by Arjuna for acting in a fashion that is not according to *kṣatriya* dharma:

> yas tvaṃ strīvad yudhā prāptaṃ sāmnā māṃ pratyagṛhṇathāḥ
>
> Like a woman, you received with conciliation, me who had arrived with war!
>
> XIV.78.6

This is a sentiment that occurs a few times throughout the poem: that women are generally more conciliatory and irenic than *kṣatriya* men. On this occasion, however, Babhruvāhana's mother, Ulūpī, a snake deity with whom Arjuna had once dallied, appears and admonishes her son—who is in fact also Arjuna's son—to fight. It is really only when women become enraged and vengeful—like Draupadī—that they encourage their menfolk to seek violent solutions: yet a woman's advocacy of violence is always a reciprocal response and never primarily active. The same message is echoed in another part of the Aśvamedha *parvan*, when the horse strays into a different kingdom and the resident king challenges Arjuna by saying, 'this horse is pastured as if among women' (*ayaṃ cāryate vājī strīmadhya iva*) for it is unguarded: implying that women are not martial in their vigilence (XIV.83.6).

In the beginning of the Sabhā *parvan*, when Yudhiṣṭhira enquired of the visiting Nārada, 'how is a wife fruitful?' (*kathaṃ vai saphalā dārāḥ*; II.5.100), he received the reply that *ratiputraphalā dārāḥ* 'a wife has fruit in sexual pleasure and sons'.

This idea of fruitfulness is again depicted in Book Three, where the girl Lopāmudrā becomes *gārhasthye* 'fit for a householder'—this being one of the conventional stations of life—and she is married off by her father (III.95.1). She had become *yuvatī* 'youthful', having attained menarche. Later on, she says to her husband, *alpāvaśiṣṭaḥ kālo'yam ṛtau mama* 'little time remains in my season': meaning that she is fertile and if to become pregnant must be inseminated.[5]

5. Concerning reproduction, to mark her new status as fertile and reproductive, a woman will take the *sīmantonnayana* 'the parting of the hair'—being marked by pigment—"one of the 12 Saṃskāras (observed ... in the fourth, sixth or eighth month of pregnancy)." Monier-Williams.

Concerning the functioning of 'fruitfulness', that is, conception, physiology was well understood and there was no mystery as to ovulation and the process of *ṛtu*, the menstrual 'cycle'. In the case of Lopudrā's husband, 'having impregnated the womb', *ādhāya garbham*, 'during intercourse', *samaye*, the foetus developed for 'seven autumns', *sapta śāradān*, and was born (III.97.21–22).[6]

The reputed purity of women in the Mahābhārata as it relates to their reproductive ability is a vital theme in the narrative progression. Promiscuity does not receive a positive valence, although men do on a few occasions form liaisons with women or feminine beings other than their principal wife. Sītā, in the *Rāmopākhyāna,* when her sexual integrity is in question, is reverbed by the aerial deities in her claim to marital fidelity (III.275.22ff.). She responds by saying that 'known by me is the way of men and women' (*viditā hi me gatiḥ strīṇāṃ narāṇāṃ ca*; III.275.22). Then she performs a truth act in support of her claim to pure virtue, whereupon deities in the sky, including Brahmā, reiterate her assertion of honor.

This married chastity is a source of great power for women, akin to celibacy in its potence and integrity, and it functions as a field for feminine heroism. Women's intelligence, particularly as it applies to a practical knowledge of dharma, functions as a powerful component of their behavior in heroic literature.[7] It is as a mother of sons that women perform this role, for the mother is more important to a man—at least in terms of his direction—than is a wife. A wife can be replaced or substituted, a mother cannot.

Yet, the opposite does not hold, as when the great seer Mandapāla makes the interesting comment about women at the close of the Khāṇḍavadāha *parvan*, to the effect that,

> naiva bhāryeti viśvāsaḥ kāryaḥ puṃsā kathaṃcana
> na hi kāryam anudhyāti bhāryā putravatī satī
>
> Never is trust to be practiced by a man, thinking, "this is my wife":
> for a wife, being with sons, does not consider her duty.
>
> I.224.31

This implies her marital duty. Certainly, Mandapāla is not a *kṣatriya*, but it is unusual for a wife to give priority to her sons rather than to a husband.[8] Loyalty for a wife is primarily to the spouse; for the husband, it is to his mother, or more really, to his male fighting kin.

6. Presumably these 'autumns' refer just to 'seasons', in the sense of lunar cycles.

7. See below, Ch. V.

8. See McGrath 2004: 186n25, where, for a woman, the husband is more important than the son.

1. *Kuntī*

Kuntī, as a girl, had been promised by her father Śūra to a son of his father's sister, his cousin: this was Kuntibhoja, who was childless (I.104.2–3). This was a simple case of fostering, without any prospect of marriage. Previously known as Pṛthā, she thence took the patronym of Kuntī. She was the elder sister of Kṛṣṇa's father.

The youthful Kuntī had been so restrained and controlled in her life, *saṃśitavratā* 'one whose vows are rigid', that she won the favor of a distempered visiting brahmin to whom she had been assigned in the household. From him—as she had been so diligent in her service—she received the favor of being able, with mantras, to summon any deity to her presence and to control him (III.289.18).

Kuntī, unlike other women in the poem, possessed this unusual capacity of being potentially divine in will. In effect, she selected deities in order to bear sons, the great heroes of the poem. This supernatural capacity set Kuntī apart from all the other women heroes of the Mahābhārata: to be able to associate with a deity on such terms of intimacy and volition was inimitable.

Thus, one day,

> vrīḍitā sābhavat bālā kanyābhāve rajasvalā
>
> The girl—menstruating whilst in virginity—was ashamed.[9]
>
> III.290.3

When she does summon a deity, Sūrya, the Sun, 'out of curiosity' (*kautūhalāt*), he allows her to look upon all the other and attendant deities, *apaśyat tridaśān rājaputrī* 'the king's daughter looked upon the Thirty" (III.290.20).[10] Only the truly heroic ever witness such a sight of divine presence: ordinary mortals are unable to bear the majesty. The Sun then allows her to conceive whilst simultaneously maintaining her original and unimpaired virginity (III.291.16).[11] During this *hieros gamos* 'he placed a foetus in her' (*tasyāṃ garbhaṃ dadhau*; I.104.10).

Kuntī is profoundly different from other women in the poem, set apart by her powers, and her femininity overarches all the other women

9. She is ashamed because the blood signifies that she is not pregnant, and at her age she should be bearing children.

10. Kuntī recapitulates this event for Kṛṣṇa at V.142.19ff.

11. Mādhavī possesses a similar gift of recurring virginity (V.114.21). Gālava exploits this capacity by using her as a means of providing temporary or brief husbands with sons, so that he may repeatedly acquire a *śūlka* 'bride price': this happens three times. Gālava had previously accepted the girl as a wife, on being 'given' her by her father, Yayāti, without ado (V.113.15).

in the narrative. Even Draupadī, who is the most dynamic of the women heroes, possesses none of these supernatural capacities.

Pregnant, Kuntī conceals her condition from everyone but a *dhātreyikā* 'a foster sister, confidante, wet-nurse, female slave' (III.292.2). This is 'because of fear of her kin' (*bāndhavabhayāt*).[12] Living in the *kanyāpura* 'young women's apartments', she was 'skilled in caution' (*nipuṇāṃ parirakṣaṇe*):

> jānatī cāpy akartavyaṃ kanyāyā garbhadhāraṇam
>
> Knowing pregnancy then [as] not to be done by an unwed woman.
>
> III.292.8

Kuntī, *rudatī putraśokārtā* 'weeping, afflicted with grief for her son', abandons the infant child to float away on a river, *vilapya karuṇam* 'having lamented pitifully' (III.292.22–23). This is Karṇa who is soon discovered and adopted by a doting couple.[13] This son possesses supernatural earrings and an invulnerable cuirass upon his torso which sets him apart from all the other heroes and mortal beings (I.104.11). No other woman in the poem bears such a child.

During the trial of arms, when Karṇa appears and bests the Pāṇḍava brothers, Kuntī recognizes him as her firstborn and 'swoons' (*moha ... jagāma*; I.126.27). When he is made king of Aṅga by Duryodhana, *snehāc channā prītir avardhata* 'her hidden affection grew because of love' (I.127.22). She maintains her anonymity concerning her son's maternity though, even though Karṇa was the firstborn of the next generation and hence the possible future king: yet this potential remains tragically un-apparent.

Her marriage followed the custom of the *svayaṃvara*, which was held for her by her foster father Kuntibhoja. There, Kuntī 'found' (*avindata*) her husband Pāṇḍu, although Pāṇḍu had actually won her (I.105.1–2). Later, in the forest, when her husband became anxious that they would have no children—for he was cursed to die if he ever enjoyed sexual intercourse—he insisted that she find a brahmin to impregnate her.[14] It is noteworthy that he prefers a brahmin rather than a *kṣatriya* as a potential mate for his wife. He tells her a story about a similar situation

12. 'Because of fear from that side of the family' (*bandhupakṣabhayāt*; I.104.13).

13. Radhā, the foster mother, is childless, although *apatyārthe paraṃ yatnam akarot ca viśeṣataḥ* 'she made especially great effort for the purpose of a child' (III.293.2). Only after discovering Karṇa and taking him as her own does she conceive and bear other sons (III.293.11).

14. A deer, whom he had shot in the forest as it copulated, cursed him (I.109.18ff.)

where a *vīrapatnī* 'wife of a warrior', *varayitvā* 'having chosen' a suitable mate, becomes pregnant three times. Kuntī is similarly soon to conceive thrice. She determines to invoke her mantric capacity in order to call down any deity of her choice.

It is ironic that Pāṇḍu is unable to reproduce with Kuntī, for he is once described as *strībhogānāṃ viśeṣajñaḥ* 'a knower of the particulars of pleasure for women' (I.109.22). He is one who is destined to die *kāmamohita* 'deluded by desire' (I.109.25), and overwhelmed *maithunadharmeṇa* 'by the dharma of sex' (I.116.9). It is as if his excessive lust has made him infertile, causing his sexuality to become accursed.[15]

As a co-wife for Kuntī, Mādrī was acquired by Bhīṣma; yet Kuntī remained the *mahiṣī* the senior 'queen'.[16]

Yudhiṣṭhira, at one point in the poem, says of her, *ūḍhāt prabhṛti duḥkhāni śvaśurāṇām ... aśnute* 'beginning with marriage, she obtained sorrows from her in-laws' (V.81.42). He compounds this by saying, 'one does not die from sorrows if she lives' (*na nūnaṃ mriyate duḥkhaiḥ sā cet jīvati*), implying that her grief had been so much in surfeit of theirs and that it was she who had in fact sustained them. Yudhiṣṭhira is unqualified in his devotion to her.

> suyodhanabhayād yā no'trāyatāmitrakarśana
> mahato mṛtyusaṃbādhād uttaran naur ivārṇavāt
>
> She rescued us, Kṛṣṇa, from fear of Duryodhana;
> like a passing boat from a great sea crammed with death.
>
> V.81.39

Once her husband is deceased Kuntī stays in the company of her five sons. Supposedly dead after the fire in the house at Vāraṇāvata, together they live a clandestine and itinerant life (I.137ff.). At this time Bhīma is the one who protects her most closely and often actually carries her upon his back. As she sleeps one day upon the earth, he admires her at length and sings her praise, addressing her serially as *svasāram* 'sister' of Kṛṣṇa's father, *sutām* 'daughter' of a king, *snuṣām* 'daughter-in-law', *bhāryām* 'wife', and *sukumāratarāṃ strīṇām* 'most delicate of women'. He finally says, *suṣuve yā sutān* 'she bore sons'. Thus all the social aspects of her femininity are touched upon during this gentle encomium (I.138.16–19). Women only speak in similar terms when they lament a male death.

15. He actually perishes in the act of copulation: *sa tayā saha saṃgamya bhāryayā* 'he having made love together with his wife' (I.116.12). This is the co-wife, Mādrī.

16. From her, "the oldest living male child fathered by the king or his oldest son", receives the "royal dignity." Scharfe 1989: 27.

During these days Kuntī is very much a figure of authority, instructing her sons how to behave and telling them what to do. She is the one to determine that Bhīma should go and destroy the *rakṣas* Baka, who periodically ate brahmin families (I.150.4). All that she has to say is, *kuruṣva* 'act', and Bhīma accomplishes the commission; and when Yudhiṣṭhira queries her decision, she quickly responds by saying,

> buddhipūrvaṃ tu dharmasya vyavasāyaḥ kṛto mayā
>
> The dharmic resolution was intentionally made by me!
>
> I.150.19

For she is *satyavādinī* 'a speaker of truth' (I.156.2), and at one point Yudhiṣṭhira says to her:

> bhavatyā yan mataṃ kāryaṃ tad asmākaṃ paraṃ hitam
>
> Whatever is considered by you to be a duty—that is our highest good![17]
>
> I.156.9

Similarly, when Kuntī declares that the five brothers should share their day's acquisitions—thinking that this is food, for they are disguised as impoverished brahmins who beg—she realizes immediately her error. She thus instructs them to all partake of the bride whom Arjuna had just won, Draupadī: thus reduplicating her own quinquelateral sexual relations.[18] Her royal authority is such that her speech is law. Kuntī becomes troubled by the prospect of a woman with five husbands, but how can her speech cause *anṛtam* 'unlaw', she asks? (I.182.5).[19]

It is remarkable and unmatched that the widow Kuntī possesses such irreversible and indubitable authority over her five warrior sons. When Yudhiṣṭhira explains to his imminent father-in-law that Draupadī

17. Sax 2002: 143 remarks that in the *pāṇḍav līlā* in Himalayan Garhwal, "So closely is Kuntī identified with truth and virtue that the normal epithet for her is 'Truthful Mother Kunti' (*satī mātā kuntī*)." In the dance she is played by an elderly woman. He adds (150), "the gods are unable to defeat Kunti's sat because she is so pure. She is an ideal mother, always serving others selflessly." She is "a supremely virtuous, benevolent, and self-sacrificing mother, as distinguished from Draupadi, who is represented as dangerous, bloodthirsty, and destructive," (151).

18. Kuntī, like Draupadī, and unlike other women in the epic, has intimate or sexual relations with five male figures: Sūrya, Dharma, Indra, Vayu, and Pāṇḍu.

19. The opposite of dharma in this discussion or conception of an event, is *anṛta*. Yet one is not simply a negation of the other, but a very different idea. It is an unusual counterpoint, for *ṛta* generally concerns more the natural order of things, whereas dharma concerns more the cultural or social order.

will be taking not one but five husbands, he says, *evaṃ caiva vadaty ambā mama* 'thus my mother told me' (I.187.29). Earlier he had stated,

> gurūṇāṃ caiva sarveṣāṃ janitrī paramo guruḥ
>
> The mother is the highest guru of all gurus.
>
> I.187.15

'She is proclaiming the word', he adds (*sā cāpy uktavatī vācam*); meaning that the word of the mother is final, that is the ultimate dharma as far as he is concerned. This is a unique moment in the kinship structures displayed throughout the poem, for nowhere else does the speech of a woman have such force in a marriage contract. It is generally the saying and doing of the father that determines the operation of matrimony. The dharmic force of Kuntī's utterance is unquestionable and intrinsic to her heroic stature.

It is at this point in the poem that the deity-hero Kṛṣṇa makes his entry and begins the association with the Pāṇḍavas that is so vital for their eventual success as rulers. Kuntī is Kṛṣṇa's aunt, the sister of his father, and the Pāṇḍavas are his cousins; and it is Kuntī who brings Kṛṣṇa into this allegiance, an alliance that is to prove crucial to the eventual victory of the Pāṇḍavas. It is this affiliation through the feminine side that enables them to triumph at Kurukṣetra. To the contrary, on the masculine side, via the brother of the father—Dhṛtarāṣṭra—the affiliation is thoroughly negative: and the ensuing conflict between the cousins is the source of war, a rivalry between Duryodhana and Yudhiṣṭhira.[20]

When Draupadī arrives at their humble household on that first evening after she had joined the family, it is Kuntī who instructs her on how to serve their food. This is first offered to the deities, then to brahmins and other members of the household, and finally the meal is to be distributed among the brothers and themselves. This is Draupadī's first action in the company of her new kin: *yathāvad uktaṃ pracakāra sādhvī* 'the good woman acted according to what was said' (I.184.7). Drupada's son, spying on these proceedings, describes Kuntī as *arcir ivānalasya...jānitrī* 'a mother, like the glow of fire' (I.185.7).

Speaking to King Drupada after the ceremonies of the *svayaṃvara* have been completed, Yudhiṣṭhira declares to his father-in-law that Draupadī is the joint *mahiṣī* 'queen', of the five brothers (I.187.22). This is the first moment that Draupadī has been so titled: for, as he says, *evaṃ*

20. This rivalry between cousins also occurs between Kṛṣṇa and Śiśupāla; in this case the former simply decapitates the latter (II.42.21).

hi vyāhṛtaṃ pūrvaṃ mama mātrā 'for such was declared by my mother previously'. Again, the authoritative voice of Kuntī determines protocol and order in the family. This *samaya* 'accord, agreement' is established between the brothers, as it is initially determined by the mother's speech.

After the actual wedding has taken place at the sacred fire according to convention and the brothers have celebrated with their new bride, Draupadī, appropriately clothed, approaches Kuntī, who then proceeds to address her, listing a series of wifely imperatives: *bhava, kuru, gacchantu*...

> kurujāṅgalamukhyeṣu rāṣṭreṣu nagareṣu ca
> anu tvam abhiṣicyasva nṛpatim...
>
> Be anointed after the king among the cities and
> kingdoms and principal Kuru forests...
>
> I.191.9

With all these imperatives, which commence with a statement of *yathā* 'as', Kuntī is making a speech act, and proclaiming in a voice of authority and injunction. She begins, *yathā indrāṇī harihaye* 'as Indrāṇī is to Indra', listing other famous and divine or semi-divine wives, *tathā tvaṃ bhava bhartṛṣu* 'so be you among [your] husbands'. The *yathā-tathā* form continues throughout the address. This is not simply advice nor maternal injunction, but a speech act which possesses efficacy: this is to become their domestic and courtly constitution.

She says, 'bear warrior sons', be *subhagā* and *bhogasaṃpannā* 'fortunate and endowed with pleasure'; 'be the *yajñapatnī*' 'sacrificer's wife'. 'Let your years eternally go correctly' *yathānyāyaṃ śaśvad gacchantu te samāḥ*, honored by the gurus, the old, the young, the wise, and by guests who arrive; be generous to brahmins at the *aśvamedha*.

> anu tvam abhiṣicyasva nṛpatiṃ dharmavatsalam
>
> Be royally consecrated after the dharma-loving king...
>
> I.191.7

> ...āpnuhi tvaṃ kalyāṇi sukhinī śaradāṃ śatam
>
> ...O lovely one, being joyful acquire one hundred autumns!
>
> I.191.11

'Obtain whatever jewels on earth' (*pṛthivyāṃ yāni ratnāni... tāny āpnuhi tvam*; I.191.11). Of course, the final admonition is to produce a son:

> yathā ca tv abhinandāmi vadhv adya kṣaumasaṃvṛtām
> tathā bhūyo'abhinandiṣye sūtaputrāṃ guṇānvitām

As I honor you now, a bride dressed in linen,
so I shall honor you further, virtuous, having produced a son.[21]

I.191.12

This communication of Kuntī's possesses a formality to it: it is as if she is enjoining, according to protocol, her new daughter-in-law in the manners of correct queenship. It is a queen advising her eventual successor how to behave and informing her as to precedence. It is a crucial speech and adheres to form.[22]

When Kṛṣṇa takes his leave of the court at the beginning of Book Two, he first visits his aunt, Kuntī, then his sister, Subhadrā, and finally, Draupadī: the procession is, aunt, sister, then cousin-by-marriage.[23] The meeting with Kuntī is described:

vavande caraṇau mūrdhnā jagadvandyaḥ pitṛṣvasuḥ
sa tayā mūrdhny upāghrātaḥ pariṣvaktaś ca keśavaḥ

He—honored by the world—with his head saluted both feet of his father's sister.
Kṛṣṇa was embraced and sniffed by her on his head.

II.2.2

Later, as the brothers and their wife prepare to depart for the forest, Draupadī, full of grief, salutes Kuntī and the 'other women there' (*anyās tatra yoṣitaḥ*; II.70.1). Draupadī is of course still in a state of undress, and her single item of clothing is stained. A great cry is heard from the assembled in the *antaḥpura* as Kuntī speaks to her daughter-in-law with a voice that is *śokavihvalayā* 'afflicted with grief'. 'You understand the order of women' (*strīdharmāṇām abhijñāsi*), she says, and *na tvāṃ saṃdeṣṭum arhāmi bhartṝn prati* 'I do not need to direct you, concerning your husbands' (II.70.5). She adds,

sādhvīguṇasamādhānair bhūṣitaṃ te kuladvayam

21. This is also a pun, for *sūtaputra* is Karṇa, and in many traditions, Karṇa and Draupadī have an unrequited affinity towards each other. See McGrath 2002: 2n4, 30n13. Kuntī, being the unbeknownst mother of Karṇa, might be discreetly encouraging her new daughter-in-law here, or at least referring to a situation which is now only present in other textual traditions. Certainly, the audience would have been privy to this nuance of the word.

22. There is definitely a community of women within the family unit, but it is not based, as in the case of men, on descent from a common father. Benveniste 1969: I.222, "Le contraste ancien entre «frère» et «soeur» repose sur cette différence que tous les frères forment une phratrie issue mystiquement du même père; mais il n'ya pas de «phratries» féminine." In the Mahābhārata, such *phratries*, among women, are organized according to principles of marriage rather than consanguinity.

23. This same procedure also occurs at II.42.50–52.

> Both families are adorned by the composition of your good qualities.
>
> II.70.5

As her sons set off towards the forest and a life of asceticism, Kuntī formally laments their passing, simultaneously praising them: the verb is *vi√lap*, 'to bewail, lament'. This is a key verb in Book Eleven, the Strī *parvan*, "The Book of Women," where the women mourn all the dead heroes scattered about the battlefield of Kurukṣetra.[24]

> syāt tu madbhāgyadoṣo'yaṃ yāhaṃ yuṣmān ajījanam
>
> For this would be my ill fortune—I who gave birth to you.
>
> II.70.15

In this speech of farewell, Kuntī is grieving as if her sons had actually died, and the lament that she sings takes such a form: praising them, listing their attributes, mentioning their birth and former opulent life, and how *daivam* 'fate' has taken them from her (II.70.13–20).

> vyasanaṃ vaḥ samabhyāgāt ko'yaṃ vidhiviparyayaḥ
>
> Ruin has come to you. What is this reversal of destiny?
>
> II.70.14

Once the twelve years of exile has actually commenced for her sons, Kuntī stays on at the court of Hāstinapura and becomes part of the retinue surrounding King Dhṛtarāṣṭra, and associates closely with his wife Gāndhārī. Vidura—a half brother of her deceased husband—had insisted that Kuntī remain in his house and not enter the forest with her sons, saying that she should remain at court:

> āryā pṛthā rājaputrī nāraṇyaṃ gantum arhati
> sukumarī ca vṛddhā ca nityaṃ caiva sukhocitā
>
> The good Kuntī, a king's daughter, does not deserve to go to the forest;
> old and delicate and always used to goodness.
>
> II.69.5

Technically Kuntī is a widow, and yet there is an aura of a co-wife about her during this period, due to the fact that a man should always take care of his brother's widow. Yudhiṣṭhira later sends greetings to her, via the emissary Saṃjaya, asking him to address 'the old women' (*vṛddhāḥ striyo*; V.30.30).

When Kṛṣṇa, in the role of *dūta* 'ambassador', next visits the court at Hāstinapura in Book Five, one of the first things that he does, after a

24. See below, Ch. V.5, for more on the theme of lamentation.

brief formal audience with the old king, is to visit Kuntī, his *pitṛṣvasāram*, his 'father's sister', paternal aunt.

> kaṇṭhe gṛhītvā prākrośat pṛthā pārthān anusmaran
>
> Kuntī, having grasped his neck, remembering her sons, cried.
>
> V.88.2

She enquires about them, sons whom she has not seen for almost a decade and a half, and she tells Kṛṣṇa how once,

> bālā vihīnāḥ pitrā te mayā satatalālitāḥ
>
> Those children, deprived of a father, were constantly fondled by me.
>
> V.88.9

She describes and praises her sons at length, inquiring as to their well-being, and includes here, as her own, the two sons of Mādrī. Then she asks after Draupadī, who chose the companionship of her husbands rather than that of her own sons. There is 'none dearer to me than Draupadī', she tells Kṛṣṇa, not even her sons (*na priyo mama kṛṣṇāyāḥ*); which is an unusual thing for a mother to assert in the epic. Despite her great portion in life, Draupadī, says Kuntī, is *duḥkhabhāginī* 'one whose lot is sorrow' (V.88.45). The sight of Draupadī being abused in the *sabhā*, she says, was 'more sorrowful' (*duḥkhataram*) than anything she had seen in her life.

Now she tells Kṛṣṇa of her own 'various sorrows' (*nānāvidhāni duḥkhāni*), of how it is to live in an alien court, a widow without her sons or daughters-in-law (V.88.54ff.). This is a long, plaintive lament of a widow, one who is resident among what is fast becoming an alien people. It is a most mournful speech, with the word *duḥkha* repeatedly uttered: for the status of widows in epic society—as in much of India today—was not easy.[25]

> duḥkhād api sukhaṃ na syāt yadi puṇyaphalakṣayaḥ
>
> If the pure fruit is destroyed there can be no happiness, because of sorrow!
>
> V.88.59

25. In the *kṛta yuga*, as depicted in I.102, 'there were no widows' (*nābhavan vidhavāḥ striyaḥ*; I.102.10). When society is perfectly balanced this condition of womanhood does not occur, implying that widowhood is a state of *adharma*. In Book Two, Kṛṣṇa asks Yudhiṣṭhira, *kaccid dārān manuṣyāṇāṃ tavārthe mṛtyum eyuṣām ... bibharṣi* 'whether you support the wives of those men gone to death in your service?' (II.5.44). This notion of paternalism does not occur elsewhere in the poem.

She makes a truth act, having made claim to the fact that *na me viśeṣo ... āsīt dhārtarāṣṭreṣu pāṇḍavaiḥ* 'there was no partiality on my part between the Pāṇḍavas and the sons of Dhṛtarāṣṭra'. 'By this truth' (*tena satyena*), she says, 'may I see you, Kṛṣṇa, with the Pāṇḍavas, surrounded by dead enemies and by fortune' (V.88.60). This speech, like much of what Kuntī says when she declaims authoritatively, has efficacy and the statement comes to pass. Such power of implicit causality—via speech—stems from her probity and also from the great heroic grief which she has suffered.

Curiously, she blames her father wholly (*pitaraṃ tv eva garheyaṃ nātmānam* 'I should reproach my father, not myself') for having given her away into fostering: 'tricked by father and by fathers-in-law' (*sāhaṃ pitrā ca nikṛtā śvaśuraiś ca*). Due to this she became *atyantaduḥkhitā* 'extremely sorrowful'. 'What fruit is there to my life?', she asks Kṛṣṇa (*kiṃ jīvitaphalaṃ mama*; V.88.63).

Her 'widowhood' (*vaidhavyam*), her loss of property, conflict, nothing is so grievous as *putrair vinābhavaḥ* 'separation from sons'. She says,

> arthatas te mama mṛtās teṣāṃ cāham ...
>
> In fact, they are dead to me, and I to them ...
>
> V.88.71

As with Draupadī, sorrow is the signal emotion marking Kuntī's life: this is the field of her struggle.

A woman without immediate male kin is in a dangerous position, for there is no one to protect her: widowhood is a marginal and uncared-for situation. When the mother of Pāṇḍu, Kausalyā, lost her son, after his obsequies had been accomplished, she and her own mother-in-law, Satyavatī, and her sister, Ambikā, the mother of Dhṛtarāṣṭra, set off towards the forest to live a life of mendicance. Unlike Kuntī, they departed from both court and poem.[26] This left Kuntī the most senior woman in the royal family, and yet:

> parāśrayā ... yā jīvāmi dhig astu mām
>
> I live—one who is dependent upon others—damn me!
>
> V.88.73

However, it is not the sorrow due to the loss of the kingdom, nor the hu-

26. 'Satyavatī, with both daughters-in-law, went to the forest' (*vanaṃ yayau satyavatī snuṣābhyāṃ saha*; I.119.11). This is an unusual depiction of widowhood at its onset.

miliation of the dice match, nor the banishment of her sons, but the sorrow caused by *sā bṛhatī śyāmā ekavastrā sabhā gatā* 'that tall dark woman wearing a single cloth, gone to the hall'. Draupadī, the *strīdharmiṇī* 'virtuous woman', being so abused and without any man to protect her, caused Kuntī the most despair—Draupadī, who was *kṣatradharmaratā* 'devoted to the law of *kṣatriyas*' (V.88.86).

Kṛṣṇa consoles her, appealing to her great dignity and rank and to all her especial qualities that set her apart from other women at the court and in the epic: *kā nu sīmantinī tvādṛg lokeṣv asti* 'what woman, other than you, is there in the worlds?' (V.88.90).

When Kṛṣṇa leaves Hāstinapura to return to the Pāṇḍavas, one of the messages that Kuntī gives to him is to congratulate Draupadī on her conduct with Kuntī's sons. Tell Draupadī, she instructs Kṛṣṇa, 'you have proceeded correctly with all of my sons' (*me putreṣu sarveṣu yathāvat tvam avartithāḥ*; V.135.12). She refers to Draupadī as 'the daughter-in-law of her deceased husband', a polite formality. It is as if her widowhood has curtailed the in-law relationship which Kuntī had enjoyed with the wife of her sons. Now, as she lives within the household of her brother-in-law, that affiliation is no more practicable and has been expunged by grief.

Kuntī repeats to Kṛṣṇa, at this second interview, what she had said earlier, that the molestation and insulting of Draupadī—during her period—grieved her more than the calumny of the dice match or the banishment of her sons: 'that tall dark woman weeping in the *sabhā*' (*sā bṛhatī śyāmā sabhāyāṃ rudatī*; V.135.15–21). The *avajñāna* 'contempt' shown towards Draupadī then was unforgiveable; it was something that was emblematic of the vast disorder which now stood imminent for the kingdom.

She reiterates the injunction which Kṛṣṇa is to give to Arjuna, *draupadyāḥ padavīṃ cara* 'travel the path of Draupadī', for she was someone who conducted herself rightly, even though she lacked protectors (V.135.19). The implication is that her husbands must stay with her and protect her: a situation which is in direct opposition to what Kuntī herself now experiences, the solitude and marginality of a widow.

When Kuntī at last meets up with her firstborn in person and is able to talk with him, her son is thoroughly rejecting of her. She had approached him with the hope of allaying Karṇa's anger and facilitating a move towards peace.

> kasmān na kuryād vacanaṃ pathyaṃ bhrātṛhitaṃ tathā

> Why would he not perform my good speech that is for the benefit of his brothers?
>
> V.142.25

Karṇa, on seeing her—he is standing in the river and praying to his father, the Sun—introduces himself as the son of his foster parents. This Kuntī denies, saying that, *kaunteyas tvaṃ ... nāsi sūtakūle jātaḥ* 'you are a son of Kuntī, born not in the clan of a charioteer!' (V.143.2).

She confesses that she bore him before she had become married and that he is her *pūrvajaḥ* 'firstborn', and that, 'you are a Pārtha, son!' (*pārthas tvam asi putraka*). She encourages him to make peace with his brothers. Karṇa fully rejects her, for he was *avakīrṇa* 'cast down', by her, and although a *kṣatriya*, he has not received the appropriate rites. He says that she is worse than an enemy, and that,

> na vai mama hitaṃ pūrvaṃ mātṛvat ceṣṭitaṃ tvayā
>
> No effort by you was made—like a mother—for my good.
>
> V.144.8

He denies that she has any interest in him, but is merely acting for her own self-service, yet he does accept—like a good son should and must do—her request that he not kill any of his brothers except for Arjuna. Kuntī, having listened, is 'trembling from sorrow' (*duḥkhāt pravepatī*). She wishes him, 'good health and well-being' (*anāmayaṃ svasti ca*; V.144.26). This is the only time in her life that she speaks with Karṇa.[27]

She does not tell her other sons about their relationship to Karṇa until after the war is over and he is dead. Then, after all the lamentation and the cremation has been accomplished she informs Yudhiṣṭhira and the others of how Karṇa was her firstborn. He exclaims,

> aho bhavatyā mantrasya pidhānena vayaṃ hatāḥ
>
> O ... by the secrecy of your speech, lady, we are slain!
>
> XI.27.17

Again, the audience observes a reference to how potent a SPEAKER she is, even in this case, where the statement of how charged her speech is actually on the level of metaphor; for it was Karṇa who was in fact slain. This is the tragic bearing of Kuntī's life.

Not long after this, Kuntī again pleads with Yudhiṣṭhira, trying to

27. Both Karṇa and Draupadī are displaced and rejected from their rightful positions in the epic, each one taking an opposite side. Kuntī stands behind this unfolding drama as mother and mother-in-law.

mitigate her error in not telling him about Karṇa. Yudhiṣṭhira, in an instant of uncharacteristic wrath, because of his mother's pretence, 'cursed women throughout the world—they shall not bear secrets' (*śaśāpa ... sarvalokeṣu ca striyaḥ / na guhyaṃ dhārayiṣyantīti*; XII.6.10). Again, one observes that the point of this utterance is directed at the inherent power which exists within the public language of women, even in this slightly negative aspect.

After the horse sacrifice is accomplished and great wealth has been distributed by Yudhiṣṭhira to the various assembled brahmins, the sage Vyāsa gives away his portion to Kuntī, who at this point in the epic is the most distinguished of the royal women (XIV.91.27). She, far more than Draupadī, possesses seniority.[28]

Some time later, as she is about to retire from political life and embark on a renunciant existence in the forest accompanying Dhṛtarāṣṭra and Gāndhārī, Kuntī makes a final summary speech to her assembled kin, both men and women. Her decision to abandon her sons and their wives in order to enter the forest and enter upon a life of austerity is perhaps a reaction to her guilt concerning Karṇa, and conduces to this departure.

She recounts how she aided and supported them over the years and also how she fulfilled her role as queen when Pāṇḍu was alive. She tells how *pītaḥ somo* 'soma was drunk' by her, and how *bhuktaṃ rājyaphalam* 'the fruit of kingship was enjoyed'.[29] Now, however, she continues,

> nāhaṃ rājyaphalaṃ putra kāmaye putranirjitam
>
> Son—I do not desire the fruit of kingship—won by my sons.
>
> XV.23.19

Sovereignty is something of the past for her, despite the implication that she might well be in a position to enjoy great political power. Kuntī appears to be giving herself a rank that is potentially superior to that of her son, Yudhiṣṭhira. As *rājamātā* she would have enjoyed great authority, if not power, had she remained at court. According to protocol—for she has no strict relation with Dhṛtarāṣṭra—she does not need to de-

28. Sax 2002: 135, describing the *pāṇḍav līlā* in Garhwal, speaks of how "a very old woman danced into the square, possessed by Kunti." That is, the performer is *actually* possessed in spirit as she dances, *by* Kuntī. He describes her role in the drama as "elderly, maternal ... associated with motherhood, sexual modesty, nurturance, and especially virtue."

29. The reference to the Vedic soma drink is, of course, an anachronistic and faux archaic reference, unless it is—alternatively—an actual marker as to the real antiquity of parts of the epic.

part like this and assume the life of a recluse; it is presumably grief that drives her away.

Kuntī finally leaves the court at Hāstinapura and joins the old king and his wife as they set off towards the forest. She says, in conversation with Yudhiṣṭhira, that she will be *śvaṣrūśvaśurayoḥ pādāñ śuśrūṣantī* 'devoted to the feet of her parents-in-law', although technically they constitute her brother-in-law and sister-in-law (XV.22.16). Kuntī leads the formal procession in first place as they set out on foot; this marks an end to her social person as she now takes up the life of an anchorite.

> kuntī gāndhārīṃ ... skandhāsaktaṃ hastam ... udvahantī
>
> Kuntī—leading Gāndhārī—whose hand was fixed upon her shoulder.
>
> XV.21.9

Then came Dhṛtarāṣṭra, his hand upon that of Gāndhārī, followed by Draupadī, Uttarā and Citrāṅgadā and other women of the household. Ulūpī is not part of this rite as she is inhuman, a *nāgakanyā* 'snake-girl'. The assembled women of the town, of all castes and not only *kṣatriya*s, lament the departure of the old king and his two ladies (XV.21.11).

Without their mother, the Pāṇḍavas become,

> kuntyā hīnāḥ suduḥkhārtā vatsā iva vinākṛtāḥ
>
> Very unhappy without Kuntī, like destitute calves.[30]
>
> XV.24.15

In the forest that night Kuntī sleeps beside Gāndhārī, who sleeps beside her husband; all of them are on the ground, lying upon *kuśa* grass. The next evening, after Gāndhārī and her husband have bathed, Kuntī leads them both, *vṛddhaṃ śvaśuram* 'the aged father-in-law' and his wife, out of the Gaṅgā (XV.25.6). There, at an *āśrama*, she becomes *valkalājinavāsinī* 'one who wears a black deerskin and bark clothing', as do the old king and Gāndhārī (XV.25.15). The ancient sage Nārada informs Dhṛtarāṣṭra that Kuntī—whom he refers to as *vadhūs tava* 'your wife'—after her demise, *bhartuḥ salokatāṃ ... gamiṣyati* 'she will go to the same heaven as her husband', presumably meaning Dhṛtarāṣṭra and not Pāṇḍu (XV.26.18).

As a remarkable appendix to the above, there occurs a small scene during this latter part of the epic, when her sons and daughters-in-law come to visit her in the forest. It is Sahadeva who approaches her first, a son who is not actually hers, but born of her co-wife Mādrī.

30. Later the Pāṇḍavas are referred to as *mātṛnandanāḥ* 'delighters of their mother', a most distinctive epithet (XV.21.1).

sasvanaṃ prarudan dhīmān mātuḥ pādāv upaspṛśan
sā ca bāṣpāvilamukhī pradadarśa priyaṃ sutam

Weeping loudly, the wise one touched the feet of his mother,
and that one, whose face was confused with tears, saw her beloved son.

XV.31.9

When Kuntī had first set off towards the forest, she had specifically asked her eldest son, now king Yudhiṣṭhira, to take especial care of Sahadeva.

sahadeve mahārāja mā pramādaṃ kṛthāḥ kvacit
eṣa mām anurakto ...

O great king, never be careless with Sahadeva:
he is the beloved of me ...

XV.22.10

This favoritism is not manifest elsewhere and it is for a son who is undistinguished other than for beauty and diligence, and for the fact that it was he who had struck down Śakuni in the great battle (IX.27.58); Śakuni being the *mūlam* 'root' of all the wrong that had beset the family. Later, as the brothers are about to leave the forest and return to the city, Sahadeva tells Yudhiṣṭhira that *notsahe'haṃ parityaktum mātaram* 'I am not able to abandon my mother', implying that his love for her is so great (XV.44.37).[31]

Then, as Yudhiṣṭhira laments for his mother after she had died by fire in the forest, he mentions that,

sahadevaḥ priyas tasyāḥ putrebhyo'dhika ...

Sahadeva was more beloved than her other sons.

XV.46.18

This love of Kuntī's for Sahadeva is an intriguing adjunct to her story, and possesses no ostensible rationale. Perhaps it refers to something lost during the preliteracy of the text, for it signals a love that appears to have no obvious import.

2. *Gāndhārī*

Gāndhārī was betrothed by her father, Sabala, to Dhṛtarāṣṭra: *dadau* 'he gave' her. She went to the marriage compliantly even though her hus-

31. When Kuntī meets Kṛṣṇa in the Udyoga *parvan* and sings a long encomium of each individual son: only Sahadave is *priyaś ca me*, 'beloved of me' (V.88.34).

band was blind, and she became his *mahiṣī*, the primary queen (I.103.11–12). As a wife she was so devoted that she adopted her spouse's blindness.

> babandha netre sve rājan pativrataparāyaṇā
>
> O king, devoted to faithfulness she bound both her own eyes.
>
> I.103.13

Similarly, sustaining this quality of fidelity even further,

> vācāpi puruṣān anyān suvratā nānvakīrtayat
>
> The pure one did not name another man by word.
>
> I.103.17

That is, she never spoke of another man in person.

Her name derives from the place; the Gandhāras lived in the northwest of India.[32] Gāndhārī had arrived at Hāstinapura with her brother, Śakuni, who was to become a key influence—as maternal uncle—on the life of her eldest son Duryodhana.[33] 'Having given the sister' (*dattvā sa bhaginīm*), he returned to his own city (I.103.15). She of course was *parayā lakṣmyā yuktām* 'joined with great fortune', meaning wealth.

Having become pregnant, Gāndhārī aborted her condition after two years of non-fruition, having heard that her sister-in-law Kuntī had born the boy Karṇa.[34] Vyāsa managed the survival of the rejected foetus, the 'piece of flesh' (*māṃsapeśī*), and secured the production of a hundred sons: for the *garbha* 'embryo' had broken into a hundred pieces, which he incubated in a hundred jars of ghee (I.107.10–22). Duryodhana was the firstborn.[35]

Whilst she had been pregnant, Dhṛtarāṣṭra had consoled himself with the charms of a lower caste woman, a *vaiṣyā*. To her was born Yuyutsu, who, as regent to Parikṣit, the grandson of Arjuna, became the sole survivor of his grandfather's line to continue into the next generation. In time, Dhṛtarāṣṭra married off—that is, arranged matrimony for—the

32. Pāṇini is said to have come from there: Gandhara in the northeast of Peshawar, giving its name to Kandahar.

33. Just as Kṛṣṇa, the maternal uncle, was to be a key influence on the lives of Kuntī's sons.

34. There is an ambiguity here, for perhaps it was not the birth of Karṇa, but Yudhiṣṭhira who precipitates this response of Gāndhārī: the babe, however, is *arkasamatajasam* 'splendid like the sun', which is indicative of Karṇa (I.107.10).

35. Yudhiṣṭhira was born before him, however (I.107.24).

hundred sons of Gāndhārī. This strange and strangely engineered super-fertility of hers is a core aspect of the nature of her heroism; such a claim cannot be made of other women in the epic.

> sarveṣām anurūpāś ca kṛtā dārā ...
>
> He made suitable wives for them all.
>
> I.108.17

The daughter of their marriage, Duḥśālā—born at the same time as the hundred—was married off by Dhṛtarāṣṭra to Jayadratha, king of Sindhu, *saubalānumate* 'with the consent of Gāndhārī' (I.108.18). It appears that a mother needs to agree to the arrangement of a daughter's wedding, but not to that of her sons.

Immediately prior to the dicing scene in the Sabhā *parvan*, when Yudhiṣṭhira arrives at the court, and after meeting with the old king, he sees Gāndhārī, *snuṣābhiḥ saṃvṛtām* 'surrounded by daughters-in-law' (II.52.27). These daughters-in-law having observed the accomplishments and fortune of the accompanying Draupadī, 'were not pleased' (*nātipramanaso'bhavan*; II.52.32).[36] The audience never really hears of the wives of Gāndhārī's sons, it is as if their marriages are obscured and occluded by the poets; all the marital emphasis is directed at the Pāṇḍavas and their simultaneous polygamies and polyandry.

At the close of the first dicing match, when the old blind king is speaking with Yudhiṣṭhira, he tells the latter to 'regard' (*paśya*) both himself and Yudhiṣṭhira's 'mother', Gāndhārī (II.65.11). One observes again that terms for mother and father are often used in this manner: referring to close affiliation though not actually bearing the full genetic import of the term.

After the conflict of Kurukṣetra is over and Gāndhārī has lost all but one of her sons, such is the immense psychic power of the queen that the Pāṇḍavas fear to approach her, Yudhiṣṭhira especially. 'She could burn even the three worlds with her terrific heat' (*ghorena tapasā ... trailokyam api sā dahet*; IX.62.11). She is so dharmically charged that her wrath is potentially wholly destructive; this is typical of certain women heroes in the poem, and this anxiety that men possess for such glances is often repeated. Says Yudhiṣṭhira,

36. On that first evening at the court of king Dhṛtarāṣṭra, as the Pāṇḍavas retire to sleep they are sung to by women, an uncommon practice that an audience does not hear of elsewhere in the poem. 'The Pāṇḍavas, being sung to by the women, slept' (*upagīyamānā nārībhir asvapan kurunandanāḥ*; II.52.35). Perhaps these were the aforementioned daughters-in-law?

> mānasenāgninā kruddhā bhasmasān naḥ kariṣyati
>
> With the angry fire of her mind she will reduce us to ashes.
>
> IX.62.12

Trying to mollify her wrath, Kṛṣṇa tells to her, 'there is no one in the world like you' (*tvatsamā nāsti loke*; IX.62.56). He begs her not to scorch the whole world with her furious glances. Gāndhārī, of course, wears a bandage or veil which covers her eyes, effectively stopping out her vision: her one act of renunciation when she married Dhṛtarāṣṭra.

However, it was via her 'divine eyesight' (*divyena cakṣuṣā*) that she was able not only to observe the slain upon the field of Kurukṣetra, but also to describe them individually during the course of her long lament (XI.16.1ff.). Having lived 'yoked with terrific austerity' (*ugreṇa tapasā yuktā*), she thereby derived an enormous mental energy, which facilitated this preternatural ability. This potence had been augmented by the favor of Vyāsa, who had augmented her insight so that,

> dadarśa sā buddhimatī dūrād api yathāntike
>
> That wise one observed even from afar, as if it were proximate.
>
> XI.16.4

In this she was like the poet Saṃjaya, who was similarly favored with divine insight by the *ṛṣi* Vyāsa: Gāndhārī also sees by virtue of immediate inspiration. Even though actually blind—because of the veil—her knowledge is derived from the visible world and is not audial in origin. Just like Saṃjaya, she too uses the exclamatory imperative when she describes a scene before her, directing the attention of her interlocutor, or of the audience of the poem: she exclaims, *paśya* 'look!' (XI.16.18).

> yā paśyāmi hatān putrān pautrān bhrātṝṃś ca keśava
> evam ārtā vilapantī dadarśa nihataṃ sutam
>
> O Kṛṣṇa, I see sons, grandsons, brothers slain!
> Thus afflicted, lamenting, she saw her dead son.
>
> XI.16.59

The body of Duryodhana causes her to collapse, overtaken by grief. She sings a formal and traditional lament for him with Kṛṣṇa as her immediate audience, and then proceeds to describe her other fallen sons, as they lie about the field in various states of death. She portrays the widowed women who are also there, weeping for the bloody corpses of their men, surrounded by scavenging animals, birds, and canines. All this is given in direct visual terms: Gāndhārī is singing in the same manner that a poet would, being inspired and having access to a world of insight which replicates material and objective reality, particularly that reality which is visible.

It is this visual capacity which sets Gāndhārī apart from all the other women in the poem and which uniquely distinguishes her. No other woman possesses this ability of poetic and dharmic insight: such is the primary field for Gāndhārī's heroism.

After the war, when Yudhiṣṭhira has taken control at Hāstinapura, Draupadī and Subhadrā and the other Pāṇḍava women *gāndhārīm anvavartanta* 'attend upon Gāndhārī' as if she was their mother-in-law (XV.1.8). Similarly, even Kuntī 'attends to Gāndhārī as if she were a guru' (*gāndhāryāṃ guruvṛttim avartanta*).[37] All the Pāṇḍava women, including Ulūpī and Citrāṅgadā, treat Gāndhārī most respectfully, as if they were *kiṃkarās* 'servants' (XV.1.21), whilst 'she was affectionate [to them] as if they were her own offspring' (*prītimaty āsīt tanayeṣu nijeṣv iva*; XV.2.3). Yudhiṣṭhira even announces that she and Kuntī are equal in his mind (XV.6.11). Yet she remains senior in the royal household and is repeatedly described as *sarvadharmajñā* 'knowing all dharma', as well as *kālajñā* 'a knower of time'.[38]

She and her old, blind husband are constantly together in the narrative as Dhṛtarāṣṭra makes plans to retire towards the forest with his wife to assume the station of *vānaprastha*: the penultimate state in the *āśrama* system, where a husband and wife leave the household and family and live simply in a pastoral and ascetic setting.

At their departure, both Kuru and Pāṇḍava women raise a cry of lament, for this is a moment—socially and politically—that is similar to the moment of death. The formula 'crying like ospreys' is used, the phrase which occurs when women lament for dead heroes: *tāsāṃ nādo rudatīnāṃ ... āsīt ... kurarīṇām ivoccaiḥ* 'the roar of them was like the high wailing of ospreys' (XV.21.11). Gāndhārī, along with her husband, is departing from society for ever (XV.21.4).

On the second night in the forest, the old king and Gāndhārī descend to the river to perform *śaucam* 'ablution' together (XV.25.4). At this stage in their joint life they are in no way separated in their various daily activities; at night they sleep side by side upon the earth. Some years later, the royal husband and wife, along with Kuntī, ritually surrender themselves to be consumed by a forest conflagration (XV.44.31). Despite

37. The lemma *guru* bears the meaning of 'any venerable or respectable person (father, mother, or any relative older than one's self)'. Monier-Williams.

38. Although *kāla* does bear the equal nuance of 'death'.

her unique powers of vision, Gāndhārī's life, like that of Kuntī, was also marked by terrific misery and emotional pain.

3. Damayantī

When Damayantī comes of age, she is so beautiful that even the deities long for her, *devānām api sundarī* 'beautiful, even to the deities' (III.50.13).[39] She is like Śacī, the wife of Indra, surrounded by a hundred companions. All this occurs *vayasi prāpte* 'when youth was obtained', referring to her sexual maturity or first menstruation.[40]

The narrative of Damayantī is told by the *ṛṣi* Bṛhadaśva to Yudhiṣṭhira. It is a parable about the folly of gambling and the devotion of a wife who saves her beloved spouse from his crazed misfortune.[41] Damayantī is thus a model to whom Draupadī is supposed to be morally akin: a strong and irreproachable wife whose love redeems her husband's madness. There is a difference in their position, however, insofar as Draupadī is ferocious whilst Damayantī is not, the latter woman being almost entirely beneficent.

The song of Damayantī is given, just as the songs of Sītā and Sāvitrī are performed, as a means of alleviating and mollifying the distress that Yudhiṣṭhira feels: these women heroes are mirrors for the honor and devotion of Draupadī.[42] Yudhiṣṭhira is being reminded about how extraordinary his wife is and he should thus be aroused from despondence. It is remarkable that the poets use model women for this

39. Flueckiger 1996, Ch. 7, describes the recording of "a *paṇḍvānī* performance, which happened to be on the Nal and Damayanti episode, from a middle-aged blind singer of the Marar (vegetable-seller) caste", in 1983. She discusses three other performances of this episode recorded later, in 1993 (160ff.), beginning with the statement that, "These Chhattisgarhi performances reflect numerous regional variations and localizations, but on the level of plot, the performances follow the general contours of the Sanskrit narrative amazingly closely. Kings and princes from all over the world arrive in hopes of being chosen by the exquisite princess (the *svayamvar* characterized, in one Chhattisgarhi performance, as a 'beauty competition', to which 'kings from America, England, Australia, everywhere', arrived)." (161).

40. The name Damayantī is connected with the root √*dam* 'to subdue, overpower, tame'. Damayantī is gifted in this capacity to control and subdue affairs, particularly as they relate to her husband, Nala. She is the one to restore him and her family to the kingdom. See Doniger 1999: 140ff., where she examines this account and makes comparisons with Greek Penelope.

41. Flueckiger 1966: 168 comments that the "narrative of Nal and Damayanti [is] a love story in which love is first characterized by the heroine's self-choice and then her determination to hold onto that choice against overwhelming odds." This is "an ideal love ... not only of erotic passion but also companionship." In Koskikallio 2005: 113–135, von Simson examines the tale in terms of a "calendar myth."

42. The Rāmāyaṇa episode is sung at III.257–275; that of Sāvitrī at III.277–282.

purpose and that Yudhiṣṭhira is not emotionally supported with *kathā*, tales of martial prowess and adventure.[43]

It is a bird, the *haṃsa* 'goose', that is the go-between for the prospective lovers, suggesting to Damayantī that she would make a good 'wife' (*bhāryā*) for Nala; and similarly, the bird describes him to her (III.50.27). Soon she is languishing for her desired one: she becomes *kṛśā* 'thin', *vivarṇavadanā* 'pale-faced', *dīnā* 'miserable', sleepless and despondent (III.51.2–4). Thus it is not long before they marry.[44]

For twelve years she has a joyous marriage with Nala. When he becomes possessed by a demon and loses all of his property in a dicing match she instantly takes control and summons the *mantrins* 'counselors'. When Nala ignores her, however, she, 'one who understands place and time' (*deśakālajñā*) then calls her 'charioteer' *sūta*—always a key figure for royalty—and consigns her two children to his care, instructing him to return them to her father's household (III.57.9–21).[45]

Damayantī, unlike Draupadī, lacks wrath and fury, for she is compassionate and mild. Draupadī has a cruel, remorseless quality about her, in her unmitigated desire for vengeance; and perhaps this love story bears a message not only for Yudhiṣṭhira but also for his wife, who, one presumes, is part of Bṛhadaśva's audience.

Thus, Nala's opponent in the dicing game, when Nala lost everything, tells him to stake Damayantī. Unlike Yudhiṣṭhira, he refuses. Then, wearing only one item of clothing, he sets off towards the forest with Damayantī similarly clad, following. When even his single item of clothing is lost, she still keeps by him, saying,

> vane ghore mahārāja nāśayiṣyāmi te klamam
>
> O king, in the terrible woods, I shall drive away your exhaustion!
>
> III.58.26

She is fully portrayed after the model of the *pativratā* 'the devoted, virtuous wife'. Even when Nala strips off half her clothing in order to cover his own nakedness and then leaves her alone and sleeping in the jungle, she remains completely dedicated to him and uncritical. Wailing in her grief, she is likened to a *kurarī*, the bird that is usually translated as an

43. There is the *Rāma-kathā*, but this arguably also concerns a woman. I am indebted to Pradip Bhattacarya for this observation.

44. See above, Ch. II.3, for a description of her marriage process.

45. The name of the charioteer is Vārṣṇeya, also an epithet of Kṛṣṇa, who is the charioteer of Arjuna. The children of Draupadī and her husbands, during their departure from the court at Hāstinapura, had been sent off to be fostered by their cousin Kṛṣṇa's family.

'osprey', the creature that is typically the emblem of feminine despair and mourning (III.60.19).[46]

Attacked by a giant snake, which is about to consume her, Damayantī is saved by a hunter who kills the serpent. He, however, is soon lusting after her, and she, with a truth act, causes the man to fall lifeless to the earth: such is the heroic power of her virtuous speech (III.60.37–38). As we have observed elsewhere, the domestic purity of women is capable of achieving preternatural force. Just as male heroes at times become supernatural in their power, so too do some of the women in the epic gain unnatural energy: such potence is typically verbal, whereas for men it is physical, as when they perform great feats of weaponry. With Gāndhārī, it is her glance that possesses energy, with Damayantī, it is her speech. Draupadī never obtains to such unnatural gifts, for she is absolutely human.

Alone in the forest, *nābibhyat* 'she did not fear', but utters a long, plaintive and lyrical monologue directed at Nala, pitiful and full of love, without bitterness, concerning the manner in which he abandoned her, daughter of a king, daughter-in-law of a king, and wife of a king. Again, this is a mirror of Draupadī and reflection of her language (III.61.12–55). In it, she sublimely praises the beauties and terrors of the forest and countryside as much as she does her absent husband. Once again, unlike Draupadī—whom an audience can assume is there beside Yudhiṣṭhira listening to this parable—Damayantī bears neither violent emotion nor rage nor contempt; she is purely devoted and lacking in resentment.

Damayantī's passage through the woods and terrain and her admiration for its visual beauty is one of several moments in the Mahābhārata where landscape is praised and given an aesthetic quality by the poets.

> imaṃ śilocccayaṃ puṇyaṃ śṛṅgair bahubhir ucchritaiḥ
> virājadbhir divaspṛgbhir naikavarṇair manoramaiḥ
>
> This auspicious mountain—with many beautiful, variously colored, shining, lofty sky-touching crests ...
>
> III.61.35

An appreciation of terrain and topography for its harmony and loveliness is rare in this epic and is often connected with places where ascetics have established a refuge and where the feminine lives in unhindered propriety. The detailing of the many kinds of tree and fauna and the physical aspects of place are something that occurs more frequently in

46. *Prakīrṇakeśyo vyathitāḥ kuraryeva duḥkhitāḥ / petuḥ putrān pitṛn bhrātṝñ śocamānā mahītale* 'Possessing disheveled hair, troubled, distressed, like ospreys grieving, they fell upon sons, fathers, brothers, upon the earth' (III.170.56).

later classical poetry, as with Kalidāsa for instance, or in the Third Book of the Rāmāyaṇa, where all the marvels and brilliance of the *āraṇya* are depicted. In the Mahābhārata, such scenes are often connected with virtuous young women, as with Śakuntalā in her forest refuge.[47]

Coming across an *āśrama* 'hermitage', Damayantī is greeted by the ascetics who—because of her radiant appearance—ask her if she is *āraṇyasya mahatī devatā* 'the great deity of the forest'? She replies to them, telling her story, much of which is praise for Nala (III.61.70ff.). They inform her that she will soon be with her husband once again and vanish into the air. It is telling that these supernatural figures consider her to be even more potent than they are.

When she comes across 'a great caravan' (*mahāsārtham*), she is *unmattarūpā, śokārtā, kṛśā, vivarṇā, malinā* 'distracted, afflicted with grief, emaciated, pale, filthy' (III.61.110). The men of the traveling band think that she is a *yakṣī*, or *rākṣasī* 'wood-spirit, demon', so far has Damayantī fallen from her former royal and human status and appearance and assumed the likeness of a natural force.

There is a beautiful and piteous moment when Damayantī pleads with an *aśoka* tree to dispel her grief and bring back her estranged husband. She plays with the word 'grief' (*śoka*).

> viśokāṃ kuru māṃ kṣipram aśoka priyadarśana
>
> O lovely *aśoka* tree, quickly make me griefless!
>
> III.61.99

The grief and sorrow which many women in the Mahābhārata receive is a common theme that runs throughout the poem. The despondency of epic women is often deeply inherent to their life and is, I would propose, a vital component to their heroic being. Women in this epic are generally figures of extraordinary mental suffering, demonstrated in particular by Draupadī and Kuntī: this duress is woven primarily upon strands of kinship.

The narrative continues through various adventures, during which time Damayantī remains utterly intent on finding Nala and renewing her marriage. Her devotion is pathetic and relentless, the best paradigm of wifely virtue. Eventually she reaches the city of the Cedis and is taken in by the queen, who having been attracted to Damayantī's superb looks, appoints her to be a maid.[48] 'You shine like lightning

47. See below, Ch. VI.1.

48. Just as Draupadī had been favored and taken in by the queen of the Virāṭas, who was similarly attracted by her looks. Physical attraction among women is a tenuous but constant thread in the poem.

among clouds' the queen remarks, concerning her beauty (*bhāsi vidyud ivābhreṣu*; III.62.23).[49]

A servant sent by Damayantī's father identifies her, and sings a long series of verses describing her beauty (III.65.10–20). She is dark, her face is like a full moon, she is a deity, with eyes like the petalled lotos. He does add, however, that 'the husband is indeed the highest ornament of a wife' (*bhartā nāma paraṃ nāryā bhūṣaṇaṃ*; III.65.18). Damayantī has a *piplu* a 'mole or freckle' situated between her eyes: and it is by this sign that she is ultimately recognized by her father's brahmin.[50]

> asyā rūpeṇa sadṛśī mānuṣī neha vidyate
>
> Such a woman with her beauty is not found here on earth.
>
> III.66.5

Damayantī remains completely loyal to Nala; nothing can detract her from that affiliation, for no matter how callously he has treated her she remains true to him. This is the ideal *kṣatriya* woman, undeviating in her dedication to her husband despite wretchedness and despair. Eventually she is returned to her father's household, where, on hearing about what seems to be the presence of Nala in another city, she herself determines to hold a second *svayaṃvara*. It is her choice, not her father's to do this, and it is unique for a woman previously married to retry such a ritual (III.68.21). She, of course, hopes that Nala will enter the lists again so that she might be able to select him one more time.

On hearing of this, Nala exclaims to himself, *strīsvabhāvaś calo loke* 'woman's being is unstable in the world!' (III.69.6). This is exactly what Damayantī has not displayed: it is Nala who has toppled. Not long after this statement, however, he says,

> vaiṣamyam api saṃprāptā gopāyanti kulastriyaḥ
> ātmānam ātmanā satyo jitasvargā na saṃśayaḥ
>
> Eminent women, even having obtained misfortune, protect themselves: virtuous women doubtless conquer heaven!
>
> III.72.25

The term *jitasvarga* 'one who conquers heaven' is a term typically employed to denote a hero who dies in battle, one who has surrendered his life in order to sustain good *kṣatriya* values and acquire fame. Such a 'virtuous woman', Damayantī the *satī*, thus partakes of the semantic field usually associated with male heroics. Says Nala,

49. Lightning is observed during monsoon, the fertile time of the year.

50. This is reminiscent of a third eye, which is borne by certain deities, namely Śiva. Again, Damayantī is being portrayed as almost preternatural.

rahitā bhartṛbhiś caiva na krudhyanti kadācana
prāṇāṃś cāritrakavacā dhārayantīha satstriyaḥ

Women abandoned by husbands are never provocative.
Virtuous women, protected by reputation, preserve life on earth.

III.72.26

After the couple finally unite once again—and this is after a separation of three years—even then she defends her honor and integrity, saying that *manasā* 'even in thought' she had never deserted him. She then makes another truth act, this time in defence of her virtue, uttering the statement three times:[51]

eṣa muñcatu me prāṇān yadi pāpaṃ carāmy aham

May this release my life—if I perform an error!

III.75.7

Here, *eṣa* refers consecutively to the wind, the sun, and the moon, who are being invoked to witness her excellence and honesty.

Damayantī, *samavāptakāmā* 'her desires fulfilled', shone 'like a night with a risen moon' (*śītāṃśunā rātrir ivoditena*); and she was like 'the earth having received water' (*toyaṃ prāpya vasuṃdharā*; III.75.26–27). Both these images are charming, lyrical, and intimately fertile, and should remind Yudhiṣṭhira of his dear wife.

This fairly lengthy account—one of the most famously distinct micro-narratives within the overall body of the text—is not simply a fable about the strength of monogamy, but concerns the power that women as wives possess vis-à-vis men. They are *plava* or *nauḥ*, a 'raft', 'boat', who can save their men from troubled seas. Despite the deluded folly of these menfolk—particularly in their compulsion for gambling—such women, Draupadī, Damayantī, and later, Sāvitrī, are powerful and capable and their strength—especially their verbal strength—is a great support for the male, if not an actual saving. Only Draupadī, however, demonstrates an unconditional rage, a remorseless and implacable drive; but then, no other woman in the poem suffers like her. Anger is typically not an emotion that good women and good wives project, and if they do, it is always compounded with grief.

This short poem of love ended with Nala having to reclaim his wife from her father's household, a requirement that reflected upon his misdemeanor towards Damayantī. Then, when he has ejected his

51. One recalls the importance of Sītā's hypothetical virtue in the Rāmāyaṇa and the consequences of that doubt.

wicked brother from the throne, 'an outcaste king' (*rājāpasadaḥ*), he tells him that Damayantī *na tvayā śakyā ... vīkṣitum* 'is not to be looked at by him' (III.77.20). Once again, the queen is reserved only for the eyes of the king and their most private staff: it is not exactly seclusion, yet she is reserved.

Of all the micro-narratives in the epic, the song of Damayantī and Nala is perhaps the most common of popular Mahābhārata tellings throughout India today. Even in the contemporary subcontinent, Damayantī remains an ideal of pure and yet practical femininity, capable of sustaining the weaknesses of her husband and of enabling him to eventually triumph.[52]

4. *Sāvitrī*

Sāvitrī is first described, even before she is born, by the goddess Sāvitrī, who promises *kanyā tejasvinī* 'a dazzling girl' to the king who is about to become her father (III.277.17). This word *tejas* is a word that is more generally an attribute of heroes, or in some cases, ascetics. As we shall see, Sāvitrī is exceptionally capable in her worldly life, and almost usurps the masculine position at times. In time, the king's senior wife, the *mahiṣī*, soon becomes successfully impregnated and the child is born; she grows to marriageable age and is *pratimāṃ kāñcanīm iva* 'like a golden image' (III.277.26).[53]

The problem is that men avoid Sāvitrī, for she is too splendid and too pure: *tāṃ ... na kaścid varayāmāsa tejasā prativāritaḥ* 'no one chose her—prevented by the splendor' (III.277.27). Such intense goodness is off-putting for the men of her community even though she is a princess. It is as if Sāvitrī is quasi-divine and men are fearful of engaging with that quality in case it turns negative: the feminine can at times be seriously daunting for men in its possible duality of mood. Also, as Jamison has noted, "the brotherless maiden is an unappealing marriage prospect for other reasons, since she is structurally likely to be a *putrikā* or 'appointed daughter'. Her firstborn son would be claimed by her own family, as a male heir able to perform ancestor worship for her sonless father."[54]

52. Fleuckiger 1996: 174–175 describes how at a performance of the Nal Damayanti song, the poet, Manmohan Sinha—a forty-five year old high school graduate who was also a construction worker during the day—"ends the narrative performance with the line: 'The woman was left alone in the jungle'." The poet was tired and it was late. "The women in the audience were aghast ... Manmohan answered simply, 'Well, you know the story.'"

53. There are few references to statuary in the Mahābhārata. Carved stone images are not known in the subcontinent until the time of the early Mauryas, the capitals of the Aśokan columns being considered the earliest pieces. Curiously, in this same episode, the audience hears of a child who *karoty aśvāṃś ca mṛnmayān* 'makes clay horses' (III.278.13).

54. Jamison 1996: 302. She observes (305n96), "As she is the *only* daughter of Aśvapati, her potential status of 'appointed daughter' may have put people off as well."

Sāvitrī herself eventually elects to marry a man whose life is destined to only continue for one more year.[55] As his ultimate day on earth approaches she performs a *vrata* 'a vow' or 'vigil', and then—which is unusual for *kṣatriya* women—'having offered an oblation to the blazing fire' (*hutvā dīptaṃ hutāśanam*), she waits. When the final dawn arrives, she, the *vadhū* 'wife', insists on accompanying her husband to the forest, which means stepping outside of the *āśrama* for the first time since she was wed: that is, one year. To do this, however, she needs to have the permission of her father-in-law (III.280.27–28). They, of course, are unaware of their son's condition and of his imminent terminus.

Satyavat, the husband, soon loses consciousness and dies and Yama 'Death', carrying a noose, comes to claim his spirit, which has the form of 'a thumb-sized man' (*aṅguṣṭhamātraṃ puruṣam*; III.281.16). Yama addresses her as a *pativratā* 'virtuous wife', and now commence the heroic moments of Sāvitrī: for with her sagacious speech and knowledge of dharma she succeeds in detaining Yama and confounding him, so that he becomes verbally obligated to her.

She insists on following Yama as he sets off with the thumb-sized man, the soul of her husband. Yama tells her to 'turn back' (*nirvarta*) and 'go' (*gaccha*), to which she refuses, citing dharma to the effect that a wife must always follow her man. Yama, impressed by her loyalty, speaks the usual formula given by a deity who is about to offer a favor, *tuṣṭo'smi* 'I am pleased'; and he asks her to 'choose a favor' (*varaṃ vṛṇīṣva*; III.281.25).

This process is repeated: Sāvitrī following, being spurned and citing dharma in response, and explaining why she continues to follow. Yama offers further favors, impressed by her attention to the law and her devotion to her husband. He tells her,

> yathā yathā bhāṣasi dharmasaṃhitaṃ
> manonukūlaṃ supadaṃ mahārthavat
> tathā tathā me tvayi bhaktiruttamā
>
> As you speak according to dharma,
> dignified, good words, agreeable to mind,
> so great is my love for you.
>
> III.281.50

She succeeds in gaining five favors in all: choosing first to benefit her father-in-law, then her own father, and only in the end does she ask to

55. "Here Sāvitrī not only chooses for herself ... but conducts the search. The candidate(s) are not brought to her; she must go into the world, unprotected by her parents. However, the exchange aspects of the marriage remain conventional. Though she *chooses*, her father *gives*." Jamison 1996: 247.

save her husband's life. Again, the scale of affection reveals the order or priorities of her rightful affiliation.

Later when her husband recovers and they are talking, she tells him, *na smarāmy uktapūrvaṁ ... anṛtāṃ giram* 'I do not remember previously uttered improper speech', for she has always spoken truthfully throughout her life. This is something that Yudhiṣṭhira has similarly essayed: thus the poets are placing her in an equal position to the *dharmarāja*. Sāvitrī is a model for him, she is an ideal mirror for the king to reflect upon in his present exiled despondence and become more aware of the causality which lies inherent in his own speech: he who is putatively the most dharmic of heroes. As with Damayantī, the intelligence and adept language of Sāvitrī is what saves a situation from calamity and the Pāṇḍava should attend to this lesson.

Having thus described her verbal integrity she proceeds to make a truth act with the usual formula *tena satyena* 'by this truth', in order that Satyavat's parents do not die—something which is worrying him—as he and Sāvitrī have not returned home from the forest that evening.

The parents, however, had already begun to search for their son, visiting all the local hermitages. As Sāvitrī is *sādhvī vadhūḥ* 'a good wife', they remain optimistic for his life. The refrain that goes about the hermitages is:

> yathāsya bhāryā sāvitrī tapasā ca damena ca
> ācāreṇa ca saṃyuktā tathā jīvati satyavān
>
> As Sāvitrī his wife is joined with good conduct and
> restraint and austerity, so Satyavat lives!
>
> III.282.10

This statement in itself takes the form of a truth act, and is pendant upon the extraordinary moral valor and vitality which Sāvitrī has demonstrated: something which is elemental and likened to a natural force.

Thus her succinct and informed speech has won her husband back, and Death is most generous to her; Yama must therefore necessarily return not only the life of Sāvitrī's husband, but he must also extend the lives and fortune of Satyavat's parents and return the sight to his father's eyes as well as give the father a hundred sons. He is also obliged to enable Sāvitrī to bear a hundred sons herself and to live for four hundred years together with her husband. Like so many of the women heroes in the poem, Sāvitrī is not actually human but partakes of supernatural qualities.

The account conveys a remarkable exchange of words, which Sāvitrī has brilliantly achieved via prudent and judicious speech. More than perhaps any other women in the poem, in terms of efficacity at least, Sāvitrī is a truly great SPEAKER. Throughout this episode, the message that Yudhiṣṭhira and the audience receives is that Sāvitrī is endowed with extraordinary spiritual and emotional vigor: her purity and mental clarity, as well as her knowledge of the correct dharma of a wife, enable her not only to sustain the life of her husband, but also that of her parents-in-law and the clan itself, as she herself produces a century of sons. Her shrewd and brilliant use of language saves everyone.

Her name derives from Savitṛ, the name of 'the sun before rising', 'mother' in the feminine.[56] She is thus a force that is undisclosed and yet absolutely vivifying and thoroughly beneficent; someone who—with her wisdom—can even turn back death. No other woman in the poem achieves such heroic powers of verbal effect: she is almost akin to a *ṛṣi* in this respect.[57]

> evam ātmā pitā mātā śvaśrūḥ śvaśuraiva ca
> bhartuḥ kulaṃ ca sāvitryā sarvaṃ kṛcchrāt samuddhṛtam
>
> Thus by Sāvitri all was uplifted from danger: her husband's clan, her father and mother-in-law, and her own mother and father, and her self also.
>
> III.283.14

5. *Ambā*

Unlike the accounts of Damayantī and Sāvitrī and Sītā, the life of Ambā is not given in a micro-narrative within the epic, but is a sub-plot that runs in and out of the main course of the poem, one which has important consequences for the development of the poem itself.[58]

Having been spurned by the man to whom she had pledged herself, after her *rākṣasa* marriage has gone awry, she sets out on a life of embittered wandering:

> pṛthivyāṃ nāsti yuvatir viṣamasthatarā mayā
>
> There is no young woman on earth more unfortunate than me!
>
> V.173.1

This is similar to the cry of Draupadī, to that of Kuntī, or later, of

56. Monier-Williams, quoting Sāyaṇa. The root is sū 'to give birth'.
57. Aklujkar, in Sharma 1991: 324–333, examines later variations of Sāvitrī's story.
58. See McGrath 2000 and Doniger 1999: 281ff., where she reviews Ambā's story.

Gāndhārī: women in the Mahābhārata suffer intensely on the grounds of feeling and affection. Ambā was to have wed King Śālva, whom, she says, *mayā varayitavyo'bhūt ... svayaṃvare* 'was to be selected by me at the *svayaṃvara*' (I.96.49). She is now without kin, without the man to whom she had given herself, and even repelled by Bhīṣma, her abductor, for he had taken a terrific vow of celibacy.[59]

Who, she asks herself, is culpable: herself, Bhīṣma, or her father who arranged the *svayaṃvara*? She should have leapt from the chariot, she says (V.173.4). This is something that never occurs, however, at least, not in the poetry: women submit to such formal appropriations. Ambā begins to decry the world and those who have led her into this outcaste situation: *dhik*, she repeatedly exclaims, 'damn!', and she includes her 'stupid father with his deluded mind' (*mandaṃ pitaram mūḍhacetasam*) in this list (V.173.5). Even Dhātā, the 'Creator', receives her condemnation. Bhīṣma she considers to be the root cause of her deplorable condition, however, and her resolution to revenge herself supplies the force for the rest of this minor narrative.

She leaves the town where she had been rejected and joins a group of male ascetics in order to learn the arts of austerity. They are initially troubled and hesitant about accepting her into their community and advise her to return to her father. They say,

> patir vāpi gatir nāryāḥ pitā vā ...
>
> Either a husband or a father is the way of a woman ...
>
> V.174.7

They also add that,

> tvām ihaikākinīṃ dṛṣṭvā nirjane gahane vane
> prārthayiṣyanti rajendrās ...
>
> Having observed you, alone in the solitary and impenetrable forest,
> kings will demand you in marriage ...
>
> V.174.10

This is what had happened to Śakuntalā and to Draupadī. Ambā replies that she is unable to return to her family's house, for,

> avajñātā bhaviṣyāmi bāndhavānāṃ na saṃśayaḥ
>
> Doubtless, I shall be despised by my kin.
>
> V.174.11

59. Dumézil 1979: 83–86, draws attention to the parallelism which exists between Ambā and Brynhildr, who are both involved in "le drame de la «maldonne»."

A royal seer then arrives at the *āśrama* and hearing of Ambā's story he speaks to her, *tāṃ kanyām aṅkam āropya* 'having placed the girl on his lap', a gesture of great familiarity; for he is in fact the 'father of her mother' (*mātur…janakas*; V.174.17). He advises her not to return to her family, but to go and seek the great hero Rāma Jāmadagnya. This is the shady arch-hero of the poem, who had instructed several of the greatest warriors of the epic in martial skills, including Bhīṣma and Karṇa. 'I would put to death Bhīṣma in battle', Ambā says (*ghātayeyam… raṇe bhīṣmam*).

On meeting Rāma, Ambā requests that he 'kill Bhīṣma' (*jahi bhīṣmam*), repeating her wish three times. Rāma is hence obliged—by the force of her speech—to challenge Bhīṣma, who once again refuses to take Ambā back. Illustrating the irrevocability of the *rākṣasa* form of marriage, Rāma tells him,

> tvayā vibhraṃśitā hīyaṃ bhartāraṃ na adhigacchati
>
> This woman is fallen on account of you: she cannot obtain a husband!
>
> V.78.18

Bhīṣma responds by saying that no man would cause a 'woman who loves another' (*parabhāvā nārī*) to live in his house like a 'snake' (*vyāla*). This does raise the question as to the state of an unmarried woman, and in this case, Ambā has also departed from her paternal household. As we have observed earlier concerning the condition of widowhood, an unattached woman, like Damayantī perhaps or Draupadī in the Virāṭa kingdom, is particularly destabilizing for men. It is as if there exists a social tension or charge that lingers about such women, which is not the case for solitary men: feminine sexuality is irresistible. A life of renunciation is the only possible recourse here and sexuality must be abjured.

Rāma fails to punish Bhīṣma and Ambā sets off alone, determined to practice ferocious austerity in order to gain the power that will defeat her former abductor: 'contemplating death' (*cintayatī vadham*), she goes off to the forest (V.187.10). Eventually she becomes a 'river' (*nadī*), a small stream, with half of her body, the other half remaining a woman (V.187.39–40).[60] She is despairing,

> patilokād vihīnā ca naiva strī na pumān iha
>
> Deprived of the world of a husband, neither woman nor man!
>
> V.188.4

60. It is curious that in order to destroy Bhīṣma she becomes like Bhīṣma's mother, a river.

There remains only one course,

> strībhāve parinirviṇṇā puṃstvarthe kṛtaniścayā
>
> Disgusted with femininity, I am resolved on masculinity!
>
> V.188.6

Śiva appears to Ambā, drawn down by her fearful austerities: something which only males usually accomplish. Offering her a favor he accomplishes her desire to become a man: she will become a *mahāratha* 'a great warrior', born into the clan of Drupada, the father of Draupadī (V.188.13). Thus Ambā, having constructed a great pyre, ignites it and enters the fire, terminating her first life. Ironically, this is the gesture of a *satī*, a widow.

She was born again as a girl to the wife of Drupada and thus became a de facto sister-in-law of the Pāṇḍavas. Strangely, her new parents refused to admit this fact concerning her femininity and brought her up as if she were a boy, and at maturity they determined to find a wife for this girl-boy: it is as if destiny continues to elude her. Yet this is done and a marriage performed, and eventually the new young wife discovers that her husband is in fact a woman and informs her companions and servants (V.190.15). It is as if the poets are toying with every possibility of sexual difference here, including transvestism. Bhīṣma's renunciation in life has been so terrific that his dramatic counterpoint must possess an equally charged ambi-sexuality.

The woman, Śikhaṇḍinī, realizing that her father-in-law intended to attack her father out of anger at being so deceived, fled once again to the forest, always a place of neutrality.[61] A *yakṣa* with whom she meets offers to exchange his *puṃsliṅga* 'male sign' for her *strīliṅga*, 'feminine sign': that is, genitalia (V.193.2–4), and the problem of the salutary marriage is thus resolved to the relief of all parties.

Many years thereafter, Śikhaṇḍin the man eventually participates in the great battle at Kurukṣetra, fighting on the side of the Pāṇḍavas. At one point in the mêlée, Bhīṣma, having encountered Śikhaṇḍin and 'having recalled the femininity of Śikhaṇḍin' (*strītvaṃ cintya śikhaṇḍinaḥ*; VI.82.26), turns away from his opponent, for he had vowed never to strike at a woman.[62] Thus, despite his overt masculinity, the femininity of Śikhaṇḍin-Ambā is so intrinsic as to pervade true nature: this is not so much a previous life but more of a transexual state.

61. See below. Ch. VI.1.

62. Bhīṣma reiterates this refusal to strike at Śikhaṇḍin-Śikhaṇḍinī at VI.94.14ff., because of his-her femininity: he was *strīpurvaka* 'previously feminine' (VI.95.8).

Bhīṣma informs Yudhiṣṭhira and his brothers of how—using Śikhaṇḍin as a shield—they can approach him and slay him, for he refuses to strike at Śikhaṇḍin (VI.103.99ff.). A *kṣatriya* cannot strike a woman, and Bhīṣma cannot attack Ambā, for she is:

> striyāṃ strīpūrvake cāpi strīnāmnī strīsvarūpiṇi
>
> A woman and also previously a woman, with the name of a woman, formed as a woman.
>
> V.193.62

In a temporal and morphological sense, Ambā is thoroughly feminine, and the term which Bhīṣma repeatedly employs to indicate this intensity is *strī*: for *strī* is inviolable and irrefragible. Femininity is a quality which cannot be modified or in any way altered, and thus would seem to approximate to an absolute.

There is the curious later phrase, where Bhīṣma, in battle, in not striking at Śikhaṇḍin, *sa ca tan nāvabuddhavān* 'was not aware of it'. The 'it' refers to his *strītvam* 'femininity' (VI.112.80); and yet, if he is unaware of this, one wonders how her sexuality was actually constituted? Perhaps this simply refers to his celibate condition: what he has rejected returns to slay him.

Bhīṣma is felled by Arjuna, who is protected by this human and feminine shield (VI.114), and Śikhaṇḍin-Ambā is eventually killed during the Sauptika *parvan*. The message is that femininity is not to be the subject of violence and is never to be assailed by a true *kṣatriya*: Draupadī is of course the exception.[63]

Having had her maidenhood spoiled, her reputation clouded, the only recourse for a young woman, it would appear, is via the male use of weapons: bronze. Draupadī faced a similar situation, having been so humiliated in the *sabhā*, yet she had to rely on the physical revenge wreaked by her husbands and their armies and allies. She was not unattached. Ambā in her life conquered *bhīṣma*, a common noun meaning 'that which is terrific', which she accomplished by becoming a man. The message is that the horror of violence is a semantic field reserved for the male only, and so Ambā became *manyunāviṣṭā* 'intent upon anger' (V.172.19).[64]

63. "In the Balinese version [of the Mahābhārata], Shikandi, the half-man, half-woman who rode on Arjuna's chariot to undermine Bhishma's ability to fight, had turned into Srikanti, Arjuna's wife." Bose 2006: 255.

64. *Kopa, manyu, krodha, saṃrabdha*: these are terms that signify varieties of 'anger'. The latter term, *saṃrabdha*, denotes a warrior's limitless 'rage' as when he becomes berserk; *kopa* indicates 'passion' or 'to be violently moved'. *Manyu* and *krodha* refer respectively to 'mettle, anger', and 'fury or resentment'.

The account of Ambā provides the epic with an internal and inherent portrait of boundary and function: only men take up arms and destroy. For a woman to cross this line is for her to suffer extraordinary mental anguish. Violence is a solely male privilege and the power of women lies in their ability with speech. The destiny of Ambā was unusual, for its combination of austerity and for its sexual translation. The usual feminine trajectories were all foreclosed in her case, as she pursued a life of unrelenting revenge.

Without Ambā the Pāṇḍavas could not have found victory at Kurukṣetra, for the hero Bhīṣma was too great to overcome. It is ironic that this greatest of heroes is felled by one whose name, Ambā, denotes 'mother' or 'good woman'.

In conclusion to this chapter I would like to cite the small image of a city that has succumbed to attack, and where a victor enters in all triumph. This occurs in Book Three when Arjuna, having defeated the Nivātakavacas, drives his chariot through the stricken town.

The *dārās* 'wives' are 'screaming like geese in autumn' (*prākrośan...yathā śaradi lakṣmaṇāḥ*; III.169.21). The *striyaḥ* 'women' are fearful of the sound of his chariot, and 'they ran in crowds' (*prādravan gaṇaśaḥ*).

> tābhir ābharaṇaiḥ śabdas trāsitābhiḥ samīritaḥ
> śilānām iva śaileṣu patantīnām abhūt tadā
>
> The noise sent forth by the ornaments—by those trembling women—
> was like falling stones in the mountains.
>
> III.169.24

Such is the terror and horror that these women feel and exhibit due to the rout which their menfolk have suffered in battle. It is not a frequent image for the epic, and the sound of the noisy jewelry conveys this disorder most forcefully and yet with delicacy.

In medieval times in India, the defeat of a defending army was frequently accompanied by the pillage and spoliation of their city. There exist accounts of how the women on these occasions, especially Rajput women, ritually destroyed themselves by 'mass suicide' (*jauhar*). This occurred after the siege of Chitor in 1567, when the emperor Akbar triumphed, and is emblematic of such a codified response to being vanquished. The reaction of the women in the city cited in the above example touches upon this kind of self-immolation.

Towards the end of the Mahābhārata, in the Āśramavāsika

parvan—through the power of Vyāsa—all the deceased from Kurukṣetra appear and rise up from the Bhāgīrathī river. It is a vision that the sage grants to those '*kṣatriya* widows' (*kṣatriyā nihateśvarā*). He says,

> yā yāḥ patikṛtāṅ lokān icchanti paramastriyaḥ
>
> Whatever most excellent women desire—worlds formed by their husbands ...
>
> XV.41.18

He tells them to enter the waters of the river where they become *vimuktā mānuṣair dehais* 'freed of human bodies', united with the spirits or souls of their deceased male kin.

This is not exactly *jauhar* 'a rite of suicide', for the situation is supernatural: nor is it as if the women were ascending the funeral pyre of their husbands. Yet the women are giving up mortal life—emancipated, as it were, of human form—in order to join with their men. They are not ascending the cremation pyre and dying but transcending towards a state of further marital union with their deceased menfolk.

The world of kinship is the one arena where women heroes live out their time according to *kṣatriya* dharma. They dramatize this system—in moments of crisis—by reminding their menfolk about the right action of a hero. Only rarely do women cross the boundary and enter into a region of aggression which their fathers, husbands, and sons inhabit. One could assert that if the fortunes of men in this epic society are to be found in warfare and bloodshed, then the fortunes of women in the Mahābhārata occur within the compounding of marriage: battle in this model would be as much an initiation as is childbirth, for young men and women.[65]

The conversations which occur between women, either as admonition or enquiry, exhibit the values that women place upon various aspects of their femininity: but these are always within the module and locus of family. It is only men who venture outside of that form and they typically do so in order to act violently.

Draupadī traverses this margin solely—but frequently—in her language; Ambā enters the domain of coercion and weaponry after an anguished transexual shift. For Damayantī and Sāvitrī, it is speech and the intelligence which inspires a correct formulation of words that truly organizes the world where woman heroes act, supplying and supporting the fabric of their kinship. For Gāndhārī, it is her preternatural and

65. See Vernant 1974: 38: "Le mariage est pour la fille ce que la guerrre est au garçon: pour tous deux, ils marquent l'accomplissement de leur nature respective."

excellent vision that allows her to assume the strength of poetic speech and to actually inflict a physical wound. Kuntī secures her heroic status by virtue of her profoundly efficacious and authoritative language.

The fact that Kuntī, Draupadī, and Damayantī all demonstrate a quinquepartite relation with male figures—even if only in potentia in the case of Damayantī—suggests some paradigmatic form concerning how femininity connects with the male in these narratives. It is as if mythical aspects of femininity are being engaged: the nature of that myth, however, remains to be proven.[66]

If there is one epithet that can be ascribed to these women heroes, it is grief: *duḥkha* or *śoka*. How they override this emotion of vast sorrow supplies the field for their heroism. It is as if suffering is a great reservoir of emotional strength and verbal conception, and from this flows their many-potent words.

66. These represent, perhaps, the *pañcabhūta* 'five elements': water, fire, air, earth, and *ākāśa*.

IV

DRAUPADĪ

NO WOMAN IN THE POEM plays such a central role as Draupadī. Saṃjaya refers to her as *rājaputrī satyavratā vīrapatnī saputrā manasvinī* 'a princess, virtuous, wife of warriors, mother of sons, esteemed': a profusion of epithets that no other woman in the poem receives so copiously (V.23.5). Her first mention in the epic occurs during the old king Dhṛtarāṣṭra's lengthy dirge in Book One. Draupadī is described as,

> yadāśrauṣaṃ draupadīm aśrukaṇṭhīṃ
> sabhāṃ nītāṃ duḥkhitām ekavastrām
> rajasvalāṃ ... anāthavat ...
>
> When I heard that Draupadī, her throat full of tears,
> was led to the *sabhā*, distressed, wearing a single cloth,
> menstruating ... like someone without a protector ...
>
> I.1.106

Outrage thus marks her entry to the poem and her grief at being so abused. This is how the poets initially signal her presence in the narrative, long before she actually appears in person. Her next mention refers to the Sauptika *parvan*: the old king decries that the *draupadeyās* 'the five sons of Draupadī' were slaughtered whilst they slept. Again, she is marked as a woman of grief (I.1.153).

At the opening of Book Four, Yudhiṣṭhira speaks of Draupadī as *naḥ priyā bhāryā prāṇebhyo'pi garīyasī* 'our beloved wife, dearer than the breaths' (IV.3.12). He says that she is like a *mātā* 'mother', and *jyeṣṭhā svasā* 'elder sister'. Wife, mother, sister, thus all the feminine kin relations are represented by Draupadī: she is completely feminine, insofar as she stands for everything that a woman can be, except—as far as her husbands are concerned—a daughter.

As a character and as a narrative figure whose actions and speeches create the movement of the epic, she is unique. Her name is a patronym: she was born from a sacrificial fire immediately after her brother, Dhṛṣṭadyumna, had similarly risen from the ritual flames (I.155.41). He was born because king Drupada had been deprived of half his kingdom by Droṇa in battle, and Drupada wanted a son to take revenge for him and kill Droṇa, an event that subsequently occurs at Kurukṣetra. Draupadī's origins are thus intimately bound up with this act of reprisal on the part of the Pāñcāla king against a brahmin.

Like several male heroic figures in the poem she has no mother: she arises from the fire 'in a great sacrifice' (*mahāmakhe*). In her case though—and in this Draupadī is unique among epic women—there exists no human father either.[1] After her fully adult birth 'from the middle of an altar' (*vedīmadhyāt*), a bodiless voice declares:

> ... kṛṣṇā kṣayaṃ kṣatraṃ ninīṣati
>
> Draupadī is about to conduct the *kṣatriyas* to ruin.[2]
>
> I.155.44

The only other figure in the poem of whom such a statement could be made is Rāma Jāmadagnya, a fighting brahmin, who actually did destroy the *kṣatriyas* several times.[3] The prediction touches upon an aspect of Draupadī's character which is thematically constant throughout the poem: that is, her wrathfulness and fury, which lead to the ultimate holocaust at Kurukṣetra. Draupadī has a certain highly charged anger about her, which is unconditional and not to be mitigated. Her lust for revenge is distinctive among the women of the poem.[4] The editors of what has become the Mahābhārata which we now possess were brahmins, and this comment upon *kṣatriya* life is enigmatic, particularly given the conflation of Rāma and Draupadī.[5] It is as if Draupadī is in fact

1. To be born without a human mother is a sign of great inner strength and purity; usually this is a condition for males, as with Droṇa or Kṛpa or Aurva, and is rare for women. Hiltebeitel, on the myth surrounding Draupadī's cult status in south India today, writes that her "associations with fire [the altar] deepen her affinities with Śiva.... [It] is also no coincidence that it is through images of fire that the goddess is invoked in her cosmic and most salvific forms." Hiltebeitel 1988: 11–12. "Epic parthenogenesis" is fully examined by Mary Carroll Smith, in Sharma 1991: 84–100. She portrays *ayonija* 'unwomb-born' births as "strong evidence of archaic warrior motifs which go back to the Vedic soma cult and the era of Aryan expansion in North India." Ibid., 100.

2. Kṛṣṇā 'the dark one' is another name—actually an epithet—for Draupadī. Sax 2002: 138 writes: "According to the bard, Bacan Singh, Draupadi was born in order to kill the Kauravas.... [She is] an incarnation of the goddess." She "goes to the burning ground every day, eats the flesh of corpses, then bathes ..." He describes "the culminating ritual, where a woman possessed by Draupadi/Kali sucks the blood from a goat kid." When the animal is later butchered, "its heart went to Draupadi and Arjuna" (p. 141).

3. III.117.9.

4. Sax 2002, in his chapter on Draupadī and Kuntī, entitles the section "Violent Women" (p. 134ff.). "Draupadi's weapon is a scythe" (p. 137).

5. See Sukthankar 1937 for this assessment of Mahābhārata redaction.

the arch-*kṣatriya*, one who is so fierce that her energy cannot remain finite and she engenders their own self-destruction.

She arises at birth,

> nīlotpalasamo gandho yasyāḥ krośāt pravāyati
> yā bibharti paraṃ rūpaṃ yasyā nāsty upamā bhuvi
>
> A blue lotus, the perfume of which blew for miles:
> she who conveyed great beauty, of whom there is no equal on earth!
>
> I.155.43

Her typical epithet is *yaśasvinī* 'one who possesses glory' (III.46.20). This word *yaśas* is a term most frequently used to qualify male heroes: it is an object of great desire for *kṣatriyas*, akin to 'fame' (*kīrti*). The acquisition of glory supplies the founding basis upon which their lives are predicated: that is, entry into the cultural system of epic poetry.

Sudeṣṇā, queen of the Virāṭas, on first seeing Draupadī, praises her beauty in detail. This is a cliché portrayal, there is nothing particularly individual about the description, which draws upon stock formulae. Hair, breasts, buttocks, nipples, feet, thighs, eyelashes, a face like the moon: all receive the usual encomia. She closes by asking, typically, if Draupadī is a supernatural being. Kings, on becoming smitten by the beauty of a woman, often also ask this formulaic question.

> kā tvaṃ brūhi ...
> yakṣī vā yadi vā devī gandharvī yadi vāpsarāḥ
>
> Tell me what you are—
> *yakṣī*, deity, *gandharvī*, or an *apsaras*?
>
> IV.8.13

Thus Draupadī combines in her person both astounding, unearthly beauty as well as a devastating and overwhelming capacity for vengeance and devastation. She is also a figure of inordinate suffering and no one is equal to her in misery.

Let us consider the rest of her life cycle as it is presented by the poem.

1. *Marriage*

At her *svayaṃvara* all the deities attend, just as they did with Damayantī (I.178.6ff.). This is also the moment when Kṛṣṇa makes his entrance into the poem, along with his brother, Balarāma. The Pāṇḍavas, who are present, disguised as brahmins, are all smitten with love for her: *kandarpabāṇābhihatāḥ* 'struck by the arrows of love' (I.178.12). Arjuna is the actual one to win her, and at the end of her life in the Mahāprasthānika *parvan*, it is her partiality towards Arjuna that Yudhiṣṭhira cites as being causative of her decease: she is *pakṣapāto ... dhanaṃjaye* 'partial to Arjuna' (XVII.2.6).[6] On the other hand, she is described by the poets as,

> abhimānavatī nityaṃ viśeṣeṇa yudhiṣṭhire
>
> Always haughty, especially to Yudhiṣṭhira.
>
> XII.14.4

After Arjuna's success, she offers him a *śuklam varamālyadāma* 'a spotless, choice string of flowers', and as he then departs from the arena he is followed *patnyā tayā* 'by that wife' (I.179.23). Thus the marriage is accomplished without further ado: *sa tām upādāya* 'he took her'.

Draupadī is effectively married off to all the brothers when the five sons return to their mother, Kuntī, and she, not having turned to see them and thinking that they were returning with food which had been begged—for they are presently living as itinerant brahmins—says, *bhuṅkta*, 'enjoy!'[7] As we noted earlier, the imperative from the mother is sufficient for the bride to become a joint possession (I.182.2).[8]

Yudhiṣṭhira dismisses whatever dubiety arises among the brothers concerning this uncommon coparcenary act in which they are about to engage by saying, *sarveṣāṃ draupadī bhāryā bhaviṣyati hi naḥ* 'Draupadī will become the wife of all of us' (I.182.15). It is Kuntī's speech, though, which establishes the situation, he merely affirms it.

Thereafter, Draupadī lives in harmonious fraternal polyandry with the five men and bears sons to them all. In the *parvasaṃgraha* 'catalogue of the sections', this marriage is called *amānuṣa* 'not human' (I.2.88). On that first night she slept at the feet of the brothers: *kṛṣṇā tu teṣāṃ*

6. In a contemporary twentieth-century version of this part of the story, in the Third Song of the *Tharu Barka Naach* (Meyer and Deuel 1998), it is Bhīma who wins Draupadī in the svayaṃvara.

7. At I.188.16, Yudhiṣṭhira, in relating this event, declares that Kuntī said: *bhaikṣavad bhujyatām* 'let it be enjoyed as alms!'

8. "La parole d'une mère est en effet irrevocable", Dumézil 1968: I.109. Vyāsa, at I.157, tells the Pāṇḍavas a story of how once, a nameless girl who had performed austerities in order to secure a husband had been met by Śiva, who proceeded to ask her what she wanted. She replied five times, saying the same thing on each occasion, that she desired a spouse. Hence, in another life, this young woman was destined to receive five husbands. He repeats this at I.189, describing how the goddess Śrī reincarnates as Draupadī. Sax 2002: 136, records how Padam Singh Negi, "chief bard," sings about Draupadī: "In Satyug, the woman of five brothers stayed with Rama, incarnate as Sita. / In Treta Yug, drummer, she stayed with Shiva, and her name was Parvati. / In Dwapar Yug, drummer, she incarnated as Draupadi in the home of Drupad Raja ... / and in Kalyug, drummer, she incarnated as Kali."

caraṇopadhānam āsīt pṛthivyām 'for Draupadī was on the earth, the pillow of their feet' (I.185.10). Kuntī, their mother, sleeps in a similar transverse position, but at the heads of the brothers.

The situation of polyandry is so unusual that even Draupadī's father, the king, declares that such a situation, where a woman possesses five husbands—it is fine if a man possesses five wives—'never' occurs (*na kadācana*; I.187.26). He calls this 'a-dharmic, unlawful' (*adharmam*). 'Law is intangible ... and we do not know its way', Yudhiṣṭhira responds (*sūkṣmo dharmo ... nāsya vidhmo vayaṃ gatim*; I.187.28).[9]

The actual ritual of their union closes with Yudhiṣṭhira, as the eldest of the brothers, first taking the hand of Draupadī in marriage: the rite being conducted by Yudhiṣṭhira's chaplain at the sacred fire in King Drupada's court. Then, day by day, the other brothers repeat the rite, until each has been formally married (I.190.11–13). After each union Draupadī has her virginity restored, becoming a *kanyā* again.[10] This is the 'wedding' (*vivāha*) proper.

The events are concluded by further gifts of 'wealth' (*dhana*), this time in the form of chariots, horses, elephants, young slavewomen, and ornamented clothes (I.190.15–17). Draupadī is now a *snuṣā* 'daughter-in-law', and Kuntī has become the *śvaśrū* 'mother-in-law' (I.191.4). These are distinct and exacting terms, each bearing particular functions. One must recall that the war itself concerns the difficulties and conflicts of kinship: that is the core crisis of the poem—the tension within kin groups—for rivalry is not external nor "exogamous," but consanguine and a contest of fratrilines.

The brothers agree—on being advised by Nārada—never to disturb Draupadī if she is 'sitting' (*sahāsīnām*) with any one of them (I.204.28). If this was to ever occur—and intimacy is implied—the offending or intruding brother would retire to the forest for a year as a penalty. A dilemma soon arises when Arjuna is importuned by a brahmin whose cattle have been stolen. In order to reclaim the animals Arjuna needs his bow, which is stowed in the room where Yudhiṣṭhira is secluded with Draupadī. Arjuna enters and is thus obliged to retire to the forest for a year and live the life of a solitary ascetic (I.205.18ff.)

Yet subsequently all the spouses live in concordant harmony together, Draupadī always being *vaśavartinī* 'obedient'. She was happy with her menfolk, like the river Sarasvatī was always happy with

9. Perhaps one could surmise that her three senior husbands are in the place of dharma, *artha*, and *kāma* respectively: with Yudhiṣṭhira, Bhīma, and Arjuna.

10. Virginity would appear to be a term of emotion, rather that a physiological state (I.190.14). The term *vivāhādhiṣṭhātā* 'hymen', must denote a certain physical state, however, although the word is not mentioned in the epic.

elephants (I.205.2–3); and she bore five beautiful warrior sons—the *draupadeyās*—to the brothers, each one born a year apart (I.213.71–82).

2. *The* sabhā

When Yudhiṣṭhira sets off towards Hāstinapura to accept the challenge of dicing, he goes *saha strībhir draupadīm ādikṛtvā* 'with women, having placed Draupadī first' (II.52.17). As the dicing scene commences, he utters the famous description of his wife, his *priyā devī* 'beloved queen'.

> naiva hrasvā na mahatī na atikṛṣṇā na rohiṇī
> sarāgaraktanetrā ...
> śaradutpalapatrākṣyā śaradutpalagandhayā
> śaradutpalaśevinyā rūpeṇa śrīsamānayā ...
> ābhāti padmavadvaktraṃ sasvedaṃ mallikeva ca
> vedīmadhyā dīrghakeśī tāmrākṣī nātiromaśā
>
> She is neither short nor tall nor too dark nor ruddy,
> possessing eyes impassioned with love ...
> with eyes like petals of autumn blue lotus, with an odor of autumn blue lotus,
> with a form like an autumn blue lotus, like the deity Śrī ...
> Her lotus face shines like a girl recently deflowered, and like a brown goose:
> a waist like an altar, long hair not too thick, coppery eyes ...
>
> II.58.32–33 and 36

Unlike all the other women in the poem, Draupadī receives a long five *ślokas* of detailed praise. Usually descriptions are of a typical order, without individual details, and simile carries the burden of portrayal. Here, her husband describes her eyes and face and waist, her callow skin, her odor. These are not the usual formulae of feminine praise, but intensely personal points of admiration and affection, attributed to no other women in the epic.

The assembled men in the dicing hall cry out in consternation or weep, such is the error and wrong that takes place when Yudhiṣṭhira stakes his wife.[11] This is what Yudhiṣṭhira later refers to as *idaṃ ... karma pāpīyaḥ* 'this worst act' (V.29.30). Duryodhana exults when she is lost, and instructs his steward to bring her so that she might join the serving girls.[12]

11. Shah 1995: 30 writes of this moment as "an instance of a wife being equated with wealth." She notes that Yudhiṣṭhira refers to Draupadī as a *ratnabhūtā* 'a gem or jewel' (I.187.23).

12. Flueckiger 1996: 72 discusses folk interpretations of this scene. On page 167, she remarks that, "The motif of women, rather than men, winning and losing partners through

Draupadī, on being directed to enter the gambling hall, immediately raises a question of ruling: did Yudhiṣṭhira lose his own person before he lost her, and was the latter possible if the former had occurred?[13]

> kiṃ nu pūrvaṃ parājaiṣīr ātmānaṃ māṃ nu bhārata
>
> Whom did you lose first, self or me, Bhārata?
>
> II.60.7

She continues, saying that dharma 'being protected, will bear us peace' (*sa naḥ śamaṃ dhāsyati gopyamānaḥ*; II.60.13).

Instructed by Yudhiṣṭhira, she enters the *sabhā*: *ekavastrādhonīvī rodamānā rajasvalā* 'with one garment, a low sarong, weeping, menstruating' (II.60.15). There are other women in the hall—it is not a male enclave—for Dhṛtarāṣṭra's wives are there:

> bhārātānāṃ striyaḥ sarvā gāndhāryā saha saṃgatāḥ
>
> All the women of the Bhāratas, assembled with Gāndhārī.
>
> II.72.19

Draupadī runs towards them for refuge (II.60.21). It is her menstrual condition that marks this moment as pitiable, and the fact that she is unprotected by her husbands and mocked by Duryodhana and his cronies. She is, after all, a *rājaputrī* 'daughter of a king', and married to the king of kings, who has just been anointed in supreme state.

It is the severe abnegation and abjection of this scene, of Draupadī and her husbands—due to the recklessness of Yudhiṣṭhira—that drives the narrative of the poem from this point onward towards the end.[14] From this moment the wrath of Draupadī is the fuel that propels the epic towards the massive destruction of Kurukṣetra. Vidura, during his lengthy monologue in the Udyoga *parvan*, tells the aging Dhṛtarāṣṭra that:

---

dicing is common in several other Chhattisgarhi folk narratives as well (for example, in the song of Subanbali ...), a motif that presents us with an alternative to the more shastric pattern of male dicing for a woman."

13. Hiltebeitel 2001 examines this "question" exhaustively. On page 240, he writes, "Draupadī's question unsettles the authorities, brings forth higher authority where it is silenced or absent, and opens the question of authority to multiple voices, including her own and the poets'." Authority is, of course, a source, generator, and maintainer of human value and worth.

14. "A hurtful act is the transference to others of the degradation which we bear in ourselves. That is why we are inclined to commit such acts as a way of deliverance." Simone Weil 1952: 72. The ritual qualities of the dice match and its strict protocol restrain the five husbands from protecting Draupadī when she is being violated. Such are the stringent formalities of *kṣatriya* life.

striyaḥ śriyo gṛhasyoktās tasmād rakṣyā viśeṣataḥ

Women are called the happiness of the household, therefore they are to be especially protected.

V.38.11

Yudhiṣṭhira has failed spectacularly in this respect.[15]

Duḥśāsana, brother to Duryodhana, drags Draupadī by the hair when she attempts to find succour with the old king's women. 'He dragged the unprotected one, like a wind drags an afflicted plantain tree' (*anāthavac cakarṣa vāyuḥ kadalīm ivārtām*; II.60.24).[16] She begs to be freed due to her condition: 'she quietly said, I am menstruating today' (*śanair uvāca adya rajasvalāsmi*; II.60.25). He ignores her and disregards her plea, *mā mā vivāstrām kṛdhī* 'do not undress me! (II.60.30). Duḥśāsana publicly calls her a *dāsī*, 'servant', 'having shaken her forcibly' (*ādhūya vegena*; II.60.37).

This is a scene not simply of humiliation but of debasement; dharma has been completely abandoned in the interests of domination and rivalry, and the formalities of the court only temper the level of abuse with a further charge and tension. As the burgeoning conflict between rival sides of a family focusses on the subjection of Draupadī's body, she supplies this primary terrain or field for the clash of cousins as they struggle for power and sovereignty. The narrative concentrates on and circulates about her person as she represents the core of the epic, the point from which all subsequent dramatic perspective emanates.

Draupadī is not at all cowed by her experience in the *sabhā*, but criticizes her subjectors and questions their authority as well as their honesty in the gambling. Of all her five husbands, Bhīma is the only one to become angry and speak for her, and he violently berates Yudhiṣṭhira. No material loss humiliates the brothers so much as the glances of Draupadī (II.60.36).

During this episode, no one amongst her oppressors in the *sabhā*—except for Duryodhana and Karṇa—addresses or refers to Draupadī by name: she is always Kṛṣṇā 'the dark one', her familiar epithet, or Pāñcālī 'daughter of the Pāñcāla', a patronym. Karṇa insults her by calling Draupadī a 'harlot' (*bandhakī*), saying, 'one husband

15. 'Wherever a woman, a gambler, a child rules, they helplessly sink like a stone boat in the river' (*yatra strī yatra kitavo yatra bālo'nuśāsti ca / majjanti te'vaśā deśā nadyām aśmaplaveva*; V.38.40).

16. Yudhiṣṭhira later describes his degradation as being primarily *draupadyā viprakarṣeṇa* 'by the dragging away of Draupadī (III.2.7).

ordained by the deities for a woman' (*eko bhartā striyā devair vihitaḥ*; II.61.35). He then orders her and the Pāṇḍavas to be stripped.[17] Then follows the famous scene where Duḥśāsana attempts to strip her and by supernatural intervention she remains clothed.

> tadrupam aparaṃ vastraṃ prādurāsīt anekaśaḥ
>
> There appeared repeatedly another cloth of the same form.
>
> II.61.41

This miracle is described as *tad adbhutatamaṃ loke* 'that most wonderful thing in the world', which causes all the assembly to shout with amazement. Only Bhīma gallantly comes to her aid, and that is only in the form of cursing Duḥśāsana. Of all the mortal women in the Mahābhārata, only Draupadī and Kuntī possess this association with the divine and supernal world: they are exceptional in this respect. Apart from birth, this moment with the cloth is the only instance of Draupadī's link with the supernatural, for she is profoundly mortal in life.

Karṇa then orders that Draupadī be taken away as a *dāsī*, but she speaks out and addresses the hall, first apologizing that she was unable to speak dutifully to her *gurus* among the assembled Kurus. She delicately plays with the words as she speaks:

> purastāt karaṇīyaṃ me na kṛtaṃ kāryam uttaram
>
> What was to be done by me in the first place—undone—must be done later.
>
> II.62.1

Given her wrathful nature and also the state of her humiliation, it is remarkable that she can maintain her dignity and sense of decorum. Draupadī reminds the assembled men that 'hitherto, dharmic women are not led into the hall' (*dharmyāḥ striyaḥ sabhāṃ pūrvaṃ na nayanti*; II.62.9). The poets describe her, 'like an afflicted osprey' *kurarīm ivārtām*, a bird of lamentation, and Karṇa speaks again, calling Draupadī not only a servant, but *dāsadhanam* 'a chattel'.

Duryodhana, in a particularly provocative manner, exposes his left thigh to Draupadī, as if making a sexual claim upon her. The poets describe his leg as being like a rod of plantain, or a thunderbolt or elephant trunk, such is its phallic vigor (II.63.11–12). Again, Bhīma is the only husband to speak and threaten revenge with avowal: he alone

17. What is said at this point is later referred to as 'unspeakable speech' (*avācyaṃ vākyam*; V.29.40).

stands out as her protector. Yudhiṣṭhira remains silent throughout all these exchanges, making no response to the debate concerning dharma; and even when Duryodhana exposes his leg he keeps quiet. Such is the great abjection of the *dharmarājā*.

Nevertheless, the protocols of the dicing match are sustained, and the Pāṇḍavas accept their status as being subject to *dāsadharma* 'the law of servitude' (II.63.7): they have been staked and lost by their brother. Karṇa repeatedly calls Draupadī a *dāsī*, a terrific insult, given their respective ranks.[18]

The old king finally speaks and reverses much of the proceedings, including the loss of wealth, by allowing Draupadī to reclaim her husbands out of bondage. He says to her, *varaṃ vṛṇīṣva pāñcālī* 'choose a favor, Draupadī', and she of course requests the return of her husbands from subjection. This is granted and Dhṛtarāṣṭra tells her, 'you are the best of all my daughters-in-law' (*tvaṃ hi sarvasnuṣāṇāṃ me śreyasī*; II.63.33).[19] Karṇa is amazed at how a woman manages to save her husbands, and cries out that Draupadī has become the *śāntir* 'peace' of the Pāṇḍavas, and their *naur* 'boat' that saves them from becoming submerged in a sea (II.64.1–3).

Throughout the poem this is a frequent metaphor that is ascribed to Draupadī, she is the vessel that will save her husbands endangered by rough seas.[20] Draupadī possesses and exhibits the gift of oratorical persuasion: an audience perceives how—right through the course of the poem—she is an adept with right speech.

That evening after the gambling, when the Pāṇḍavas have actually departed, the old king, in conversation with Saṃjaya, his *sūta* 'poet', relates the dire astronomical and natural events that occurred when Draupadī was publicly injured and mortified in the *sabhā* (II.72.21ff.). Her physical being was so attuned to and potent with the forces of nature that during her crisis in the dicing hall there were terrible natural disasters simultaneously occurring. Meteors fell, there was an eclipse, seismic disturbances were manifest, terrific winds arose, and spontanous fires accompanied by a howling of jackals occurred at the *agnihotra* sacrifices: these are all terrible portents. He says,

tasyāḥ kṛpaṇacakṣurbhyāṃ pradahyetāpi medinī

18. On the social significance of insults in preliterate culture, see Parks 1990.

19. Another 'princess' (*rājaputrī*), at III.190.79, makes a truth act and similarly saves her husband by causing a rash king to reverse his decision.

20. Yudhiṣṭhira later refers to this, saying, 'she took the Pāṇḍavas from affliction ... like a boat from the flood of ocean' (*kṛcchrāt pāṇḍavān ujjahāra ... nair iva sāgaraughāt*; V.29.35).

Even the earth would be burned by her miserable glance.

II.72.18

For Draupadī possesses such intrinsic cosmic and dharmic force that her despoliation only conduces to a series of further organic calamities.

After the second dicing match, when it has been determined—as Yudhiṣṭhira had once again lost the game—that the Pāṇḍavas would spend twelve years living as forest ascetics, Duḥśāsana taunts the brothers with insults, and says to Draupadī, *patiṃ vṛṇīṣva* 'choose a husband', for her men have become *klībāḥ* 'eunuchs' (II.68.10–11). It is notable that he expects Draupadī to be the one to select a spouse, the convention of feminine volition being implicitly sustained.

As they set out from the court on their way towards the forest and exile, there is a great cry in the inner quarters of the palace, ostensibly the women's quarters, the *antaḥpura* (II.70.2). Kuntī makes her farewell, reminding Draupadī that she knows *strīdharma* well, saying that her daughter-in-law possesses 'good demeanor', she is *śīlācāravatī*.

As they depart, Draupadī is described as *śoṇitāktaikavasanā muktakeśyā*, possessing 'a blood-stained single garment, her hair loose' (II.70.9). She has become a most pitiable figure; as the queen of a king who had just celebrated the *rājasūya*, the paramount rite of kingship, she goes weeping, *keśaiḥ praticchādya mukham* 'having concealed her face with her hair' (II.71.6).

She curses the Kauravas who have caused this exile, or rather, she curses the Kaurava women, transmitting her own grief and humiliation to them: those women will become, in thirteen years, *kṛtodakā nāryaḥ* 'women who have performed the water oblation for the dead' (II.71.19–20). They will have husbands, she says, sons, kin, and friends all killed, fourteen years hence, when the Pāṇḍavas return from their exile. Then, it will be the Kaurava women who are bloody with menstruation and with their hair in disarray. This is a brutal and horrific curse, a speech act which comes into effect by Book Eleven of the poem. Like the words of Kuntī, the words of Draupadī possess efficacious authority and charge.

3. *The Forest*

The audience's first image of Draupadī in the forest is when she is depicted as a correct wife at a meal:

yudhiṣṭhiraṃ bhojayitvā śeṣam aśnāti pārṣatī

> Having satisfied Yudhiṣṭhira, Draupadī eats the rest.
>
> II.4.7

Vidura describes Draupadī as she was during her first days in the forest, in the evening as *rākṣasas* were coming out.

> pañcaparvatamadhyasthā nadīvākulitāṃ gatā
> momuhyamānāṃ tāṃ tatra jagṛhuḥ pañca pāṇḍavāḥ
> indriyāṇi prasaktāni viṣayeṣu yathā ratim
>
> She is confused, like a turbid river situated between five mountains:
> the five Pāṇḍavas seized that very bewildered one there—
> as five senses enamored—with regard to pleasure.
>
> III.12.17

It is a complex metaphor that is unique in the poem and perfectly captures the delicacy and strength of her polyandrous situation, and there is a charming ellipsis at play here concerning the nature of *rati* 'pleasure'. When they set off again it is 'having put Draupadī first' (*kṛṣṇāṃ puraskṛtya*), which is an unusual order: they follow her rather than vice versa (III.12.68).

It is not long after this scene when the audience first hears of Draupadī's great capacity for wrath and anger as they listen to a supremely eloquent speech. Now she is no longer the quiet young and nubile bride, but a mother, a queen and wife; one whose power has been usurped and her sons sent into fostering. During the dicing scene she appeared distraught and pitiful although fully self-possessed and her rage had not yet had the necessary time to mature and acquire its compulsion.

In the *araṇya* 'forest' one evening, not long after they have arrived, Kṛṣṇa appeared. Arjuna sings his praises in a lengthy hymn and then Draupadī begins her encomium of the god-hero (III.13.43ff.). She likens him to Prajāpati, the creator, and says that he is Viṣṇu himself. 'You are sacrificer and to be sacrificed', she says of him, (*yaṣṭā tvam asi yaṣṭavyo*; III.13.44). He is truth itself and eternal, and the sun and moon rest upon him; even the immortality of the deities is founded upon him, she says.

This eulogy continues for ten eloquent and grandiose lines, and its content is reminiscent of what is spoken during Book Eleven of the Gītā, insofar as it expresses a cosmic and theophanic view of Kṛṣṇa.[21]

21. One wonders how Draupadī has knowledge of this aspect of Kṛṣṇa, for unlike Arjuna she has never been witness to such revelation. One could speculate that this passage is perhaps an introjection by the Bhārgava editors; see Goldman 1977.

divaṃ te śirasā vyāptaṃ padbhyāṃ ca pṛthivī vibho
jaṭharaṃ te ime lokāḥ puruṣo'si sanātanaḥ

Heaven is pervaded by your head, O lord, and earth by your feet,
these worlds are your stomach: you are the eternal Man.

III.13.47

Draupadī praises his absolute divinity, not his heroic mortality, saying that his body represents the perpetual universe. One can imagine a complaisant Kṛṣṇa sitting there enjoying such lyrical adulation, until the tone drastically shifts.

Then the real Draupadī—the Draupadī of popular myth—embarks on a furious tirade, one of the longest dramatic speeches in the whole epic.[22] She has become a woman of complex and profound vehemence, one thoroughly capable in the drama of public performance. This is a tour de force and there is nothing gentle, submissive, nor dubious in her words.

'How', she says, given the extraordinary and supernatural potence of Kṛṣṇa, could she have been allowed to experience what she did in the *sabhā*? 'Wife of the sons of Kuntī, friend of Kṛṣṇa, sister of Dhṛṣṭadyumna, how could she, be dragged to the *sabhā*'?

strīdharmiṇī vepamānā rudhireṇā samukṣitā
ekavastrā vikṛṣṭāsmi duḥkhitā kurusaṃsadi

Devoted to feminine propriety, trembling, sprinkled with blood,
wearing one piece of cloth, grievous: I was dragged to the hall of the
Kurus!

III.13.54

As her invective gathers, she becomes bitterly irate:

dṛṣṭvā ca māṃ dhārtarāṣṭrāḥ prāhasan pāpacetasaḥ

The wicked sons of Dhṛtarāṣṭra, laughing, having seen me!

III.13.55

'They desired to enjoy me as a servant' (*dāsībhāvena bhoktum mām īṣūs te*), she says. 'I am the daughter-in-law, by right, of Bhīṣma and of Dhṛtarāṣṭra', she adds (*bhīṣmasya dhṛtarāṣṭrasya ... snuṣā bhavāmi dharmeṇa*; III.13.57).[23]

Her outrage during the course of this speech is not to be discounted,

22. It is sixty-five verses: III.13.43–108.
23. One is a great uncle-in-law, the other is a putative grandfather-in-law.

and it is the first time that this fervent persona of Draupadī is fully expressed. Her fury is not only being *dāsīkṛtā balāt* 'because of force made servile', but also because her menfolk and male kin did nothing, whilst Kṛṣṇa, this fabulously omnicompetent deity, was not even aware, let alone present!

'I accuse the Pāṇḍavas', she says (*garhaye pāṇḍavān*), and she insults both Arjuna and Bhīma by name, citing their great and famous exploits and yet their utter failure to support her against Kaurava violation. She then begins to refer to rightful or conventional practice concerning women, 'this perpetual way of dharma' (*śāśvato'yaṃ dharmapathaḥ*).[24]

> yad bhāryāṃ parirakṣanti bhartāro'pabalā api
>
> Since husbands, even weak ones, protect a wife.
>
> III.13.60

Draupadī then enters into a historical recapitulation of the deeds of Arjuna and Bhīma, especially those of the latter, when he killed Hiḍimba and Baka.[25] She refers to herself as a 'beloved wife' (*priyā bhāryā*) and daughter-in-law. Why were her potent husbands so pusillanimous, she cries, when,

> kule mahati jātāsmi divyena vidhinā kila
>
> I was born in a great lineage, indeed, by divine ordinance!
>
> III.13.107

The poets describe her at this point as *kruddhā* 'fierce', a word indicating a quality of wrath that is extreme: it is a heroic term often used on the battlefield (III.13.111). She then pitifully claims that she is without anyone to protect her:

> naiva me patayaḥ santi na putrā madhusūdhana
> na bhrātaro na ca pitā naiva tvaṃ na ca bāndhavāḥ
>
> O Kṛṣṇa, I have no sons and no husbands,
> no brothers and no father, neither you nor kin.
>
> III.13.112

24. See below, Ch. V, for a more extensive analysis of this topic.

25. This reads like a compressed micro-epic that a performance poet could expand or contract at will, depending on how much time was available and how inclined his audience were to hearing the material. See Nagy 1996a, 1996b, on this process. Flueckiger 1996: 164, discussing the contemporary song tradition of Chhattisgarh, comments: "These days anyone can sing *paṇḍvānī* ... Harijans, whom we call Satnamis, used to sing *paṇḍvānī*.... You can tell the story [*kathā*] in two minutes or two days."

The worst thing of all, she says, was the laughter of Karṇa (III.13.113). Draupadī then emotionally crumples, weeping and sobbing, claiming that she is without husbands. It is this solitary wretchedness which has given the figure of Draupadī such great valence in modern Hindu culture.[26] Her unalleviated wrath and bloodthirsty need for revenge, however, attunes her more towards the negative aspects of the *Devī* 'goddess'.[27] This speech supplies the first manifestation of that wrathful and ruthless side of Draupadī, a tone that is to run throughout the rest of the poem, generating and sustaining its movement.

Throughout the speech she repeatedly addresses Kṛṣṇa as Madhusūdhana, one of his epithets meaning 'killer of the demon Madhu'. She punctuates her long declamation with repetitions of this term and her closing word is also 'Madhusūdhana'. 'Juice, nectar, something sweet and delicious', is another way of construing *madhu*. Thus she is simultaneously claiming him to be the 'destroyer of sweetness': in effect this is what has happened, for Kṛṣṇa, who is this supreme cosmic power, has condoned the destruction of sweetness and happiness, and it is this which Draupadī is so ferociously damning with her speech, subtly emphasizing—by means of anaphora—the ironic nuance of this name.

Kṛṣṇa's only exculpation of himself is to say that he was absent and that he was busy elsewhere. The poets add a further touch of 'paronomasia' (*śleṣa*) when Kṛṣṇa declares *asāṃnidhyaṃ ... mamānarteṣv abhūt tadā* 'but it was my absence among the Ānartas' as his only mitigation (III.14.14). This is the name of a people in northern Kāṭhiavāḍ—in contemporary Gujarat—but the word can also be heard

26. Mankekar 1999: 40 discusses the effect of the televised version of the Mahābhārata on women in Delhi: "Several women appropriated the example of the public disrobing of Draupadi [not in the Critical Edition text, but only in the appendix] to reflect on their own subordinated positions, and in the process formulated powerful critiques of gender inequalities in their families and communities." "The creators of the televised Mahabharat saw Draupadi as ... a marker of (Hindu) Indian 'civilization'.... For both the presenters of the disrobing as well as the viewers, however, Draupadi also embodied 'Women's rage', in particular, the rage of a woman wronged.... Draupadi came to embody ... not just Hindu womanhood, but ... Indian Womanhood.... Viewers, especially women, also perceived Draupadi as an icon of women's vulnerability." Ibid., 224.

27. See Kinsley 1986. Hiltebeitel 1989: 339, writes concerning twentieth-century cult worship: "Draupadī is also regarded as a goddess, with her own cult centred at the medieval capital of Gingee ... although it is recalled in her cult's folklore that she is an incarnation of Śrī, she is in many ways more a multiform of Durgā or Kalī. In her cult, her epic roles are deepened ... so that the actions of the male heroes now largely revolve around her." Sax 2002: 135, observes how "the dangerous and sexually active Draupadi is explicitly identified as Kali and is sometimes the recipient of dramatic blood sacrifices."

as a *guṇa* form—the vowel augmented—of the term *anṛta* 'untruth, disorder'.[28]

He does promise that she shall be 'a queen of kings' (*rājñāṃ rājñī*; III.13.116), and that she will be avenged and her tormentors slain.[29]

When this episode concludes and the Pāṇḍavas set out once again on their golden chariot yoked with amazing horses, Draupadī is with them, standing in the vehicle. This is a most unusual sight for an audience to visualize, the heroes and their woman departing on a single chariot (III.24.1–2).

Her second major speech in the poem comes not long after this, after they have lived one year in exile, when Draupadī and her husbands are sitting 'at evening' (*sāyāhne*) in the forest. She is described by the poets as,

> priyā ca darśanīyā ca paṇḍitā ca pativratā
>
> Affectionate and lovely and sage and devoted to her husbands.
>
> III.28.2

She addresses Yudhiṣṭhira, the *dharmarāja*, and initially complains about the scene in the dicing hall, about how abused she was by Duryodhana, whom she insults in detail along with his cronies; Karṇa, in particular, she loathes. Draupadī has an extremely acerbic and astringent tongue when it comes to invective: *pāpaḥ, nṛśaṃsaḥ, durātmā, duṣṭātmā, pāpapūruṣa, durmatiḥ, duṣkṛtakarmaṇaḥ* 'wicked, cruel, bad, rotten, wicked man, fool, ill-doing' ... the list is relentless and vitriolic (III.28.3–9).

Then, she suddenly changes her tone, from anger to grief:

28. Kṛṣṇa's role in this epic has been much discussed by Matilal 1989 and Hiltebeitel 1976, among many. His use of deception, dramatic ellipsis, and of sheer misconduct, tends to further the process of narrative. In dramatic counterpoint to Kṛṣṇa there is Vyāsa, who appears at certain significant moments and advises on how the story actually is and how it shall proceed. Vyāsa has an agnatic relation to the Pāṇḍavas, and Kṛṣṇa's relation is that of affiliation: they both exist on the periphery of events, almost hors de texte, and at crucial moments influence the sequence of historical progression. As a trio, Arjuna, Draupadī, and Kṛṣṇa all possess the epithet or title of 'black one, dark one' (*kṛṣṇa/ā*). In this triform organization, Arjuna plays the active role and Draupadī's role is one of gravity: she is all potential. The role of Kṛṣṇa is one of ambiguity, of detour: he causes the narrative to always jump aside onto another course or trajectory.

29. Draupadī makes the claims for revenge, having suffered an ordeal. Kṛṣṇa forecasts the punitive and vengeful order of events that will restabilize the kingdom and cancel her abuse. Arjuna is the one who practically and actually accomplishes all this. It is as if these three Kṛṣṇa/ās are aspects of one energy or force, and Draupadī functions in the primary and feminine position.

idaṃ ca śayanaṃ dṛṣṭvā yac cāsīt te purātanam
śocāmi tvāṃ mahārāja duḥkhānarhaṃ sukhocitam

Having seen this bed which was once yours,
I grieve for you—O king—used to happiness, undeserving of sorrow!

III.28.10

'This grief oppresses me', she says (*śoko mām rundhayaty ayam*). She remembers and recounts to Yudhiṣṭhira his throne and former opulence; now, he is filthy and wears clothing made of bark (III.28.14).

Next, she laments their present diet, compared to previous luxury, and goes on to verbally excoriate Bhīma and then Arjuna for their weakness and lack of temerity. She continues to berate all her husbands for their deficient valor, citing their former prowess and invincibility as heroes. During this particular movement of her wrath—and one must recall that the Mahābhārata is sung or chanted—she repeats again and again the refrain, *kasmān manyur na vardhate* 'why does anger not arise?'

Draupadī, in this long and bitter aria, then turns to her own self, detailing her own nobility. She proceeds to engage Yudhiṣṭhira at length on the subject of dharma and on the nature and possibility of action. This dialogue between the two continues for several hundred *śloka*s; and in one of Yudhiṣṭhira's rebuttals he condemns *krodha* 'anger' as the basis of policy. This is of course directed specifically at Draupadī, who completely personifies anger at this point.[30]

Her lengthy harangue on *nīti* 'policy' closes with a few maxims. She particularly contemns the man of conciliation, implying her husband and interlocutor:

vyasanaṃ vāsya kāṅkṣeta vināśaṃ vā yudhiṣṭhira
api sindhor girer vāpi kiṃ punar martyadharmiṇaḥ

Yudhiṣṭhira, one should desire the misfortune or ruin of him [the conciliator];
even if [he was] a river or a mountain—so how much more of a human being?

III.33.52

This formal duo ends when Bhīma enters the discussion and introduces the subject of *artha* 'property' and 'desire' *kāma* (III.34.2ff.). Yudhiṣṭhira, responding to his brother, speaks of how, after the dicing, *abhavac charaṇaṃ draupadī naḥ* 'Draupadī was our refuge' (III.35.6).

30. He says, *kṣamā bhavo hi bhūtānām* 'conciliation is the origin of beings' (III.30.32). This speech is analyzed below, in Ch. V.3.

At this point, Vyāsa appears—as he does—out of nowhere, a deus ex machina. He advises Yudhiṣṭhira on the appropriate course of immediate affairs, instructing him to send Arjuna off in order to acquire cosmic weaponry from the deities.

When Arjuna is about to set off towards the abode of Indra in order to obtain these extraordinary munitions, Draupadī approaches him and makes her farewell. She says,

> māsmākaṃ kṣatriyakule janma kaścid avāpnuyāt
> brāhmaṇebhyo namo nityaṃ yeṣāṃ yuddhe na jīvikā
>
> May we obtain no birth in the clan of *kṣatriyas*!
> Constantly honor Brahmins, whose livelihood is not in battle!
>
> III.38.21

Not many *adhyāyas* previous she had been extolling the *kṣatriya* virtue of violent action; and now, as her most favored husband departs, she speaks in a fashion that goes contrary to that view. There will be no delight in living without him, she says, for all of them (III.38.23–24). 'Obtain fortune', she adds (*svasti prāpnuhī*), and 'praise to the Creator and Ordainer' (*namo dhātre vidhātre ca*), the two divine figures whom she had extolled earlier on, when speaking with Yudhiṣṭhira.[31]

Whilst Arjuna is absent securing this weaponry from Indra, Draupadī tends to the other husbands and others who are present, 'like a mother'. It is extraordinary how she runs the gamut of emotions with such simple and mediate facility; she is a figure of great affective range.

> patīṃś ca draupadī sarvān dvijāṃś caiva yaśasvinī
> māteva bhojayitvāgre śiṣṭam āhārayat tadā
>
> Draupadī the glorious, like a mother, having fed
> the husbands and all the twice-born, then took the remainder.
>
> III.47.10

She remembers Arjuna fondly, her *madhyamaṃ patim* 'middle husband' (III.79.11). 'Without him, the forest does not please me' (*tam ṛte ... vanaṃ na pratibhāti me*), she says disconsolately. 'I see this earth void—as it were' (*śūnyām iva paśyāmi ... mahīmām*). The natural beauty of the place no longer delights her.

Yet the constant reiteration that the audience hears throughout the poem concerning the discomfiture of Draupadī in the *sabhā*, and the

31. There is the moot question: are these two deities are central in her personal devotions, or are they deities that figure more prominently among women in this *kṣatriya* culture?

frightful consequences of that incident, is repeated again and again all through the epic until the confrontation at Kurukṣetra.[32] Her brother, visiting once whilst they are at Kāmyaka in the forest, makes such a statement.

> duryodhanas tava krodhāt devi tyakṣati jīvitam
> pratijānīma te satyaṃ mā śuco varavarṇini
>
> Queen, Duryodhana will forsake his life because of your anger,
> we truly promise you! Do not grieve, O beautiful woman!
>
> III.48.31

He and his companions continue, describing the unavoidable bloodshed that will one day ensue, and the scavengers that will consume the corpses of those who mistreated her in the assembly hall (III.48.32–36). This promise of revenge, with its ghastly images—of flesh and blood and decapitation—recurs throughout the poem, to be accomplished during the four battle books; the imagery is vividly revisited during Book Eleven, the Strī *parvan*.

Once, as she and the remaining husbands make their way towards Mount Gandhamādhana, Draupadī collapses, *vepantī kadalī yathā* 'shaking like a plantain' (III.143.4). Yudhiṣṭhira wonders how they can continue with their pilgrimage, given her fatigue and physical exhaustion, and he takes his fallen wife into his lap and 'laments' for her.[33] Bhīma calls upon his son, the *rākṣasa* Ghaṭotkaca, who simply appears, and he instructs the demon to carry Draupadī.[34]

Soon, once they arrive at the *āśrama* of Nara and Narāyaṇa, they are greeted by the ascetics, and,

> kṛṣṇāyās tatra paśyantaḥ krīḍitāny amaraprabhāḥ
> vicitrāṇi naravyāghrā remire tatra pāṇḍavāḥ
>
> The Pāṇḍavas, men-tigers, spendid as immortals, sported,
> watching the charming amusements of Draupadī.
>
> III.145.43

It is unusual for an audience to hear of Draupadī having fun, for she is generally either wrathful or afflicted by the constant harshness of *vanavāsa* 'living in the forest'. This is a rare snapshot of her at ease.

Draupadī, at this Kāmyaka hermitage, becomes intoxicated with the

32. At III.48.5 this is referred to as *draupadyās taṃ parikleśaṃ* 'that vexation of Draupadī'.
33. The verb is *pari*√*div* (III.144.9).
34. He had been born to the *rākṣasī* Hiḍimbā, in a time prior to Bhīma's marriage with Draupadī.

fragrance of a flower, the *saugandhika*, and demands that Bhīma bring her more. The perfume had been transported by a strong breeze from afar, and so Bhīma sets off northward to obtain more of the blossom for his wife, *draupadyāḥ priyam anvicchan* 'desiring the love of Draupadī (III.146.16).[35] She, however, had already given the original flower to Yudhiṣṭhira. These flowers are *mahārhāṇi divyāni ... bahurūpāṇi virajāṃsi* 'precious, divine, multifold, dustless' (III.153.1).

When Bhīma eventually locates the forest from whence the flower has blown, *jagāma manasā priyām* 'with his mind he went to his beloved' (III.150.28). Such wording of emotion and affection—the language of intimacy—is rare in this poem, and if it does occur, it is often formal and typical, as if cliché. Bhīma and Arjuna are the only two husbands of Draupadī ever to receive any ascription of the sentiments of love.

When Yudhiṣṭhira discovers that Bhīma has gone off in order to acquire flowers for Draupadī, he questions her. As she replies, the poets describe her:

> priyā priyaṃ cikīrṣantī mahiṣī cāruhāsinī
>
> The beloved sweetly smiling queen, desiring love ...
>
> III.153.12

Here, briefly, and almost like a shadow, the reader senses something of how Draupadī manages her five men, of how in control of her affections she is, and of how she modulates her dealings with the husbands: moving from one to another, always varying, tacitly shifting, sustaining a certain coquetry and yet always being without duplicity.[36]

Some time after this episode, Draupadī again implores Bhīma to amuse her with another favor. More than with any other of her husbands, Draupadī has an often fond and playful relation with Bhīma, which is particularly evident in Book Four. On this occasion the poets say:

> tataḥ kṣiptam ivātmānaṃ draupadyā sa paraṃtapaḥ
> nāmṛṣyata mahābāhuḥ prahāram iva sadgavaḥ
>
> Then that scorcher of enemies as if personally reviled by Draupadī,
> like a good bull the great-armed one did not bear the blow.
>
> III.157.25

35. Bhīma is a complex figure. He is a great protector of family, due to his enormous strength; yet, he is also the most horrific and ghastly of all the brothers and the most brutal, and is oftentimes described as Yama, 'Death' personified. At III.158.10, Yudhiṣṭhira himself rebukes his brother for his appallingly bloodthirsty and indiscriminate violence. It is telling that Draupadī is so attracted to this husband.

36. There is virtually no lying or verbal untruth in the Mahābhārata: the epic generally lacks that form of misdirection.

In the eleventh year of their *vanavāsa* Kṛṣṇa again comes to visit the Pāṇḍavas. Having greeted the brothers he then addresses Draupadī, congratulating her on her *śiśavaḥ suśīlāḥ* 'well-disposed infants' (III.180.23). This is the first mention of any children that an audience receives. Kṛṣṇa remarks that it is a pity that they have no 'maternal uncles' (*mātulāḥ*) to find joy in, for the children are staying with his own clan, the Vṛṣṇis.[37]

He praises the good *kṣatriya* qualities of the boys, their bravery and truthfulness. Without Kuntī or Draupadī, the youngsters are being brought up by Subhadrā, Draupadī's co-wife with Arjuna: she being the sister of Kṛṣṇa and the cousin by marriage of Draupadī. Pradyumna, Kṛṣṇa's son, is also fostering the children; he is similarly mentoring Abhimanyu, Arjuna's son by Subhadrā, and is *guruvat* 'like a guru' (III.180.29). Draupadī does not respond to any of these statements, and the silence is telling.

In conversation with Satyabhāmā, the *mahiṣī* 'first wife', or 'queen' of Kṛṣṇa, Draupadī talks about her polyandric situation, something which obviously fascinates her interlocutor. Satyabhāmā asks why the Pāṇḍavas, who are *vaśagās* 'obedient', are never troubled by their situation (III.222.4). She enquires about the *bhagavedana* 'that which confers connubial felicity', which Draupadī must have access to: that is, sex. For Satyabhāmā would like to possess such attractions for her own husband.[38] Perhaps Satyabhāmā is thinking of the wife of Jaratkāru, for she 'served her husband in unusual ways' (*bhartāraṃ ... upācarat upāyaiḥ śvetakākīyaiḥ*; I.43.10).[39]

Draupadī, who is described as a *pativratā* 'devoted to her husbands', is offended (III.222.7).[40] She decries the use of aphrodisiacs as being unsalutary, and says,

37. Shah 1995: 18, on the importance of the *mātula*, notes, "he was the nearest relative of status who could safeguard their interests from their agnatic relation's conflicting self-interest. Both Śakuni and Vāsudeva are frantic in their efforts to safeguard the share of their nephews the Kauravas and the Pāṇḍavas in the Kuru patrimony." Lévi-Strauss 1963, Ch. II, discusses "the avunculate" at length.

38. Sax 2002: 142 describes how in Himalayan Garhwal, "Draupadi is also thought to exhibit a kind of hypersexuality. Throughout Garhwal, women appeal to Draupadi, the sexually active wife, and not to Kunti, the aged mother, when they wish to become pregnant. Most of them equate polyandry with an excessive sexual appetite." He notes that in an adjoining region, the upper Tons valley, fraternal polyandry is still practiced.

39. Literally 'with the manners of a white crow'. Even Karṇa once makes the observation that, *īpsitaś ca guṇaḥ strīṇām ekasyā bahubhartṛtā* 'and the desired quality of all women is many husbands for one woman!' (I.194.8).

40. Conversely, the ideal of the problematic wife is given by the statement, *susāntvitāpi hy asatī strī jahāti* 'a bad wife—even conciliated—quits' (II.57.12). This proverb is repeated at III.5.19.

sadārān pāṇḍavān nityaṃ prayatopacarāmy aham

Piously, I always attend to the Pāṇḍavas and their wives.

III.222.18

'No other man is respected by me', she adds (*na me anyaḥ puruṣo mataḥ*). She continues,

ye ca dharmāḥ kuṭumbeṣu śvaśrvā me kathitāḥ purā

Whatever dharmas exist in the household were once told to me by my mother-in-law.

III.222.32

These dharmas not only concern the household management, but also refer to ritual life within the establishment.

patyāśrayo hi me dharmo mataḥ strīṇāṃ sanātanaḥ

I consider the perpetual dharma of women as resting upon the husband.

III.222.35

It is the connection between the mother and son which maintains households, not the relation between wife and husband: Draupadī has received her injunctions as to household management from Kuntī, and it is the latter who has supplied the domestic constitution. We have observed above how authoritatively Kuntī speaks and how her sons respect the absolute literality of such prescription. The husband is the *deva* 'deity', and the *gati* 'the way', but it is the mother-in-law who directs this devotion, who interprets the wishes of the son-husband.

As we see—via the manner in which women instruct their menfolk in what is correct dharma and practical conduct—it is the women who maintain and sustain the families within the confines of a household.[41] The men, advised by their women, are active externally in the world, and as *kṣatriyas* that necessitates 'carnage' (*daṇḍa*) and conflict.[42]

It is by such great dedication, says Draupadī, that 'my husbands are obedient to me' (*bhartāro vaśagā mahyaṃ*; III.222.37). There is a nice

41. See below, Ch. V.

42. All these lines about how the husband is the arbiter of family and married life are very much a rhetoric modified by actual practice. If we presume that most if not all of the audience at the declamation of the epic—during archaic times—were male, then the axis of the poem's message is clear. If these epic poems were being recited—and this is at a later "stage" in the poem's formal historical trajectory—at occasions of pilgrimage where women would be present if not actually predominant, then the poet-audience axis is very different. Which of these two is actually the case for our text can only remain hypothetical.

play on the nature of equation here, the dialectics of marriage: for as we have observed, the devotion to the husband is in fact a dedication to the mother-in-law, Kuntī, who is *pṛthivīsamām* 'equal to the earth'. Draupadī tells her interlocutor, *svayaṃ paricarāmy ekā* 'only I attend upon her' (III.222.38).

She describes to Satyabhāmā how she ran the various feasts at the palace of Hāstinapura and how it was her responsibility to keep control of the treasury.

> prathamaṃ pratibudhyāmi caramaṃ saṃviśāmi ca
>
> I awaken first and I lie down last.
>
> III.222.56

That is 'my fascination' (*saṃvananaṃ mama*), she says at the close of the first half of this long speech on wifely conduct.

'You shall cut your husband from his lovers' (*bhartāram ācchetsyasi kāminībhyaḥ*) only by good conduct, Draupadī goes on to inform Satyabhāmā (III.223.1). He is 'divine', she says (*daivata*): yet deities in the Mahābhārata, as the audience well knows, are subject to many kinds of propitiation and deceit.

> duḥkhena sādhvī labhate sukhāni
>
> A virtuous woman obtains good things with difficulty.
>
> III.223.4

Beware of the indiscretion of the 'co-wife' (*sapatnī*), Draupadī adds. The audience hears no more on this potentially thorny subject, however, and the speech closes with the final admonition to 'honor the husband, wearing lovely odors and unguents, ornaments and costly flowers' (*mahārhamālyābharaṇāṅgarāgā bhartāram ārādhaya puṇyagandhā*; III.223.12).

That is, ultimately show deference, yet use every charm possible in order to be attractive. Nevertheless, the primary source of domestic dharma derives from the mother-in-law. In the case of Kuntī, who is a widow and alone, she manages to sustain this great authority which she possesses without deference to a husband.

4. *The Court of Virāṭa*

At the outset of this chapter, before they have arrived at the court of King Virāṭa, Yudhiṣṭhira is in counsel with his brothers and they are planning how they shall maintain their disguise as they return to urban life, now that the period of exile concludes. Concerning Draupadī, he says,

> sukumārī ca bālā ca rājaputrī yaśasvinī
> pativratā mahābhāgā kathaṃ nu vicariṣyati
>
> A young princess and famed daughter of a king:
> virtuous, illustrious—how will she live?
>
> IV.3.14

Draupadī without hesitation determines that she will work as a 'maid-servant' (*bhujiṣyā*), a 'domestic servant who works in the women's apartments' (*sairaṃdhrī*). She plans to work for the queen, Sudeṣṇā. Once in the town, she proceeds,

> vāsaś ca paridhāyaikaṃ kṛṣṇaṃ sumalinaṃ mahat
>
> Having put on a single, large, black, very dirty garment.
>
> IV.8.2

Later, Draupadī, on being praised in detail by Sudeṣṇā the queen, gives her name as Mālinī, and says that she used to be the servant of Kṛṣṇa's senior wife.[43] Sudeṣṇā continues to praise Draupadī's beauty, saying that men and especially her husband will find her irresistible. Sudeṣṇā remarks,

> vṛkṣāṃś cāvasthitān paśya ya ime mama veśmani
> te'pi tvāṃ saṃnamantīva pumāṃsāṃ kaṃ nu mohayeḥ
>
> Look at the trees bent down, which are in my quarters!
> Even they seem to honor you! What man might you not confound![44]
>
> IV.8.22

Ignoring this supernatural event, Sudeṣṇā wonders how her husband will be when he observes Draupadī's hips and her *vapur amānuṣam* 'unearthly body'. She says, 'always, whatever man would see you ... he would become taken by the deity of love' (*yaś ca tvāṃ satataṃ paśyet ... sa ca anaṅgavaśo bhavet*; IV.8.25). It is unusual for a woman in Mahābhārata to be speaking about the possible infidelities of another woman; once again, Draupadī is exceptional.

Draupadī simply avows her fidelity to five *gandharva* husbands, thus admitting to preternatural qualities and unusual marital practice. The queen makes no comment upon this.

43. See above, Ch. I. for this speech. The name *mālinī* means 'garlanded'. It is telling that the garment that she puts on at this moment is *kṛṣṇa* 'black', which is similar her usual epithet, *kṛṣṇā*: such is the signification of her disguise!

44. One recalls that trees are a standard metaphor for heroes in the Mahābhārata.

When the *senāpati* 'general', Kīcaka, takes a fancy to Draupadī, problems arise. He is completely smitten by her and flatters her in the usual fashion, asking if she is a deity: *kā devarūpā* 'who is this divine form?' He says, *tyajāmi dārān mama ye purātanāḥ* 'I am giving up my former wives', because he suddenly wants Draupadī so much.

She repels and spurns all advances, insulting him and saying,

> dayitāḥ prāṇinām dārā dharmaṃ samanucintaya
>
> Remember dharma! Wives are beloved of men
>
> IV.13.14

Addressing him as *sūtaputra* 'son of a charioteer', she begins to instruct him in proper dharma and good conduct, saying that she is *durlabhām ... vīrair abhirakṣitām* 'difficult to obtain, protected by warriors'.[45] She repeats what she said to queen Sudeṣṇā, *gandharvāḥ patayo mama* 'my husbands are *gandharvas*, sons of deities' (*devasutā*). No one appears to pay attention to these extraordinary claims.

The *senāpati* approaches the queen and involves her in his designs, requesting that she send Draupadī to his household in order to secure some cordials. Draupadī resists the order but goes, having first made a truth act, an act of illocution which, as we have seen, is a kind of speech that women perform in order to preserve their moral integrity.

> yathāham anyaṃ pāṇḍubhyo nābhijānāmi kathaṃcana
> tena satyena māṃ prāptāṃ kīcako mā vaśe kṛthāḥ
>
> As I do not acknowledge any other man but the Pāṇḍavas,
> by this truth may Kīcaka not obtain me to his will.
>
> IV.14.18

'She worshipped the Sun a moment' (*upātiṣṭhata sā sūryaṃ muhūrtam*), which is a most unusual thing for Draupadī to do and something which she never does again. The poets also refer to her in this instance as *abalā*, which means 'woman', but the term also connotes 'weakness'.

When Kīcaka tried to molest her, 'she threw him on the ground' (*bhūmau ākṣipya*), a somewhat manly feat to do to a warrior (IV.15.6). He then seizes her by the hair and tosses her down and strikes her with his foot. This is in the presence of king Virāṭa, as well as Yudhiṣṭhira and Bhīma, none of whom say anything. The scene is as awful as that of the dicing episode in the *sabhā*.

Draupadī then gives one of her virulent and ferocious speeches. She is horrified that a mere *sūtaputra* should kick her with his foot—something

45. Another 'son of a charioteer' is, of course, Karṇa, with whom, in many vernacular non-Sanskritic traditions, Draupadī is intimately linked.

that is particularly insulting to do to any person—and she repeatedly refers to herself as 'an esteemed wife', again and again saying,

> ... māṃ māninīṃ bhāryāṃ sūtaputraḥ padāvadhīt
>
> The son of a charioteer, struck me—an esteemed wife—with his foot!
>
> IV.15.15

Draupadī continually reiterates the valor and heroism of her husbands, yet they do nothing for her despite the degradation of this moment. There is a cynical and pungent irony in this, seeing that two of the husbands are present as witnesses.

> kva nu teṣām amarṣaś ca vīryaṃ tejaś ca vartate
> na parīpsanti ye bhāryāṃ vadhyamānāṃ durātmanā
>
> Where is the splendor, virility, and intransigence of them,
> who do not preserve a wife being struck by a wicked man?
>
> IV.15.22

Women like her, she says, *dadyur na yāceyur* 'they should give and should not ask', which is very much a *kṣatriya* sentiment.[46] Such women are *brahmaṇyāḥ satyavādinaḥ* 'pious, truthful'. She praises the pride and strength and martial vigor of the men to whom she is married: where are those *mahārathāḥ* 'chief warriors' now, she asks?

This scene full of pathos is reminiscent of the earlier *sabhā*, thirteen years previous, which opened the period of clandestine exile for the Pāṇḍavas. It is as if there is a dramatic framing taking place—marking the onset and the closure of exile—by virtue of this repetition.[47]

She calls her splendid, powerful, warrior-husbands *klībā* 'eunuchs', playing with this oxymoronic sense, and questions their implacable virility and their *tejas* 'potence' (IV.15.21). She even questions King Virāṭa, who has condoned the viciousness which has been done to her and Kīcaka's complete disregard of dharma, and—ignoring Virāṭa—she calls upon the assembled to give judgment.

Yudhiṣṭhira successfully silences her, for their disguise is now in jeopardy. The poets refer to Draupadī here as, *mahiṣīṃ priyām* 'beloved queen', reminding the audience as to the status of the players in this part of the narrative: high royalty, but incognito.

'Go,' Yudhiṣṭhira instructs her, 'go, do not stay here!' (*gaccha mātra*

46. The ideal model is that *kṣatriyas* give and brahmins receive: hence wealth circulates and an economy is created.

47. See Witzel 1987, Minkowski 1989, and Malinar, in Koskikallio 2005, on the concept and use of 'framing' techniques.

sthāḥ; IV.15.31). For at this point if their identity is discovered they must return to the forest for another twelve years: such was the pact with Duryodhana. She departs with the statement that,

> atīva teṣāṃ ghṛṇinām arthe'haṃ dharmacāriṇī
>
> I, extremely virtuous, am in the service of those who are compassionate!
>
> IV.15.35

Here she implies that her two husbands, present at her molestation, once again allowed her to be abused and to suffer without protection. Once again they have publicly failed her for reasons of political expedience. She departs, 'having let down her hair' (*keśān muktvā*), 'her eyes crimson from rage' (*saṃrambhāl lohitekṣaṇā*).

> sā hatā sūtaputreṇa rājaputrī samajvalat
>
> She, a princess, struck by a charioteer's son, blazed![48]
>
> IV.16.1

Such is the indignity and its consequent sorrow, which is so intrinsic to Draupadī's life.

True to character, Draupadī now reflects on how to secure the death of Kīcaka (IV.16.1ff.). She resolves to depend upon Bhīma and she approaches him in the night when all sleep. The poets portray her as a completely white cow of three year's age, or a cow-elephant approaching a great bull; having embraced him as a creeper clings to a flowering tree, and having woken him as a wife of a king of beasts wakens a sleeping lion. They lavish much metaphorical detail upon this moment, counterposing similes of intimacy with the real desire for death and revenge.

> sā lateva mahāśālaṃ phullaṃ gomatitīrajam
> bāhubhyāṃ parirabhyaitaṃ prābodhayad aninditā
>
> She—like a vine having embraced a great blossoming *śāla* tree near the shore of the Gomatī—the virtuous one awoke him with both arms.
>
> IV.16.7

'Rise, rise', she says (*uttiṣṭha*), asking why he lies there, *yathā mṛtaḥ* 'as

48. The verb √*jval* 'to blaze' is typically employed to describe the sacrificial fire, as oblations are offered into it causing it to flare. One recalls Draupadī's origins out of a sacrificial hearth.

if dead!' (IV.16.9). Again, the poets signal to the audience that he speaks to her as his 'queen, chief wife' (*mahiṣīṃ priyām*), despite the discredit of their present clandestine and banausic life.

She complains to him of her subjection and humiliation in the Kuru *sabhā*, at being dragged to the assembly by a servant and spoken to as a slave; and she reminds Bhīma of how Jayadratha had abducted her when they were in the forest. Now, thirdly, she has been publicly kicked by a mere *senāpati*. No other woman in the poem undergoes so much degradation like this.

Her indignation is furious, and proceeds for over a hundred verses, beginning with her contempt for Yudhiṣṭhira: at how, because of his gambling, he allowed her to sink to such a humble position, where she is presently denigrated.

> aśocyaṃ nu kutas tasyā yasyā bhartā yudhiṣhiraḥ
>
> Of her—what is not to be lamented—whose husband is Yudhiṣṭhira!
>
> IV.17.1

The audience hears of her disgusted wrath, at how someone of the affluence and stature of Yudhiṣṭhira should be so overruled by inferiors. 'Despise your elder brother', she says (*bhrātaraṃ ca vigarhasva jyeṣṭhaṃ*; IV.17.10). She categorizes Yudhiṣṭhira's former fabulous wealth—forsaken because of his gambling—and enquires why Bhīma does not now see her, *śokasāgaramadhyasthām* 'stood amidst an ocean of grief'?

> pārthivāḥ pṛthivīpālā yasyāsan vaśavartinaḥ
> sa vaśe vivaśo rājā pareṣām adya vartate
>
> That king, to whom princes and rulers were subordinate,
> now acts powerless, at the behest of others!
>
> IV.17.24

Draupadī speaks best when she is inflamed with anger, then her lines run on with vast eloquence and drama as she excoriates her objects, usually the husbands. 'I speak from sorrow', she admits (*duḥkhād ... bravīmy aham*; IV.18.1). This is her most profound voice, and the reason why so many contemporary Indian feminists have taken Draupadī as their archetype.

> idaṃ tu me mahād duḥkhaṃ yat pravakṣyāmi bhārata
>
> This is the great sorrow which I shall describe, O Bhārata.
>
> IV.18.1
>
> śoke yudhiṣṭhire magnā nāhaṃ jīvitum utsahe

Submerged in the grief of Yudhiṣṭhira, I am not able to live!

IV.18.8

Draupadī suddenly changes her tone and endears herself to Bhīma by telling him of how all the women in the *zenana* gossip about how he and she are lovers and sleep together. She then abruptly continues with her tirade, lambasting individually each of her other husbands, commencing with Arjuna. She turns her wrath upon him, recalling his former deeds and exploits and, as she did with Yudhiṣṭhira, she compares his present lowly station with his previous boldness: now he has become a 'young dancing-master of girls'. When she sees this, she says, 'my mind becomes dejected' (*sīdati me manaḥ*).

pārthaṃ ... paśyāmi tūryamadhyasthaṃ diśo naśyanti me tadā

I see Arjuna standing among his instruments—then my orientation is destroyed.

IV.18.22

This great royal hero of matchless prowess, of whom,

striyo gītasvanaṃ tasya muditāḥ paryupāsate

Ecstatic women now attend upon the sound of his song.

IV.18.12

Draupadī then turns to Sahadeva and Nakula, similarly lamenting their downfall. 'How can I live', she asks Bhīma (*kiṃ nu jīvāmi*) 'seeing such degradation?'

vikriyāṃ paśya me tīvrāṃ rājaputryāḥ

Look at me, the extreme transformation of a king's daugher!

IV.19.2

'I look to the arising of my husbands' (*pratīkṣāmi bhartṝṇām udayam*), she adds.

sāhaṃ dāsatvam āpannā na śāntim avaśā labhe

I have acquired servitude: helpless, I obtain no peace.

IV.19.15

There is a tremendous intimacy in this nocturnal scene, with its confessions of love and its despair and its intense animosity to the other husbands who have accepted, once again, her disgrace without demur.

ārtayaitan mayā bhīma kṛtaṃ bāṣpavimokṣaṇam
apārayantyā duḥkhāni na rājānam upālabhe

That release of tears, Bhīma, was made by me—distressed,
unable to resist sorrows—I do not reproach the king.

IV.20.14

It is probably the most private and revealing of all of Draupadī's speeches, being more informed by despondency than outrage, and being more intimate than any other scene in the poem where she is the speaker. Her language after the dicing scene was more tinged with ire than with pity; here the tone comes *snehāt saṃvāsajāt* 'from love born of sexual congress' (IV.18.4). Nowhere else in the poem is this degree of Draupadī's private affection so touched upon and exposed.

Her anger and contempt soon dissolve again as she turns to weeping for her own lamentable situation, decrying how *daivam* had brought her to such a point (IV.19.5ff.). She, who was so royal and luxurious, is now a handmaid: 'know that unbearable sorrow of mine', she cries (*idaṃ tu duḥkhaṃ ... mamāsahyaṃ nibodha tat*; IV.19.21). 'She weeps gently' (*ruroda śanakaiḥ*) and Bhīma joins her with his own tears, having put her coarsened hands upon his face.

Draupadī soon rallies, however, and redirects her wrath once more against Kīcaka, plotting her vengeance and his death. She reminds Bhīma of how he had saved her at III.154, when the *rākṣasa* Jaṭāsura abducted her, and of how he had helped to save her from Jayadratha's intended capture. 'Kill this bad man!', she says (*jahīmam pāpam*).

tam evaṃ kāmasaṃmattaṃ bhindhi kumbham ivāśmani

Crack him, deluded by desire, like a pot upon a stone!

IV.20.32

She threatens to commit suicide if Kīcaka lives for one more day: *viṣam āloḍya pāsyāmi* 'having licked poison, I shall drink [it]'. What *kṣatriya* husband can resist such a claim? Women *kṣatriya*s, just as the men, must always be prepared to give up their life for the maintenance of *kṣatriya* dharma. This is a principle even today, particularly among the *rājput*s, which has prevailed for centuries.[49]

śreyo hi maraṇaṃ mahyaṃ bhīmasena tavāgrataḥ

For my death is better in front of you, Bhīma!

IV.20.33

49. See Harlan 2003.

'I shall do as you say', Bhīma tells her (*kariṣyāmi ... bhāṣase*, accepting her commission; IV.21.1). Draupadī clings to her husband, who soothes and embraces her, whilst in his mind approaching Kīcaka. So they pass the remainder of the night, and so ends this vivid and dramatic scene between the couple, charged with so many particular and various emotions. An audience must have been thrilled by the range and depth of this scene, for so many different and intense sentiments have been displayed and sung.

The next day, Kīcaka offers Draupadī great wealth if she will accept him as her lover. She then arranges for a rendezvous between them: there, her husband will batter him to death. 'Tear him out', she says to Bhīma, 'as an elephant tears out a reed' (*naḍaṃ nāgeva uddhara*; IV.21.28). 'Make the honor of the clan!' (*kuru mānaṃ kulasya*), she says, reminding him of appropriate conduct.

Draupadī never has compunction concerning death or revenge, being utterly without qualm when it comes to punishing those who have offended her. Bhīma, similarly, will later destroy the life of Duryodhana and of Duḥśāsana in retribution for how they treated Draupadī. Of all the husbands, he is actually the only one to take personal vengeance for her sake: he is the actual agent of the vendetta which courses through the central narrative of Mahābhārata.

Kīcaka becomes elated at the prospect of the tryst, not realizing that 'Death was embodied as the maid', Draupadī (*sairandhrīrūpiṇaṃ ... mṛtyum*; IV.21.19). When he is reduced to a 'ball of flesh' (*māṃsapiṇḍa*), mangled, without arms or legs or head like a tortoise, Draupadī is 'joyous' (*prahṛṣṭā*).

The sons of the *senāpati*, witnessing the remains of their father, determine to take Draupadī to the cremation ground and incinerate her along with Kīcaka. She of course, screams for her husbands as they drag her off, 'having lifted her up and bound her' (*tāṃ samāropya nibadhya ca*; IV.22.10). It is Bhīma, once again, who comes to her rescue, and slaughters—using an uprooted tree as a bludgeon—one hundred and five of her assailants. Exulting, he slips away back towards his kitchens, and Draupadī, delighted, *mṛgī bālā* 'a young doe', returns from the cremation ground towards the town (IV.23.12).

> tāṃ dṛṣṭvā puruṣā rājan prādravanta diśo daśa
>
> Men, O king, having seen her, run to the ten directions.
>
> IV.23.13

They flee, 'trembling from fear of the *gandharvas*' (*gandharvāṇāṃ bhayatrastāḥ*), having heard that her husbands, supposedly *gandharva*, had punished those who sought to violate and immolate her. Greeting Bhīma, she in a grand manner,

> taṃ vismayantī śanakaiḥ saṃjñābhir idam abravīt
> gandharvarājāya namo yenāsmi parimocitā
>
> Smiling softly she said this to him, knowingly:
> hail to the Gandharva king—by whom I am freed!
>
> IV.23.15

The Virāṭa queen now treats her differently, as does the king, aware that his régime is possibly endangered: *rājā bibheti ... te gandharvabhyaḥ* 'the king fears because of your *gandharvas*', Sudeṣṇā comments, and now refers to Draupadī as *rūpeṇāpratimā bhuvi* 'without equal in beauty on earth'.

There is a conflation of death and beauty here, something which is intrinsic to Draupadī's person: she elicits male desire and yet she is always profuse and prolific in her rage and encouragement of bloody vengeance when that desire runs out of hand. No other woman in the epic compounds such intense duality in her person: the sinister and the gentle.

Towards the end of this *adhyāya*, when the territory of the Matsyas is being raided by the Kauravas and their cattle being driven off, Uttara, the crown prince—somewhat of an effete fop—is called upon to save the Virāṭas from defeat. He responds rather grandiosely, saying how wonderfully he will fight, and that he should be considered to be like Arjuna himself!

Draupadī overhears this fabulous claim, which 'she did not tolerate' (*nāmarṣayata*; IV.34.1). She approaches him 'modestly, gently' (*vrīḍamānā ... śanakair*), and proposes that the disguised Arjuna should act as Uttara's charioteer. There is a playfulness and lightness to this brief scene, in nice contrast to the previous act, where Draupadī was presented in such a distraught, virulent, and pitiless light.

Finally, at the close of the Vīrāṭa *parvan*, during the dicing match between Virāṭa and Yudhiṣṭhira, when the former loses his temper and throws the dice at Yudhiṣṭhira, causing blood to flow, it is Draupadī who instantly secures a bowl in which to catch the fluid, knowing that if it touched the earth there would be trouble. For Yudhiṣṭhira is an anointed king, and if Arjuna had learned that the sacred blood of his brother had been spilled he would have had to wreak a terrible revenge.

'He looked at Draupadī', and,

> sā veda tam abhiprāyaṃ bhartuś cittavaśānugā

> She, obedient to the thought of her husband, knew his meaning.
>
> IV.63.46

She is always astute, sensitive to the constantly varying needs of her menfolk, which only darkens the pathos as to how she herself is treated.

5. *Prior to War*

The poet Saṃjaya, who is entrusted with the position of emissary in Book Five, tells his king how he had been introduced to Arjuna and Kṛṣṇa when he had been on his mission. They, along with their wives, Draupadī and Satyabhāmā, were apart in the *śuddhānta* 'the private quarters' (V.58.3). The two heroes were garlanded and decorated with sandal paste, and were *madhvāvasvakṣībau* 'drunk with spirituous liquor'. Arjuna's feet lay in the laps of the two women, and Kṛṣṇa's lay in the lap of Arjuna. This is a rare sketch of an exclusive and private scene, unusual for the epic. Such languorous images of Draupadī in the poem are rare, and they give great chiaroscuro to her character.[50]

In the Udyoga *parvan*, assembled together with their ally Kṛṣṇa, the Pāṇḍavas discuss the possibility of war and future policy. Draupadī is present and contributes her point of view to the debate. She has only one recommendation, and that is, *teṣu na kartavyā kṛpā* 'compassion is not to be made among them' (V.80.12). She favors a tough and aggressive policy of war and has no interest in appeasement.

> tasmāt teṣu mahādaṇḍaḥ kṣeptavyaḥ kṣipram ...
>
> Therefore, a great club is to be hurled among them, quickly!
>
> V.80.14

Hesitation about the use of cruelty is never a problem for Draupadī. As usual she speaks with steady measurement and tempo in her diction: there is always authority and gravitas to her words and her speech always suits the addressee.

'What woman is there like me on earth?', she asks of Kṛṣṇa (*kā sīmantinī mādṛk pṛthivyām asti*; V.80.20).[51] She describes her birth and ancestry, and the fact that she had born five sons to this distinguished lineage into which she had married, and where she now stood as *mahiṣī* 'chief queen'. Then she reminds Kṛṣṇa about how she was dragged by

50. There are few mentions in the Mahābhārata of alcohol consumption or the rituals of drinking so often associated with Indo-European warrior elites. See Kristiansen and Larsson 2005: 225–226.

51. 'A woman who wears her hair parted (as a pregnant woman)', *sīmantī*: Monier-Williams. Such is typically a sign of married status.

her hair into the *sabhā* and insulted whilst her husbands watched in silence. She became like a slave of the wicked, there in the middle of the hall, whilst the Pāṇḍavas showed no anger!

As she recounts this episode once again, she speaks with extreme drama, going so far as to imitate the words of the old king, and the tension of her speech is heightened by a reiterated use of the present tense: she is enacting the whole scene for them, and not simply recounting it. She mimics Dhṛtarāṣṭra,

> varaṃ vṛṇīṣva pāñcālī varārhāsi ...
>
> Choose a favor, Draupadī: you deserve a favor!
>
> V.80.27

She subtly pleads with Kṛṣṇa, saying he was alive during all this and, 'you were longed for by me in my mind' (*manasā kāṅkṣito'si me*; V.80.26). 'Protect me!' she begs him (*trāhi mām*). She denigrates Bhīma and Arjuna both, using the term *dhik*, which can be loosely translated as 'damn', not a word that women in the Mahābhārata often apply to their husbands.

The poets then make much of how she collected her very black and perfumed hair, which was glowing like a snake, in her left hand and, *gajagāminī* 'moving like an elephant', approached Kṛṣṇa. She addressed him with tearful eyes, saying, 'this was pulled by the hand of Duḥśāsana, it is to be remembered' (*ayaṃ ... duḥśāsanakaroddhṛtaḥ smartavyaḥ*; V.80.36).

If Arjuna and Bhīma wish for compassion towards the Kauravas, she says that her father and his sons and also her own sons, led by Abhimanyu—the son of one of her co-wives—'they will fight with the Kurus' (*yotsyanti kurubhir*). She wants to see,

> duḥśāsanabhujaṃ śyāmaṃ saṃchinnaṃ pāṃsuguṇṭhitam
>
> The dark severed arm of Duḥśāsana, covered in dust.
>
> V.80.39

Her voice trembles and she quivers as she weeps, sprinkling her breasts with a gush of passionate tears.

Kṛṣṇa, completely swept up by her impassioned and moving remonstrance speaks of the destruction which is about to occur, and says, *satyaṃ te pratijānāmi* 'I truly promise you!'

> acirād drakṣyase kṛṣṇe rudatīr bharatastriyaḥ
> evaṃ tā bhīru rotsyanti nihatajñātibāndhavāḥ
> hatamitrā hatabalā yeṣām kruddhāsi bhāmini

> You shall soon see, Draupadī, the weeping Bhārata women!
> Thus, O timid one, they shall weep—kin and relatives killed.
> You are angry, O passionate one, at ones whose force and friends are slain!
>
> V.80.44–45

This promise is fulfilled in Book Eleven, the Strī *parvan*, when the battlefield is described by the poets. However, Draupadī's sons are also among the fallen.

Before the respective armies assemble at Kurukṣetra, Draupadī is left at Upaplavya, 'surrounded by women, slave girls and slaves' (V.149.55). Like all women in the poem, she has nothing to do with the actual and bloodthirsty conflict upon the field.[52]

6. *After the War*

After all the killing at Kurukṣetra is done, there occurs the supplementary horror of the Sauptika *parvan*, during which Aśvatthāman kills the brother of Draupadī and her five sons whilst they sleep at night. Thus Draupadī's revenge is nullified and once again she collapses with grief (X.11.6).[53]

Lying weeping in the arms of Bhīma, she again makes the ultimate threat, that if Yudhiṣṭhira cannot secure the death of Aśvatthāman, she will commit suicide by entering *prāya* 'death by meditative starvation' (X.11.15). This is an act that women do not usually make in the Mahābhārata, and is a threat that male *kṣatriya*s perform: Droṇa, Duryodhana, and Yudhiṣṭhira, for example, make such a proposal. Women generally, if in a situation of duress, will threaten to 'enter the fire', or to use 'the rope': *prāya* is only invoked by Draupadī. In her facility for brutality, which includes this commitment against her own person, Draupadī, as we have also noted above, behaves in a somewhat un-feminine manner. Her outrage is such that she goes beyond the

52. Kartikeya Patel, in Sharma 2002: 65, comments on "the menstruation festival (*raja parba*) of the Goddess in ... Orissa.... The participants often point to the story of goddess Draupadī who was disturbed during her menstruation: what followed was a great battle and almost total annihilation of the tribe of the Kurus. Just as the disturbance of Draupadī's menstruation caused the destruction of the Kuru lineage, the disturbance of mother earth's menstruation period would cause the destruction of crops and other vegetation." In Harivaṃśa LXXIII.17, there actually occurs the unusual image of a menstruating earth: *mahī navatṛṇacchannā śakragopavibhūṣitā / yauvanastheva vanitā svaṃ dadhārārtavaṃ vapuḥ* 'The earth, covered in new grass, adorned with cochineal insects, like a beautiful young woman produced its own wonderful mense.'

53. She had also lost her father, Drupada, who had been killed by Droṇa, Aśvatthāman's father.

usual margins of feminine conduct, perhaps because she has been so uniquely abused. However, this is perhaps due to her having no human parentage, except in a nominal sense, and thus her status as a woman is similarly not absolutely differentiated.[54]

On being conciliated by Yudhiṣṭhira, she assuages her promise on the condition that a jewel—with which Aśvatthāman was born and which was located on his forehead—be brought to her. The ever-faithful Bhīma immediately sets off to secure the gem. Then, receiving this jewel, she surrenders her vow, and offers the stone to Yudhiṣṭhira, and thus her grief is tempered (X.16.33). It would have been unacceptable if she had died in *prāya*, for this is in fact a most effective form of intimidation, which functions by humiliating those who are being threatened by undercutting and subverting their moral stature.[55]

At the horse sacrifice, which occurs towards the conclusion of the poem, Draupadī is 'invited'—as a queen should be—to sit down close to the immolated victim whilst the priests burn the selected parts; she participates verbally in the rite (XIV.91.2–14).[56]

Then, once her mother-in-law has departed, Draupadī lives with her husbands, bereft of all her sons. She stays with the women of the court, including Subhadrā, her co-wife, whose son had also been killed.

When Yudhiṣṭhira sets off towards the forest in order to meet up with the old king and his wife and Kuntī, Draupadī accompanies him:

> draupadīpramukhāś cāpi strīsaṃghāḥ śibikāgatāḥ
> stryadhyakṣayuktāḥ prayayur visṛjanto'mitaṃ vasu
>
> An assembly of women, led by Draupadī, in palanquins,
> joined with women attendants, set off, distributing endless wealth.
>
> XV.30.12

There, Saṃjaya, who has retired with the old king and his retinue, is asked by the assembled ascetics to describe the visitors from Hāstinapura. He describes Draupadī as *iyaṃ ... madhyaṃ vayaḥ kiṃcid iva spṛśantī* 'this one, touching as it were middle age': an uncommonly realistic observation (XV.32.9). She is seated with Subhadrā and Ulūlpī, along with a wife of Bhīma—sister of the king of Magadha, Jarāsaṃdha—and

54. See above, Ch. III.5, where Ambā is born into this family and her parents—Draupadī's nominal parents—seek to obscure her sexual identity. It is as if there are problems of sexual difference at work in this *kula*: that is certainly the subtext.

55. Gandhi made successful use of a similar threat in order to intimidate his opponents.

56. Jamison 1996: 65ff. describes this aspect of the ritual as it is given in the Veda: the details are sexually vivid, something that the epic poets choose to elide.

with Uttarā, and the wives of the sons of Dhṛtarāṣṭra: thus Saṃjaya describes the co-wives and female cousins-in-law, listing them 'in order of precedence' (*yathāmukhyam*).

At the end of the poem it is only Draupadī, of all the wives, who accompanies the five brothers as they finally depart the kingdom: she alone remains with them at death, for she of all the women in the poem is that exceptional (XVII.1.19ff.).

After her death, Yudhiṣṭhira requests of Indra, who is accompanying him, to hear of what happened to his wife.

> yatra sā bṛhatī śyāmā budhisattvaguṇānvitā
> draupadī yoṣitāṃ śreṣthā yatra caiva priyā mama
>
> Where [is] that tall dark one, possessed of energy and intelligence:
> Draupadī, my love? Where is that best of young wives?
>
> XVII.3.36

In the underworld, at the conclusion to the poem, Draupadī stands between her brother Dhṛṣṭadyumna and her sons, the Draupadeyas: woman, maternal uncle, and sons (XVIII.II.41). She is finally described as *śrīr eṣā draupadīrūpā* 'Śrī—formed as Draupadī' (XVIII.4.9).[57]

It is her wrathfulness that characterizes Draupadī most definitely, and her adroit and subtle use of forceful language; and she, more than any other woman in the poem, is a figure of paramount suffering. Her constantly vital femininity, replete with sensitivity and desire, her sexuality and its potence—for she maintains five husbands—leads to Draupadī becoming the pivot of contest in the poem, the token of sovereignty and kingdom itself. Yet her *furor* remains unsatisfied.

57. Manu observes at IX.26: *prajanārthaṃ mahābhāgāḥ pūjārhā gṛhadīptayaḥ / striyaḥ śriyaś ca garheṣu na viśeṣo'sti kaścana* 'for the purpose of procreation, eminent women in houses—like the house lamps—are to be honored: there is no distinction between fortune and women.'

V

SPEAKING OF TRUTH

WOMEN IN EPIC MAHĀBHĀRATA, more than male heroes, speak what is considered to be social truth: what is right for *kṣatriyas* and what constitutes good behavior.[1] They are *satyavādinī* 'SPEAKERS of truth' or *dharmacāriṇī* 'one whose conduct is dharmic'.[2] Usually, such speeches are made when a crisis is occurring and right demeanor is in question: then, a woman will speak, clarifying the situation and exhorting a hero or king who is not acting correctly and without due regard to *kṣatriya dharma*.[3] They are the ones to comprehend the system of valence that underlies kinship.[4] Women, like brahmins, are thus *avadhyā* 'not to be killed' (V.36.64): they comprehend the nature of worth.

1. Ingalls 1995: 4, states, "The heart of the Mahābhārata, as we have it in the Critical Text, is undoubtedly the teaching of right action..." It is women who are generally the speakers or interpreters of such action. When a situation lacks dharmic equilibrium, then *śvaśrūśvaśurayor agre vadhūḥ preṣyān aśāsata / anvaśāsac ca bhartaraṃ samāhūyābhijalpatī* 'a woman, in the presence of her parents-in-law, instructs the servants, and having summoned the husband, talking, rebukes him' (XII.221.75).

2. Sidhanta 1929: 147, notes that "though the woman is necessarily in the background, she has a good deal of influence, due to her association with the hero." Harlan 2003: 97, quotes Tomar Singh Chauhan, who repeats a proverb that I myself have heard spoken in Kacch: "The *sari* is more powerful than the *sapha* (turban)." In this sense, women in the epic bear forward the idea of the Vedic deity of sacred speech, Vāc, as she is portrayed for instance, in RV X.71.1ff.

3. There is an exception to this pattern, when an actual deity, Sarasvatī, speaks to a *muni* 'ascetic', in Book Three, informing him of the duties of those who adhere to dharma: this is essentially advice for brahmins, however, not for *kṣatriyas* (III.184.5ff.). It is unusual for a feminine figure to be instructing brahmins on ritual procedure, particularly as it applies to the *agnihotrin*. Sax 2002: 155, in his study of twentieth-century village drama, notes that "Draupadi and Kunti safeguard caste honor, an exaggerated concern ... which is typical of Kshatriyas, both male and female ... Kali/Draupadi and Kunti, like the women who play their parts, are good Kshatriya women."

4. "For words do not speak, while women do; as producers of signs, women can never be reduced to the status of symbols or tokens. But it is for this very reason that the position of women, as actually found in this system of communication between men that is made up of marriage regulations and kinship nomenclature, may afford us a workable image of the type of relationships that could have existed at a very early period in the development of language, between human beings and their words." Lévi-Strauss 1963: 61.

Perhaps it is for this reason that Bhīṣma says, 'women are to be always honored and cherished' (*pūjyā lālayitavyāś ca striyo nityam*; XIII.46.5). If women are not treated correctly, then all undertakings are 'unfruitful' (*aphalāḥ*) and houses that are *jāmīśaptāni* 'cursed by a daughter-in-law' are *nikṛttāni* 'humiliated'. Such is the inherent power of a woman's diction, in potentia. In this chapter I would like to inspect this feminine verbal potence.

To begin with, there exists an intial problem insofar as human comprehension is limited and unable to apprehend fully the cosmos. For if wisdom lies in a fathoming of dharma, its intricacies and disguises, and resides in a profound understanding of how the universe functions, then some apprehension of what 'comes from the deities', *daivam*, is required.

Bhīṣma, in the Anuśāsana *parvan*, declares that,

> na ca strīṇāṃ kriyā kācid iti dharmo vyavasthitaḥ
>
> For women, dharma has established that there are no sacrifices whatsoever.
>
> XIII.40.11

It is as if the consciousness of women in the epic is more attuned to this realm of *daivam* without ritual mediation, and that they are thence more connected with how the world of right dharma functions on earth. They have a privileged relationship with dharma, which is not always accessible to men; a relationship which is in no way dependent upon sacrificial practice, being more mundane and immediate. I shall argue that this concerns speech and its projected morality.

Women will often declaim upon the subject of dharma, but at certain points—and these are usually moments of reversal—they will also discourse upon the potence and efficacy of this counterpoint *daivam*.[5] Often, at this point, there arises the question of rebirth and also the obscure nature of *karma*.[6] The model is that of human volition and the necessity of action within a context that is not only human and natural but also divine and cosmic, and where temporality is extensive and runs beyond a single human life.

Further, as Bhīṣma tells Yudhiṣṭhira,

> nāsti bhāryāsamo loke sahāyo dharmasādhanaḥ
>
> There is no companion in the world like a wife who furthers dharma.
>
> XII.142.10

5. Wood 2001: 48ff., has the interesting view that Kṛṣṇa represents *daivam*.

6. In Western systems of physiology and psychology the idea of *heredity* is the most proximate concept to doctrines of *karma* and rebirth.

Sāvitrī is perhaps the doyenne of such women. She was able to speak so truthfully that she could control the material course of life itself; she was able to transcend or reverse the course of events by virtue of her emotional and mental purity and through an understanding of right dharma, and by implication, *daivam*.[7] As she saved her husband—says the sage Mārkaṇḍeya to Yudhiṣṭhira—so too will the dharmic Draupadī preserve him: *tārayiṣyati vaḥ* 'she will rescue you' (III.283.15).

Contrary to this, in Book Five, Vidura says to his sleepless old king,

> strīṣu rājasu sarpeṣu svādhyāye śatrusevīṣu
> ... viśvāsaṃ kaḥ prajñaḥ kartum arhati
>
> What intelligent man is obliged to put trust in
> women ... kings, snakes, recitation, those who serve an enemy?
>
> V.37.53

This is an unusual juxtaposition of objects: royalty, the *veda*, deadly snakes, and women. One usually associates *veda* and kingship with authority, and snakes with death. Yet in the next line, Vidura goes on to say that 'snakes, fire, lions, princes' are *atitejasaḥ* 'most splendid'. If trust is not to be placed in those with inordinate strength or potence, this is exactly where Vidura situates his category of women, as far as wise men are concerned.[8]

An example of such a woman would be given when Satyavatī determines that her son Vyāsa should beget offspring upon the wives of Vicitravīrya. In order to sustain the family lineage—by the rite of *niyoga*—she summons Vyāsa and informs him of her project. 'Satyavatī, you know the law', he instantly replies (*vettha dharmaṃ satyavati*). He adds,

> yathā ca tava dharmajñe dharme praṇihitā matiḥ
>
> As, O knower of dharma, your mind is fixed upon dharma.
>
> I.99.36

This is quite a statement for someone whose dharmic capacity and influence is perhaps greater than any other figure in the poem! No one has more power in the poem than Vyāsa, not even Kṛṣṇa.[9]

7. See above, Ch. III.4, for an analysis of Sāvitrī as heroic.

8. Alternatively, there is the figure of Kṛtyā, 'most wonderful' (*mahādbhutā*), the only really dark feminine figure in the poem, negative in the sense of deceit or anti-dharma rather than appearance. She arises from fire and escorts Duryodhana into the 'underworld' (*rasātalam*), where the Dānavas promise him supremacy over the whole earth (III.239.22–240.24).

9. Sullivan 1990, would go so far as to assert that Vyāsa is similar to the arch-deity Brahmā in his potential.

Another good illustration of how women act in this verbally potent fashion occurs in the scene where the brothers and Draupadī are trying to convince Yudhiṣṭhira, who—out of grief for the awful ruin of Kurukṣetra—wishes to abandon sovereignty and become a renouncer. Arjuna tells the story of how a queen, the wife of king Janaka, berated her lax husband, who had forsaken his kingdom in order to take on a life of asceticism. Arjuna impersonates the feminine voice here, saying: 'how, having abandoned your kingdom ... having assumed a life adorned with skulls', she says, *katham utsṛjya rājyaṃ svaṃ ... kāpālīṃ vṛttim āsthāya*. How can he now live like a beggar, she asks (XII.18.7).

> śriyaṃ hitvā pradīptāṃ tvaṃ śvavat saṃprati vīkṣyase
>
> Having abandoned blazing fortune you now appear like a dog!
>
> XII.18.12

She, the wife of Janaka, decries his renunciant life, having put aside not only kingdom but also herself, and she questions his motives.[10] She contemns his present habit of acceptance rather than of giving, for this goes against the *kṣatriya* grain. Then she reminds him about all the aspects of wealth which he had rejected, and all the many acts of generosity and charity which he once performed, and she insults his present mendicance. 'Do not seek the power of delusion', she cries (*mā mohavaśam anvagāḥ*; XII.18.36).

> evaṃ dharmam anukrāntaṃ sadā dānaparair naraiḥ
>
> Such is the dharma always mentioned by liberal men!
>
> XII.18.37

The implication is that *kṣatriyas* are not such men. This kind of treatment of a husband by a wife is typical: the latter reminding the former of his weakness and of his need to accomplish what is appropriately dharmic. Let us scrutinize specific models of such kinds of speech.

1. *Śakuntalā*

The episode of Śakuntalā presents the epic audience with its first comprehensive narrative of a woman in the poem. In this, certain aspects of the feminine, especially in a social setting, are established.

10. Such figures, she says, *parivrajanti dānārthaṃ muṇḍāḥ kāṣāyavāsasaḥ*, 'callow, wearing a reddish-yellow cloth, they wander for the sake of charity' (XII.18.31). This is remarkably reminiscent of a Buddhist monk, although there are no overt references in the epic to Buddhist life. See della Santina 1989.

Kaṇva, the girl's eremitic and brahminical father, in describing how he came to foster her, tells of three kinds of paternity.

> śarīrakṛt prāṇadātā yasya cānnāni bhuñjate
> krameṇa te trayo'py uktāḥ pitaro dharmaniścaye
>
> In the determination of dharma it is said that fathers are three in rank:
> one who makes the body, one of whom life is given, one whose food he eats.
>
> I.66.13

In a son is the establishment of family and lineage, and yet, where maternity is culturally uniform paternity can be acceptably diverse and triform.[11] As Benveniste has observed, there is no symmetry in the relation between fathers and mothers.[12] "The vocabulary of Indo-European kinship ... has taught that—in conjugation—the situation of the man and that of the woman had nothing in common. The term for 'marriage' is different for men and women: for the former it is verbal, and for the latter nominal."[13] Thus the terms husband and wife are not merely in simple opposition for their asymmetry is extensive, as for example in,

> kulavaṃśapratiṣṭhāṃ hi pitaraḥ putram abruvan
>
> The forefathers said a son is the foundation of the clan.
>
> I.69.17

It is the action of women that weaves this tissue of *kula* 'clan', and women who in their speech actively sustain and refine the values of both kin and *varṇa*.

The scene opens with the usual depiction of the lyrical and pacific conditions that typify such a hermitage in which an unmarried women is living. Upon his unexpected arrival there, king Duḥṣanta speaks the conventional forms of address, *kāsi kasyāsi ... kim arthaṃ cāgatā vanam* 'what are you, whose are you, and for what purpose are you come to the woods?' (I.65.12).[14] He continues,

11. At I.111.27–29, six kinds of sons are catalogued as 'heirs' (*bandhudāyāda*) and six as non-heirs. 'One born to oneself, one received as gift, one purchased, the son of a remarried widow, one born of a young wife, one of an unchaste woman; a son given, one purchased, one adopted, one who approaches of his own accord, a son whom a pregnant woman brings to a marriage, a son of unknown seed (*jātaretās*), born of a lowly womb.'

12. "Père et mère, frère et soeur ne constituent pas des couples symétriques en indo-européen." Benveniste 1969: I.209.

13. Ibid., 239–240.

14. When Śaṃtanu meets Gaṅgā at I.92.30, he addresses her with a similar formulation: 'what are you and whose are you?'

icchāmi tvām ahaṃ jñātum tan mam ācakṣva śobhane

I want to know you ... tell me that, O lovely.

I.65.13

Śakuntalā describes her own conception, how she was born of a *gāndharva* union between a seer and an *apsarā*. Abandoned by her mother, she was cared for by birds and animals until her foster father, Kaṇva, the *ṛṣi*, discovered her and named and adopted her. Her name refers to the sustenance which 'birds' (*śakuni*) had formerly supplied (I.66.14).

When Duḥṣanta presses Śakuntalā to surrender herself to him—*bhāryā me bhava* 'become my wife'—in what would be construed as a *gāndharva* rite, which he says, 'is declared the best' (*śreṣṭha ucyate*), he offers her gifts, or bride price. She tells him to ask her father, for "he will offer me to you" (*sa māṃ tubhyaṃ pradāsyati*), which fits the *ārṣa* model (I.67.5).[15] He responds by insisting that she is able to offer herself, to which the clever girl replies:

yadi dharmapathas tv eṣa yadi cātmā prabhur mama
pradāne pauravaśreṣṭha śṛṇu me samayaṃ prabho

If this is the way of dharma and if I am mistress of myself,
O best of the Pauravas, hear my stipulation for giving in marriage, sir.

I.67.15

She is thus informing the king-seducer as to the conditions and later, terms, of their union: their child—a son—shall become *yuvarāja* 'crown prince'.

satyaṃ me pratijānīhi yat tvāṃ vakṣāmy ahaṃ rahaḥ

Promise me a truth, which I shall speak to you privately.

I.67.16

Śakuntalā is ignoring the bride price and determining her own covenant, to which the king gives his assent, *evam astu* 'let it be so'. The actual lovemaking is described as:

jagrāha vidhivat pāṇāv uvāsa ca tayā saha

He took her hands accordingly, and 'married' with her.

I.67.19

15. It is noteworthy that they not only negotiate marriage but the *kind* of marriage which both anticipate.

Later in this story, Śakuntalā, having been spurned by this husband with whom she had joined according to the rites of *gāndharva* marriage, speaks a diatribe to her seducer-king-spouse, in which she admonishes him about the rights and wrongs of a husband's conduct and the values of a good wife. The king's instant and overt rejection enrages her, and she becomes *saṃrambhāmarṣatāmrākṣī* 'one whose eyes are reddened with passionate wrath':

> kaṭākṣair nirdahantīva tiryag rājānam aikṣata
>
> She looked sideways, as if scorching the king with glances.
>
> I.68.21

She accuses him of lying 'like the vulgar' (*prākṛtas tathā*), and discourses upon the importance and validity of truthful speech, condemning mendacity. She threatens him, saying,

> yadi me yācamānāyā vacanaṃ na kariṣyasi[16]
> duḥṣanta śatadhā mūrdhā tatas te'adya phaliṣyasi
>
> If you do not accomplish my speech—of me imploring:
> Duḥṣanta, then your head will split a hundredfold![17]
>
> I.68.35

At one point during this long denunciation, of forty-six *ślokas*, she makes an enigmatic statement:

> sakhāyaḥ praviviktеṣu bhavanty etāḥ priyaṃvadāḥ
> pitaro dharmakāryeṣu bhavanty ārtasya mātaraḥ
>
> Those agreeable [wives] are friends in loneliness,
> they are mothers of an unhappy one, fathers in the rites of dharma.
>
> I.68.42

This is first instance in the poem where a woman declaims upon dharma, a position that women thereafter often take up. Here, the dharma is that of the kinship formation within—not so much the nuclear family—but between a man and woman themselves. The studied ambivalence in this instance where kinship terms are shifted about the person of a feminine speaker, sounds strange. Śakuntalā describes what makes for a correct wife and she advises Duḥṣanta to seek her as a wife—something she actually is—and yet tells him that she, in her agreeableness, will be like a husband for him.

16. For the implications of using the verb *yāc*, see Jamison 1996: 191. To employ this verb is to actually compel, and the reciprocal term is the verb *dā*, 'to give'.

17. This is typically how enraged *ṛṣis* threaten wrongdoers.

> ardhaṃ bhāryā manuṣyasya bhāryā śreṣṭhatamaḥ sakhā
>
> A wife is half of a man. A wife is the best friend!
>
> I.68.40

Those 'possessing wives' (*bhāryāvantaḥ*) 'perform ceremonies correctly': they are *kriyāvantaḥ*. She then turns from the subject of the good wife, and admonishes him concerning sons:

> ātmano janmanaḥ kṣetraṃ puṇyaṃ rāmāḥ sanātanam
>
> Women are the everlasting virtuous field of one's own birth.
>
> I.68.51

It is as if a woman not only gives birth to children, especially sons, but is also—conceptually—the genetrix of the husband, via the formality of marriage. Nominally, there exists the *bhartā* 'maintainer' and the *pati* 'master', and it is as if the good wife allows the man who is the *bhartā* to become a *pati*. She speaks what is 'true belief' (*satyaḥ pravādaḥ*), the kind of exhortation of a woman to a male *kṣatriya* which is common throughout the Mahābhārata.

She continues with her advocation,

> putrasparśāt sukhataraḥ sparśo loke na vidyate
>
> In the world there is no touch more joyous than the touch of a son!
>
> I.68.57

Śakuntalā amplifies this long declamation on the ethics of marriage and its conduct by saying,

> satyaś cāpi pravādo'yaṃ yaṃ pravakṣyāmi te'nagha
>
> So this speech which I shall utter is truth, O sinless man!
>
> I.69.5

She even quotes from Manu's *dharmaśāṣtra* on the nature and category of sons, adding that, *nāsti satyāt paro dharmo* 'there is no higher dharma than truth' (I.69.24), which is a rhetorical interpretation of dharma, being descriptive rather than the usual prescriptive: she is taking a supererogatory position here. She warns Duḥṣanta about *anṛta* 'wrong', but in the sense of 'natural dis-order' or 'profound error'. Dharma and *ṛta* refer to two very different systems: the latter denoting natural order, whereas the former signifies right prescription. In her speech to the king, Śakuntalā interprets all this for his benefit.

The scene closes with Śakuntalā departing and a disembodied voice from above telling the king that, *bhastrā mātā pituḥ* 'a mother is the water bag of the father' (I.69.29); that is, a most essential item which supplies him with sustenance and from which he drinks. The son—the water in this metaphor—born to the union of Duḥṣanta and Śakuntalā, is, of course, the eponymous Bharata, from whom stems the nominal idea of the epic, the *bhāratī kīrtir*, 'the Bhārata fame' (I.69.49).

2. Gāndhārī

Gāndhārī is always vociferous in her proclamation as to what should be policy for the kingdom. When Dhṛtarāṣṭra had rescinded the plan to let the Pāṇḍavas return to Indraprastha with all their wealth, it is Gāndhārī—presumably still in the *sabhā*—who speaks out against her firstborn son, Duryodhana, reproving his actions and his violent antipathy for the five cousins. She says that he will be 'certainly the end of the clan' (*anto nūnaṃ kulasya*; II.66.30), and tells her husband to ignore her son's policy. She calls Duryodhana 'a child' (*bāla*), who is 'untrained' (*aśiṣṭa*). She says,

> mā kulasya kṣaye ghore kāraṇaṃ tvaṃ bhaviṣyasi
>
> You shall not become a cause in the terrible destruction of the clan
>
> II.66.31

She is what the poet refers to as *dharmayuktam* 'possessed by right' and *dharmadarśinīm* 'one whose vision is dharmic' (II.66.28 and 36). She reminds the assembled *kṣatriyas* as to how they should act during the crisis, and concludes her oration by saying, *śamena dharmeṇa parasya buddhyā jātā buddhiḥ sāstu*, 'let wisdom be generated by equanimity, by dharma, by the wisdom of another' (II.66.35). By ellipsis, this refers to herself.

Her husband ignores her injunctions, and yet he does recall the Pāṇḍavas to a second dicing match: thence begin the initial stages in the breaking apart of the clan, *bheda* 'the breach', just as Gāndhārī had warned.

During the Udyoga *parvan*, after the first exchange of ambassadors and in private colloquy with her husband and Duryodhana, Gāndhārī overtly rejects both her son and his bellicose plans.

> aiśvaryakāma duṣṭātman vṛddhānāṃ śāsanātiga
>
> Wicked one whose desire is power! Exceeder of the injunction of elders!
>
> V.67.9

When he is 'slain by Bhīma', she adds, then, *smartāsi vacanaṃ pituḥ* 'you will recall the speech of your father'. At this point, Duryodhana's wish for war has destroyed all affection that his mother possesses for him: a situation which according to conventional kinship patterns would normally be unthinkable. Gāndhārī has placed dharma before affection.

Later, when Duryodhana rejects the offers of peace that Kṛṣṇa, as emissary, offers, the old king calls for his wife in the hope that ultimately she will be able to convince their son to adopt a strategy that is more pacific. Dhṛtarāṣṭra refers to her as *mahāprājñā* 'extremely wise'. 'If she can soothe the foolish wicked one', he says, (*yadi sāpi durātmānaṃ śamayet duṣṭacetasam*) then peace is possible (V.127.3). He turns to Gāndhārī as a last resort, hoping that her seasoned language might avert *vyasanaṃ ghoram* 'terrible ruin'.

She appears in the *sabhā*, 'a glorious princess' (*rājaputrī yaśasvinī*) and instantly starts to speak in a manner that is forceful and authoritative. This is after all the other speakers have failed to turn Duryodhana away from a policy of belligerence: Saṃjaya, Bhīṣma, Dhṛtarāṣṭra himself. She is the final voice on an ascending scale of reasoning.

She orders that Duryodhana be called, referring to him as *ātura* 'sick, suffering', and begins her monologue—which lasts for forty-three verses—by first berating her husband for allowing the situation to become so conflicted: he is *garhya* 'reproachable'. He has obtained the fruit of *rājapradāna* 'conferral of the kingdom', by allowing his deluded, foolish, and wicked eldest son to take power (V.127.13). Dhṛtarāṣṭra, has allowed *bheda* to occur 'among his own people' (*svajane*). 'Who would cause punishment to fall among his own kin?', she asks (*sveṣu daṇḍaṃ kas tatra pātayet*).

Then, on Duryodhana's entry to the *sabhā* she begins to criticize him, beginning,

> duryodhana nibodhedaṃ vacanaṃ mama putraka
>
> Duryodhana, pay attention to this speech of mine, my boy!
>
> V.127.19

This old and blinded queen proceeds to give a long, eloquent declaration upon good kingship and the follies of greed and anger, drawing upon metaphors of fire and of horses uncontrolled by their charioteer, and of fishes in a net. 'A king should first conquer himself as if he were a country' (*ātmānam eva prathamaṃ deśarūpeṇa jayet*), she says, and then turn to his ministers and enemies (V.127.28). Control and domination begins with the self:

> satataṃ nigrahe yuktendriyāṇāṃ bhaven nṛpaḥ

> A king should always be rightly in control of his senses.
>
> V.127.33

'There is no prosperity in war', she says, *na yuddhe ... kalyāṇam*. Greed is not a source of kingdom, she adds in closing, and she decries all 'avarice' (*lobha*). Her last word is, *praśāmya* 'be at peace!'

After Kṛṣṇa has concluded his embassy and returned to the Pāṇḍavas, there is much debate in the *sabhā*, with Bhīṣma and Droṇa speaking. Gāndhārī is also present and once again offers her denunciation of Duryodhana's bellicose strategy. She calls upon those present, princes and royal seers: 'let them hear—I shall speak of your transgression', (*śṛṇvantu vakṣyāmi tavāparādham*; V.146.28).

'You are of evil mind and perform excessively cruel deeds!', she says (*tvaṃ pāpabuddhe'tinṛśaṃsakarman*). She describes how the kingdom is rightfully to be governed by Dhṛtarāṣṭra, along with Bhīṣma and Vidura, and she completely goes against the hostility of Kaurava and her son Duryodhana, saying that the kingdom should justly go to the sons of Pāṇḍu. Such a public statement is a dramatic and unambiguous controversion of what has been happening at the Hāstinapura court, and Gāndhārī very much stands apart in this, siding with Bhīṣma and Droṇa and outrightly challenging her husband.

'Having put dharma first', she says (*dharmaṃ puraskṛtya*), 'let Yudhiṣṭhira the son of dharma rule' (*yudhiṣṭhiraḥ śāstu dharmaputraḥ*; V.146.35). There is no ambivalence or embellishment of her message: it is simple and brief and subversive of her son and his old weak father, her husband.

Long after this speech, after all the conflict and destruction have occurred, even though she then blames her firstborn and his companions for the annihilation of the clan and families, she criticizes Bhīma for not observing *kṣatriya* dharma during the duel which took place between him and Duryodhana, in which the former made an unorthodox blow, so breaking the legs of her son.

> kathaṃ nu dharmaṃ dharmajñaiḥ samuddiṣṭaṃ mahātmabhiḥ
> tyajeyur āhave śūrāḥ prāṇahetoḥ kathaṃcana
>
> How then could those heroes ever abandon in war, for the sake of life,
> this dharma which has been established by those great-souled
> dharmic ones?
>
> XI.13.19

She then reprimands Bhīma for drinking the blood of Duḥśāsana after killing him, saying how crude an act this was, being *anārya* 'indecent' (XI.14.12–13). At this point, the poets again refer to her as *dharmajñā dharmadarśinī* 'law-knowing and law-seeing'.

Her contempt for the Pāṇḍavas and their use of dubious, un-*kṣatriya* means to win the war, is unleashed upon Yudhiṣṭhira, and her glance, peeping out from behind her blindfold, scorches his toenails: such is the terrific dharmic 'energy', the *tejas*, that she has concentrated within herself during her artificially darkened life.[18]

> aṅgulyagrāṇi dadṛśe devī paṭṭāntareṇa sā
>
> That queen, through a gap in her blindfold, saw the tips of his toes.
>
> XI.15.6

Those toes thence came to possess *kunakhībhūta* 'unattractive nails'. Earlier on in the poem, Janamejaya had asked his poet about a similar potential, which another woman's eyes possessed: 'how did Draupadī, whose glance was terrific, not burn the sons of Dhṛtarāṣṭra?', he asked (*kathaṃ sā draupadī kṛṣnā ... dhārtarāṣṭrān nādahad ghoracakṣuṣā*; I.56.7).

Gāndhārī, on the field at Kurukṣetra after the war, with her dharmically charged vision—despite the occlusion of her eyes—observes everything. In her rage she curses Kṛṣṇa, who had been accompanying her about the field. 'I shall curse you' (*śapsye*) she says, to the effect that all his own kin shall be mutually slain when thirty six years have elapsed, and he too will perish. This speech act comes to pass in the Mausalya *parvan*. Kṛṣṇa simply agrees with her, saying that she was not cursing him but only making a visionary utterance: *jāne'ham* 'I know', he tells her (XI.25.44). Knowing dharma, for Gāndhārī, implies an insight to the future.

When Yudhiṣṭhira desires to join with his mother in the forest, along with the old king and his wife, Gāndhārī tells him that this is unacceptable. Without Yudhiṣṭhira to perform the obsequial rites, she says, the clan would be endangered: *tvayy adhīnaṃ kurukulaṃ piṇḍas* 'depending on you is the Kuru clan's ancestral food' (XV.44.25). She is the one to remind him of his most necessary sacrificial duties towards the deceased forbears, and therefore he must remain at Hāstinapura. Yudhiṣṭhira, of course, complies with her instruction as to what is right. No one has ever outrightly contradicted Gāndhārī.

3. *Draupadī*

In the *sabhā* where she had been so forcibly abjected, Draupadī had ad-

18. On marrying her congenitally blind husband, Gāndhārī had put on a blindfold, thus occluding her own vision, so that she might in no way be superior to her husband (I.103.12).

dressed the hall with great verbal aplomb and dignity, reminding them as to her status and honor. It was her first long speech in the poem and concerned dharma. She was the only one present to attempt to transform the situation of ordered violence into one of discussion.

Draupadī tells them that until her *svayaṃvara* had occurred, she had never been seen in public, and since that occasion, she had never again been publicly observed; nor had she ever been touched by another man apart from her husbands, before Duḥśāsana dragged her into their presence (II.62.4–6).

> mṛṣyante kuravaś ceme manye kālasya paryayam
> snuṣāṃ duhitaraṃ caiva kliśyamānām anarhatīm
>
> I consider the reversal of time—[how] these Kurus disregard
> a daughter and daughter-in-law, undeserving of torments.
>
> II.62.7

She refers to herself as *ahaṃ strī satī śubhā* 'I, a woman, decent, beautiful', abused in the midst of their assembly. 'Where now is the dharma of great kings', she enquires (*kva nu dharmo mahīkṣitām*).

> sa naṣṭaḥ kauraveyeṣu pūrvo dharmaḥ sanātanaḥ
>
> That ancient perpetual dharma is lost among the Kauravas!
>
> II.62.9

She continues her measured and formal denunciation, citing that she is the 'friend' (*sakhī*) of Kṛṣṇa, and 'virtuous sister' (*svasā satī*) of her brother, and wife of the sons of Pāṇḍu.

> brūta dāsīm adāsīṃ vā tat kariṣyāmi kauravāḥ
>
> Say—servant or not—that I shall do, Kauravas!
>
> II.62.11

One should recall that her great husbands, stripped of their clothing, are sitting on the floor near her in silence, having said nothing that would protect her from maltreatment. Only she stands there and defends herself, describing the ethical and legal conditions which envelop the situation. She demands that the court consider and determine the moral ground upon which her position rests (II.62.13). No one else makes such a claim.

Vidura and Gāndhārī both bewail the situation and speak to Dhṛtarāṣṭra, who addresses Draupadī as a 'dharmic wife' (*dharmapatnī*), and asks that she request a favor of him. He addresses her:

> vadhūnāṃ hi viśiṣṭā me tvaṃ dharmaparamā satī
>
> For you are distinguished of women, virtuous, an emblem of dharma!
>
> II.64.27

She asks that he free her husbands from their loss of person, sustained during the gambling match. Dhṛtarāṣṭra grants them freedom and urges her to ask him for further favors, but she desists, reminding the old king of the dharma concerning the giving of favors. Only a king can request three favors, she says knowingly (*trayas tu rājño*); for other *kṣatriyas* and their women, two should suffice (II.63.35).

As the Pāṇḍavas prepare to depart for the forest, Vidura, speaking to Yudhiṣṭhira in the *sabhā*, says of Draupadī that she is, *dharmārthakuśalā* and *dharmacāriṇī*,'skilled in policy and dharma' and 'one whose conduct is dharmic' (II.69.9).

During the initial days of forest exile, Kṛṣṇa and certain other kings visit the Pāṇḍavas. It is not long before Draupadī is berating him in particular and her husbands and male kin in general for all that occurred during and after the dicing game in the *sabhā*.[19]

She has been discoursing on how it is that husbands must protect wives and how feckless her own menfolk had been towards her in not fulfilling the dharma of husbands (III.13.60). Concerning wives, she loosely quotes a conventional aphorism from Manu:

> ātmā hi jāyate tasyāṃ tasmāj jāyā bhavaty uta
> bhartā ca bhāryayā rakṣyaḥ ...
>
> A man's self is born in her, thus she becomes a wife.
> A husband is to be protected by a wife.[20]
>
> III.13.62

On another occasion, early in the Āraṇyaka *parvan*, 'the Book of the Forest', Draupadī, in her second major speech, full of invective and contempt, questions the *kṣatriya* qualities of her husbands. Here, she begins a theme that runs throughout the poem, and it is a theme that *kṣatriya* women often take up: that is, they remind their male kin as to the true nature of warrior dharma and how to behave correctly as a *kṣatriya*.

19. Bailey, in Rukmani 2005: 69ff., has analyzed this exchange, focussing on Draupadī's use of the term *manyu* 'anger' and Yudhiṣṭhira's avoidance of that word and his preference for the term *krodha*. "*Manyu* has a slightly different semantic implication, reflecting the frenzied anger of the warrior more than the controlled anger (*krodha*) of the brāhmaṇa."

20. Manu, IX.8: *patir bhāryāṃ saṃpraviśya garbho bhūtveha jāyate / jāyāyās tad hi jāyātvaṃ yad asyāṃ jāyate punaḥ.*

'There is no *kṣatriya* without anger in the world' *na nirmanyuḥ kṣatriyo'sti loke*, she says indignantly; III.28.34).[21]

> yo na darśayate tejaḥ kṣatriyaḥ kāla āgate
> sarvabhūtāni taṃ pārtha sadā paribhavanty uta
>
> A *kṣatriya* who does not show splendor when death comes,
> O prince, all beings always insult him.[22]
>
> III.28.35

She continues, *tvayā na kṣamā kāryā śatrūn prati kathaṃcana* 'by you, submission is never to be made towards enemies', cautioning Yudhiṣṭhira about his pusillanimous conduct, advising him as to right action. She does this in an acrimonious and infuriated manner.

As is usually the case in the epic when someone is offering counsel or instruction, a digression is made for a short story to illustrate the point. Draupadī now relates the 'tale' (*saṃvāda*) of the *asura* Prahlāda and his grandson, Bali Vairocana. This is a narrative about the difference between 'patience' and 'energy' (*kṣamā* and *tejas*). It is thirty-six verses of edifying account, which Draupadī sings without personal rancor; her own voice intrudes or returns after the story is complete. In fact, there is no story as such, it is really only a speech that a grandfather offers, teaching a young man about the distinction between action, inaction, and timeliness. It is in exactly the same form that Bhīṣma speaks to Yudhiṣṭhira later on in the poem.[23]

If you are not strict, says Prahlāda-Draupadī, everyone, including the servants, will revile you: patience and mildness lead to weakness, for 'contempt is worse than death in this world' (*loke'smin maraṇād api garhitam*). She lists the *doṣāḥ kṣamāvatām* 'the errors of the gentle' (III.29.16). Concerning such a ruler, she-he comments, 'his wives go as they please' (*dārāś ca pravartante yathākāmam*).

Yet, Prahlāda says, excessive 'anger' (*krodha*) is equally destabilizing and reprehensible, and leads to debility on the part of the king. Such a 'man obtains enemies' (*śatrūṃś ca labhate naraḥ*; III.29.19). She—acting

21. Yudhiṣṭhira can be considered as a possible archetype for Aśoka, the Buddhist emperor, or vice versa: see Sutton 1997 and Fitzgerald 2004. Yudhiṣṭhira later makes the statement—not a typically *kṣatriya* statement—that, *ānṛśaṃsaṃ paro dharmaḥ*, 'compassion is the highest dharma' (III.297.71). It is a sentiment that Draupadī naturally decries.

22. Harlan 2003: 105, concerning contemporary legend in Rajastan, writes, "Thus Rajput mothers are portrayed in narratives and conversation as demanding that their sons fight, however unlikely their survival in combat may be.... Sons' blood, shed in battle, reveals the splendor of mother's milk."

23. Bhīṣma, like Prahlāda, is also *pitāmaha* 'grandfather', that is, one who has learned from long experience and whose role is frequently and appropriately to offer counsel.

out the voice of Prahlāda—goes on to describe the judicious use of both patience and energy, and in this lies the founding of good kingship.

> mṛdunā mārdavaṃ hanti mṛdunā hanti dāruṇam
> nāsādhyaṃ mṛdunā kiṃcit tasmāt tīkṣṇataro mṛduḥ
>
> By moderation one slays the delicate, by moderation one slays the harsh.
> Nothing is irremediable with moderation: thus, the moderate is more zealous!
>
> III.29.30

This is a micro-narrative which she relates with great drama, imitating two male voices, examining at length the aspects of the two kinds of action. She is reminiscent of the old counselor Vidura, a Polonius-like character who at times is guilty of great longeurs when he is admonishing Dhṛtarāṣṭra about policy. Even the opening line is a standard formula marking the onset of such speech:

> atrāpy udāharantīmam itihāsaṃ purātanam
>
> So here, they declare this ancient tale ...
>
> III.28.29

It is almost as if the poets slot in this rather formulaic dialogue simply because it fits the occasion, and that here there is a recitation of a standard piece of edifying discourse, part of a poet's moral repertoire which suits this moment in the epic nicely. Draupadī, who usually has such a powerful, dynamic, and emotionally charged tone of voice, tense and brilliant, is completely absent from this story. She merely concludes the narrative with a comment directed at Yudhiṣṭhira, that this is a moment for *tejas* on his part. She closes with,

> kāle prāpte dvayaṃ hy etad yo veda sa mahīpatiḥ
>
> For when the time has arrived, whoever knows both, he is a great king!
>
> III.28.35

Again, it is as if the poets had slipped this small account into the movement of the narrative, for there is no indication of Draupadī's persona; it is as if she is reciting or quoting a piece taken from the Śānti *parvan* on the nature of kingship. It is a small and well-framed aria, as it were, distinct from the rest of her speech. She later says, towards the end of her address, returning to her own voice once more:

> tad ahaṃ tejasaḥ kālaṃ tava manye narādhipa

> O king, I think that it is the moment for your energy!
>
> III.29.33

She terminates this long address with an admonition to Yudhiṣṭhira to be both harsh and moderate, for only in that will he be seen as a 'great king' (*mahīpatiḥ*; III.29.35).

Bhīṣma in the Śānti *parvan* speaks of similar truths when he informs Yudhiṣṭhira as to the nature of *rājadharma* (XII.59ff.). Such discourse is very much in the style of *arthaśāstra*, where a young king receives instruction as to the nature of kingship. As wives, mothers, or paramours, certain women in the Mahābhārata—like Draupadī—are in this identical position of admonishment: they offer direction to a *kṣatriya* who is falling from his duty and code.[24]

Earlier, she had said to Yudhiṣṭhira that a *kṣatriya* who is overly pacific and hesitates in the use of violence,

> apriyaḥ sarvabhūtānāṃ so'amutreha ca naśyati
>
> He perishes, here and in the other world, unloved of all beings.
>
> III.28.37

Yudhiṣṭhira calls her *mahāprajñe* 'O greatly wise one', and responds in kind, extemporizing upon this theme of anger and moderation. He responds at great length to the effect that *krodhamūlo vināśo hi prajānām iha* 'the ruin of creatures here is the root of anger' (III.29.3). His rebuttal is also a long discourse modeled on *śāstra*, which continues for fifty *ślokas* in a similar formal and impersonal manner, and is addressed to her, whom he repeatedly names in the vocative. He speaks in praise of *kṣamā*, 'patience' or 'submission'. These exchanges are not really part of the dramatic narrative, but function more as edifying interludes, drawing upon the moral discourse of others.

Draupadī responds to him again, accusing him of being deluded; she speaks another long monologue, this time of forty-two verses. Now she specifically addresses the question of dharma: what is right, not so much for them in the forest, but in the cosmos at large.

> rājānaṃ dharmagoptāraṃ dharmo rakṣati rakṣitaḥ
>
> Law, protected, protects a king who is a protector of Law.
>
> III.31.7

24. Bhīma sums up this code when he says, *kṣatriyasya tu sarvasya nānyo dharmo'sti saṃyugāt* 'For every *kṣatriya* there is no other law than conflict!' (III.36.34).

She begins by praising her husband for his good conduct and rightful life, his piety and generosity: he had always led a life that was honest, truthful, forbearing, and wise (III.31.18). Then she speaks of Dhātā, the Creator or supporter of the universe, 'the world stands in the will of the lord' (*īśvarasya vaśe lokas tiṣṭhate*), she says, 'like a wooden doll' (*yathā dārumayī yoṣā*).

> śakunis tantubaddho vā niyato'yam anīśvaraḥ
>
> Or—a bird bound by a thread—this powerless one is restrained.
>
> III.31.24

The audience is now hearing a less vituperative condemnation of Yudhiṣṭhira's kingship or husbandry, as Draupadī extends the model of her address to something far greater and more universal: humanity's place in the cosmos, specifically as it relates to dharma. It is as if she wishes to mollify her husband, having berated him so forcibly and having listened to his sober and measured reply. She praises the *kṣatriya* dharma of vigorous action and decisiveness and simultaneously criticizes her spouse for his lack of such energy, as she now retreats from her initial vehemence into metaphysical considerations which are not quite so censorious of his behavior. Mankind is *nātmādhīno* 'not dependant upon its own will', she says (III.31.26).

All this appears to be a retrogression from her former stance, where she only commended action and condemned Yudhiṣṭhira for his lack thereof. Now, it is Dhātā who is the only source and presence of agency or causality in the universe, and the idea of kingship is so amplified. Throughout the poem when things go wrong and predicaments arise, *kṣatriyas* often lament their misfortune by saying that all is due to *daivam* 'fate', although they will concurrently praise determination and intensity as good *kṣatriya* qualities. It is a paradox for readers today, this seeming contradiction, and it would appear that such good warrior qualities are really only manners, and have no efficacy in terms of volition: autonomy is reserved solely for the divine. Draupadī says,

> dhātur evaṃ vaśaṃ yānti sarvabhūtāni bhārata
>
> O Bhārata, all creatures travel the will of Dhātā.
>
> III.31.28

Again, the message of Draupadī in this second part of her speech is closely akin to the dharma portrayed in parts of the Gītā, where the 'body' (*śarīra*) is *kṣetrasaṃjñita* 'known as the field'. She speaks about the power of 'illusion' (*māyā*), which Dhātā possesses: he is one 'who slays beings with beings' (*yo hanti bhūtair bhūtāni*; III.31.31). 'This self-created paternal great-grandfather, Brahmā' (*svayaṃbhūḥ prapitāmahaḥ*) 'destroys beings with beings having made a disguise' (*hinasti bhūtair bhūtāni chadma kṛtvā*; III.31.35).

> dhātāraṃ garhaye pārtha viṣamaṃ yo'nupaśyati
>
> O prince, I accuse the Creator, who looks upon misfortune!
>
> III.31.39

So ends the second part of this protracted and complex dialogue between Draupadī and Yudhiṣṭhira, in which both parties again proclaim set pieces as if they were rehearsing from memory. This is not just angry talk but sophisticated discussion, on a level equal with informed *paṇḍitas*, although it lacks a reciprocal tension. She speaks like a *ṛṣi* 'a poet-seer', such is her intellectual range and verbal measurement.

Draupadī began with a highly authoritative criticism of Yudhiṣṭhira, which rapidly became an appraisal of how ineffectively he was implementing *kṣatriya* dharma, the primary duty of a king. Then, she progressed via refined argument to the nature of human action in universal life and condemned the Creator just as she condemned Yudhiṣṭhira. Her final words were,

> kāraṇaṃ balam eveha janāñ śocāmi durbalān
>
> Force is the principle [or motive] here: I grieve for weak creatures!
>
> III.31.42

Yudhiṣṭhira responds a second time, defending his allegiance to dharma, and says that 'you should not revile the Creator nor dharma' (*nārhasi ... dhātāraṃ dharmam eva ca ... kṣeptum śaṅkitum*; III.32.14). He adds, *ayaṃ saphalo dharmo* 'this dharma is fruitful', for such a life possesses consequence, it is efficacious.

Draupadī speaks for a third time, beginning rather coyly: *ārtāhaṃ pralapāmi* 'I. unhappy, speak plaintively' (III.33.2). 'Action, indeed, is to be done by a living being' (*karma khalv iha kartavyaṃ jātena*), she says, extending her previous argument. There is nothing but action and the fruit of action, for:

> svakarma kuru mā glāsīḥ karmaṇā bhava dañśitaḥ
>
> Perform your own action! Do not be averse! Be armed with action!
>
> III.33.8

Draupadī no longer speaks in that shrill, agitated tone with which she began her first monologue, which was more of the nature of a disquisition. She talks as one well-schooled, learned, and tempered in her sentences: this is the voice of conviction, advising her king on how conduct should be performed and according to what standards. She speaks as if in council.

Here, she distinguishes *haṭha* 'necessity' from *diṣṭam* 'destiny', yet amalgamates them. Usually in the epic, when events have proved unfortunate a speaker will decry *daivam* 'fate', and Draupadī addresses this notion, linking it to *vidhi* 'the ordained or prescribed' (III.33.15). Now, for Draupadī, these terms or forces are fact, *tat phalaṃ pūrvakarmaṇaḥ* 'that is the fruit of previous action', the outcome of what was performed in a previous life.

Once again she is shifting her arguments onto another level: human causality has acquired a temporal quality, something different from the ordination which she spoke of in her previous declamation. This is immediately modified, however, when Draupadī says that the Creator ordains according to previous action: that Dhātā mediates between lives or time. 'This body is the instrument of the Creator' (*kāraṇaṃ tasya deho'yaṃ dhātuḥ*; III.33.21). A human is thus *avaśaḥ* 'without will'.[25]

Draupadī even quotes, like Bhīṣma in Book Twelve—and this is still within an oral tradition one presumes—from the lawgiver Manu: *kartavyaṃ tv eva karmeti* 'action is to be done!' (III.33.36). Her sagacity in verbal articulation is precise and rhetorical: as the audience heard in the Sabhā *parvan*, it was Draupadī who was the first one to raise the question as to legality, concerning whether or not Yudhiṣṭhira was entitled to gamble her away having already lost himself (II.60.7).

Certainly, she says, there is *siddhi* 'fulfillment', and there is *asiddhi* 'unfulfillment', yet there must always be, prior to these, 'action' *karma* (III.33.47–48). She discounts completely the possibility of any necessity or destiny behind the failure to act: this is the one thing which Draupadī utterly decries, which for us as readers appears anomalous. For the decision not to act is surely an act of volition? This is not the case for Draupadī, for not to act, according to her reasoning, is to be quiescent, as if non-extant or unliving, defunct.

She speaks of the *dhīra* 'resolute man' and of *nara* 'man' as she

25. It could be that speaking of *daivam* in terms of human action is a *kṣatriya* manner of speaking and ideology is at work; just as Protestant reformists in the seventeenth century in Europe would speak of the doctrine of "predestination" or "election" as a way of justifying their own activity. Brahminical dependence upon the sacrifice and ritual behavior projects a very different view of the cosmos. For *kṣatriyas*, however, to invoke *daivam* is perhaps an obverse way of proclaiming their own vigorous and unmoderated pursuit of decisive action, and the use of the term has nothing to do with an aleatory view of life. A reliance upon the efficacy of human action—rather than the *yajña*—can be magnified by making the claim that such behavior is merely a reaction to what is *daivam*.

approaches the end of her speech, and returns to addressing Yudhiṣṭhira in the vocative again.

All this, she adds, she heard from a brahmin whom her father once hosted. He had learned from Bṛhaspati, the deity of wisdom and eloquence who exists as the divine sacrificer. He was, she says, instructing her brothers and she overheard this in the house; sometimes he actually spoke to her when she was sitting on her father's lap (III.33.58). Thus she closes a most learned and subtle series of speeches, words that were given in the manner of moral and metaphysical tuition. As all good teachers do, she ends with a gracious reference to her own instructor in these matters, a *gurustuti*.[26]

When Draupadī, disguised as a maid whilst in the court of king Virāṭa, is assailed by her would-be seducer and kicked when she rebuffs him, she makes a long speech decrying her fortune.[27] During this speech she cites the failure of kingship on the part of Virāṭa, who has allowed such to occur within the public sphere of his court, going so far as to say that he is not behaving like a king: *na rājan rājavat kiṃcit samācarasi* 'king, you do not in any way behave like a king!' Draupadī is, of course, still in the guise of a maidservant.

Being kicked is a particularly base and vile insult in this culture and is more a symbolic form of violence than anything forcible. She says—without hesitation—to those assembled with Virāṭa,

> dasyūnām iva dharmas te na hi saṃsadi śobhate
>
> Your dharma is of outcastes: it looks bad in the assembly!
>
> IV.15.24

Draupadī with her usual stinging and subtle animation calls upon those others in the *sabhā* to see the error and transgression of the scene, which in fact occurs. They cry *sādhu sādhu* 'good, good!', awarding the judgment to her and the blame to her violator, Kīcika (IV.15.28).

26. Bhīma contributes to this involved discussion with a long monologue of his own, asseverating the equal importance of *kāma* 'desire' and *artha* 'property'. He makes the traditional argument that *kāma* is to be pursued in youth, *artha* during middle age, and *dharma* at the latter part of one's life (III.34.2ff.). Whether this actually applies to the phenomenon of kingship, which Draupadī was addressing, is another question. Yudhiṣṭhira's rebuttal to him is, 'I prefer dharma to immortality and life' (*vṛṇe dharmam amṛtāj jīvitāc ca*; III.35.21). This is hardly something, one presumes, that the bitterly impassioned Draupadī would admire.

27. Such subjection to male lust and violence has given the figure and example of Draupadī great mythical authority for women in India today, where she is very much still a hero of feminist culture.

Once again it is the feminine voice that turns events—in a public setting—back to a system of order, once dharma has been destabilized. In this case Draupadī speaks in the assembly and calls for a decision on the part of those men present. No other woman in the poem accomplishes this kind of public suasion, not even Gāndārī, and it is notable that the king is actually swayed by the opinion of his courtiers and assembled warriors.[28]

During the night, when Draupadī goes down to the kitchens to talk with Bhīma about how Kīcaka had insulted her, and after she has given her anger its run, her speech becomes larger and more abstract, as she reflects once again upon *daivam*. This is a term that is so often associated with affairs that have gone awry, and often, when a *kṣatriya* speaker is lamenting a course of events, they turn to reflecting upon 'fate' as an adjunct to dharma. The two are connected, synchronically and, in terms of rebirth, diachronically. As Draupadī says,

> sthitaṃ pūrvaṃ jalaṃ yatra punas tatraiva tiṣṭhati
>
> Where water once stood, there it is again.
>
> IV.19.7

Even her vociferous criticism of Yudhiṣṭhira's gambling necessarily involves this association, for gambling by definition partakes of the random and of chance: the cosmos can interfere as human volition is put aside and certainly that is *daivam*. Yudhiṣṭhira's lust for gambling has given access to *daivam*, which then preponderates over that which is *puruṣāt* 'coming from the human'.

'Because of that dice-rogue', she says, *akṣadhūrtasya kāraṇāt* 'I am a servant' (IV.19.1). She adds,

> na daivasyātibhāro'sti na daivasyātivartanam ...
> daivena kila yasyārthaḥ sunīto'pi vipadyate
> daivasya cāgame yatnas tena kāryo vijānatā
>
> There is no excessive burden for destiny, no going beyond destiny ...
> Of one whom—on account of destiny—the well-conducted aim miscarries,
> the effort to be done by that knowing one is in the oncoming of destiny.
>
> IV.19.6 and 8

Draupadī draws upon her own misdoings as a child, saying, *bālayā ... mayā*

28. There is Śakuntalā, of course, but her tale is not part of the macro-narrative, the epic per se.

vai vipriyaṃ kṛtam 'the disaffection done by me as a child', offended the Creator, Dhātā, causing her present *durnīta* 'folly'.

Referring to the need to maintain their disguises and clandestine life during this final year of the exile, she says:

> tad dharme yatamānānāṃ mahān dharmo naśiṣyati
> samayaṃ rakṣamāṇānāṃ bhāryā vo na bhaviṣyati
> bhāryāyāṃ rakṣyamāṇāyāṃ prajā bhavati rakṣitā
>
> Whilst you are struggling for that dharma, a great dharma will be destroyed.
> Protecting your treaty, your wife is no more!
> When wives are protected, subjects are protected.
>
> IV.20.26–27

In the next book, the Udyoga *parvan*, as her husbands and Kṛṣṇa discuss the possibility of war, Draupadī is present and speaks at their conference. She of course propounds a tough policy of attack, and as usual, reminds them of their standing as princes and of their responsibility under *kṣatriya* dharma. Yudhiṣṭhira's tendency to favor appeasement is a proposal that she particularly abhors, and she reminds him,

> kṣatriyeṇa hi hantavyaḥ kṣatriyo lobham āsthitaḥ
>
> A *kṣatriya* who is fixed on greed is to be slain by a *kṣatriya.*
>
> V.80.16

According to dharma, it is important to slay someone who is a miscreant, she tells them. Draupadī never has any qualm about proposing the use of extreme violence.

Then, after the conflict at Kurukṣetra is over, Yudhiṣṭhira endures another moral crisis, particularly after hearing that Karṇa had been his elder brother. He censures the destruction and ruin of family and clan, and determines to take up a life of renunciation and enter the forest. All his brothers speak against this, then Draupadī addresses him.

She reminds him of how, during their forest exile, it was he who always maintained the morale of the brothers, telling them of how they would one day reclaim sovereignty and destroy their enemies. She says, *na klībo vasudhāṃ bhuṅkte* 'a eunuch does not enjoy the earth', and *na klībo dhanam aśnute* 'a eunuch does not obtain wealth'. The *klība* in question here is, by implication, Yudhiṣṭhira: the *dharmarāja* and *kururāja*!

> nādaṇḍaḥ kṣatriyo bhāti nādaṇḍo bhūtim aśnute
> nādaṇḍasya prajā rājñaḥ sukham edhanti ...

> A powerless *kṣatriya* does not shine, powerless he does not obtain wealth.
> The subjects of a powerless king do not prosper happily.
>
> XII.14.14

She continues, describing what is *paro dharmaḥ* 'the highest law' for kings, and discerning between that and what is right for brahmins: the 'protection of the good' (*satāṃ ... paripālayan*) and its obverse, punishment of the lawless. It was by violence and the bloody destruction of the Kaurava army that Yudhiṣṭhira won back his position: thus, she says, *bhuṅkṣva vasuṃdharām* 'enjoy the earth!' (XII.14.20).

'Having slain thousands of kings', she adds, he has become *mohāt ... unmattaka* 'mad from delusion'. 'I am the lowest of all women in the world' (*sāhaṃ sarvādhamā loke strīṇām*), she tells him, after all that she went through because of his dicing, and she closes by commenting on Yudhiṣṭhira's desire to retire from the kingdom in order to enter the forest,

> svaṃ tu sarvāṃ mahīṃ labdhvā kuruṣe svam āpadam ...
> praśādhi pṛthivīṃ devīṃ prajā dharmeṇa pālayan
>
> Having seized all the earth, you will make yourself a calamity!...
> Order the goddess Earth, protecting subjects with law!
>
> XII.14.36 and 38

Arjuna supports Draupadī in her admonishment, reiterating that 'the wise know rule is the law' (*daṇḍaṃ dharmaṃ vidur budhāḥ*; XII.15.2). Draupadī is always firm, if not extreme, in her wish to deploy *daṇḍa*, and her eloquent vituperation is well tempered with the nuances of what is law and right for kings.

4. *Kuntī*

Kuntī, in order to maintain the family lineage, by virtue of her especial mantric powers, called upon the deity Dharma so that he might impregnate her: such was her inimitable influence in the world.[29] The son produced of this union is Yudhiṣṭhira, the *dharmarāja*.

> āhvayāmāsa vai kuntī garbhārthaṃ dharmam acyutam
>
> Kuntī summoned unshakeable Dharma for the purpose of conception.
>
> I.114.1

29. Sax 2002: 148, describes how respected Kuntī is in the Himalayan Garhwal, where she is considered "an ocean of truth, a knower of dharma."

When Pāṇḍu wishes her to continue reproducing in this fashion, after she has already given birth to three sons, she refuses, saying that such is irregular, *āpatsv api* 'even in distress' (I.114.65). She is the one who is familiar with the process of order and right; she knows what is appropriate for a king.

When Kuntī and her nephew Kṛṣṇa are speaking at the court of Hāstinapura, when the latter is visiting on an embassy of peace, she is distressed in her assessment of the situation. Yet, on a more optimistic note, as she speaks of how her son Arjuna will destroy the Kauravas, she says, *nityaṃ dharmo dhārayati prajāḥ* 'dharma always sustains creatures'.

> dharmaś ced asti ... tathā satyaṃ bhaviṣyati
>
> If there is dharma, then truth will be.
>
> V.88.67

She instructs Kṛṣṇa to inform Yudhiṣṭhira that,

> bhūyāṃs te hīyate dharmo mā putraka vṛthā kṛthāḥ
>
> Your dharma has fallen excessively: do not act in vain, son!
>
> V.88.72

Kuntī then admonishes Kṛṣṇa to remind her other sons as to their adherence to *kṣatriya* dharma, and in particular he is to tell Arjuna that he must never forsake Draupadī, neither physically nor morally: for she has been the only one to maintain the standard of vengeance. Implicit is Kuntī's approbation of this firmness.

Kṛṣṇa, having unsuccessfully proposed a policy of peace and reconciliation, before he leaves Hāstinapura and sets off back towards the Pāṇḍavas, once again visits Kuntī. He asks if she has any message for her sons, and she repeats what she said before, 'Your dharma has fallen excessively!' 'Do not act in vain' (*mā ... vṛthā kṛthāḥ*).

> urataḥ kṣatriyaḥ sṛṣṭo bāhuvīryopajīvitā
> krūrāya karmaṇe nityaṃ prajānāṃ paripālane
>
> The *kṣatriya* was created from the chest, living by the virility of his arms:
> always fierce in action for the guarding of subjects.
>
> V.130.7

Then she gives at length—the speech lasts four *adhyāyas*—first, an *upamā*, an extended 'simile', which is really an edifying discourse or parable about King Mucukunda; followed by an account of a *kṣatriya* mother speaking to her lackadaisical son.

The story of Mucukunda illustrates good kingship, particularly as it applies to *daṇḍanīti* 'the conduct of punitive rule', or legitimate use of violence. This maintains the 'fourfold order' of society (*cāturvarṇyam*) for, she adds,

> yugasya ca caturthasya rājā bhavati kāraṇam
>
> Kingship is the cause of the fourth age.
>
> V.130.16

Kuntī expounds upon the *yugas* and their relation to kingship, and of a king's duties to the four *varṇas*. The speech is vivid and well layered with metaphor, and closes with the same lines that it opens with. It is not a monologue given in a fit of passion or grief, but is a well-rendered and firmly delivered argument, whose rhetoric is seamless and fluent.

> na hi vaiklavyasaṃsṛṣṭānṛśaṃsye vyavasthitaḥ
> prajāpālanasaṃbhūtaṃ kiṃcit prāpa phalaṃ nṛpaḥ
>
> For a king familiar with feebleness, established in mildness,
> incapable of protecting subjects, obtains no fruit at all.
>
> V.130.20

Then, she closes this first part of her speech with a severe injunction:

> pitryam aṃśaṃ mahābāho nimagnaṃ punar uddhara
> sāmnā dānena bhedena daṇḍenātha nayena ca
>
> Deliver your sunken patrimony, strong-armed one—
> by conciliation, by money, by divisive rule, and by policy!
>
> V.130.30

She ends with the admonition:

> yudhasva rājadharmeṇa mā nimajjīḥ pitāmahān
>
> With the dharma of kingship—fight! Don't submerge your
> ancestors![30]
>
> V.130.32

As usual in the Mahābhārata, it is the royal women who are the ones to be cognizant in detail and eloquent in expression when matters of kingship arise. They function in the poem as a true *mirror of princes*. As an epic which focusses on and dramatizes the practice of rule, it is these

30. Kuntī sustains the metaphor of a *kṣatriya*'s heroic action being a vessel that saves or supports others upon a turbulent sea.

kṣatriya women who are the main speakers. Arjuna and Bhīma address Yudhiṣṭhira on a couple of occasions concerning *artha*; Vidura ponders at length the old maxims relating to good rule; and Bhīṣma, of course, devotes tens of hours to the didactics which extol good kingship. It is the women in the poem, however, who justly dramatize and speak at crucial decisive moments and who impel the narrative onward with their words. They are the real knowers of kingly action and truth.

Kuntī expands upon *upamā* and speaks an *itihāsa* 'story', a tale about a mother enjoining her son to sustain *kṣatriya* dharma. This short narrative is both dramatic and instructive, and Kuntī not only imparts a message to Kṛṣṇa for her sons, but acts out the story, playing the two voices herself. She imitates both mother and son, as the former verbally impels the latter—dejected after a defeat—into action, as he raises excuses concerning his reversal in battle. She actually sings both parts of the duo.

Kuntī is not only communicating a message but actually performing it, something unusual in the poem except in the case of the poets themselves. We see in the Strī *parvan* how Gāndhārī also assumes the role and function of a poet, when she gives visual depictions of the dead warriors, describing mental imagery which happens to coincide with physical reality.

Kuntī opens her drama with the line,

> na mayā tvaṃ na pitrāsi jātaḥ kvābhyāgato'hy asi
>
> Not born by me nor by your father, where are you come from?
>
> V.131.5

She calls him a *klība* 'castrate', saying, *dhuraṃ vaha* 'bear the yoke'; *uttiṣṭha* 'stand up'; *mā bhais* 'do not be fearful'; and she calls him a *kāpuruṣa* 'coward!' He retorts with,

> kṛṣṇāyasasyeva ca te saṃhatya hṛdayaṃ kṛtam
>
> Your heart has become solid like black metal.[31]
>
> V.133.1

As with many of her speeches, this one is also well illustrated with metaphor and simile, with dogs and snakes and hawks and water, with fire

31. The 'black metal' in question, *kṛṣṇāyas*, is sometimes considered to be 'iron' rather than bronze, but this is not actually known and remains the topic of many interpretations. It could possibly refer to the crude tin, *trapu*, which is a dark metal, necessary for the manufacture of bronze, although Apte, Monier-Williams, and Böhtlingk and Roth do not consider such a gloss. The use of this term in the present *śloka* could also be merely anachronistic.

and corpses; Kuntī displays great poetic finesse in her discourse. 'Do not burn for smoke ... conquer', she says (*mā dhūmāya jvala ... jahi*). 'One who is apathetic is neither man nor a woman' (*niramarṣaś ca naiva strī na punaḥ pumān*). She exhorts him to be valiant and brave, to enjoy the virility and audacity of combat, and admonishes him not only to good kingship but to heroism, mentioning the words *vīra* and *śūra* frequently, 'warrior' and 'hero'. 'Be our boat' (*bhava naḥ plavaḥ*), she says, drawing upon this typical heroic metaphor.

> ekaśatruvadhenaiva śūro gacchati viśrutim
>
> A hero goes to renown by the death of just one enemy.[32]
>
> V.132.23

'Kingship is like a door to heaven', she says (*svargadvāropamaṃ rājyam*).

> ahaṃ hi kṣatrahṛdayaṃ veda yat pariśāśvatam
>
> I know the heart of *kṣatriya*-dom—which is perpetual.
>
> V.132.36

This is one of the most formal descriptions of *ksatriya* dharma in the poem, without the usual personal injunctions and invective that a woman—like Draupadī for instance—would display. The fact that Kuntī literally acts out the two voices gives the dialogue an even more official and objective character. Even the long discourse on *rājadharma* by Bhīṣma in Book Twelve, although the message and exempla are often similar, never takes on such a theatrical form.

Kuntī makes the unusual comment that she speaks in the voice of this mother, Vidurā, to her son, Saṃjaya: 'as a powerful man to a feeble one' (*balavān iva durbalam*; V.134.6). Even if this is not Kuntī's personal voice, the communication retains a similar trajectory. Certainly, the call for action, given the circumstances, is a *kṣatriya* message: she is certainly not instructing Kṛṣṇa to command her son Yudhiṣṭhira to sue for peace.

The son—in her story—responds by calling his mother a *netrī* 'leader' (V.134.12), and Kuntī closes her address by saying that the anecdote is called *jaya* 'Victory', and if it is repeatedly heard by 'a pregnant woman—she will give birth to a warrior' (*abhīkṣṇaṃ garbhiṇī śrutvā dhruvaṃ vīraṃ prajāyate*; V.134.18).

32. Harlan 2003: 105, on the subject of hero legends in contemporary Rajastan, notes, "The heroic death of sons, then, validates their birth from their mother's wombs and their suckling their mother's breasts, this latter act being traditionally simulated by Rajputs in past centuries both before marriage and battle."

Perhaps this is a tale that circulated among Bronze Age *kṣatriya* women, told during the period prior to confinement. Thus, *kṣatriyā sūte vīram* 'a *kṣatriya* woman bears a warrior', which are the closing words of the narrative. It is unusual that Kuntī performs the account with such facility, as if it is a familiar procedure for her.[33] None of her other speeches assume such a staged, histrionic form. This speech has the air of something practiced and traditional, a story that is typically exchanged between women: but on this occasion is given before men.

At the beginning of the subsequent *adhyāya*, there is the statement that,

> kuntyās tu vacanaṃ śrutvā bhīṣmadroṇau mahārathau
>
> Bhīṣma and Droṇa, the great warriors, having heard the speech of Kuntī ...
>
> V.136.1

These two then speak with Duryodhana, signifying that Kuntī has been performing her edifying drama in front of several men, and not only Kṛṣṇa. 'Having entered the house and honored her feet' (*praviṣyātha gṛhaṃ tasyā caraṇāv abhivādya ca*) is how this scene opens, thus implying that Bhīṣma, Droṇa, Duryodhana, and presumably others, must have also been present (V.130.1). Perhaps this is just a curious lapse on the part of the poets, and is merely an attempt at continuity after what appears to be a dramatic soliloquy taken from another tradition, like a long quote or theatrical paraphrase. The epic poets must have relished such virtuoso pieces, where a poet imitates a woman who enacts a simultaneous performance of two men.

In her final speech in the epic, given to her assembled sons and daughters-in-law, Kuntī, makes a farewell as she is about to set off—along with Gāndhārī and Dhṛtarāṣṭra—towards an eremitic life of seclusion and renunciation in the forest. In this speech she recounts how she was the one to sustain the spirits of her family during their sojourn in the wilderness. When they were fallen from happiness, she says, *kṛtam uddharṣaṇaṃ mayā* 'the gladdening was done by me' (XV.23.2).

She recounts how she raised their morale during those times of despond, repeating the phrase *uddharṣaṇaṃ kṛtam*. That is, she was the one to sustain their dharmic self-possession, and it was her constant encouragement which maintained their integrity against so much

33. Typically, one "performs" an action; these words of Kuntī are not mere recitation, but enactment.

suffering and ordeal. Kuntī, like Draupadī, was the one actually to uphold the family during their exclusion and to sustain its values.

5. *Lamentation*

Women in the Mahābhārata assume the formal role of threnody, much as they did in the cognate world of archaic Greece as represented in the Iliad.[34] Lamentation for a fallen hero is a particular form of poetry that usually only women perform.[35] Dhṛtarāṣṭra, on hearing of the death of Bhīṣma, sings a long requiem, in which he praises the martial accomplishments and skills of the departed hero and describes his life (VI.15); similarly, Yudhiṣṭhira sings a detailed elegy for his brother Karṇa in Book Eleven. Such male lamentation is not typical, however, and lacks a certain harsh unconstraint, being more controlled in its delivery than the mourning songs uttered by women.

In the Strī *parvan*, women's lamentation is the subject of the book and all decorum and shame is abandoned; the women go out of the city, disclosing themselves to the world in a state of raving and distracted grief.[36] They wander the field of Kurukṣetra trying to identify the mangled and dismembered deceased, before wild animals devour the corpses of eighteen full armies.

> vilāpo vīrapatnīnāṃ yatrātikaruṇaḥ smṛtaḥ
>
> The lamentation of the wives of warriors—where extreme mourning is recalled.[37]
>
> I.2.191

They, who were formerly modest, become *ekavastrā* 'wearing only one cloth' and *nirlajjā* 'shameless'; 'their minds struck with grief' (*śokenābhyāhatajñānāḥ*; XI.9.14–15).

> darśayantīva tā ha sma yugānte lokasaṃkṣayam

34. Alexiou 1974 has described this feminine role extensively. Holst-Warhaft 1992 has developed the model, applying it to modern Greece. See Das 2007: 49ff. for contemporary India.

35. Concerning the Rajput poetic tradition: "In short, heroic men are portrayed in many traditions as not fearing loss of life as they face that very prospect; to women is relegated the role of experiencing their loss." Harlan 2003: 106.

36. See Fitzgerald 2004: 3–25. Harivaṃśa LXXVII is devoted to the lamentation of the royal wives.

37. The sequence of grief is given as 'sons, brothers, fathers' (I.2.192). When Yudhiṣṭhira grieves a few *ślokas* later, it is for 'fathers, brothers, sons' (I.2.196). Kinship is different for men and women, in terms of their ascending scales of affection.

> It was as if they were causing the ruin of the world to appear at the end of a *yuga*.
>
> XI.9.13

Yudhiṣṭhira, approaching the scene,

> ... strīṇāṃ ... kurarīṇām ivārtānāṃ krośantīnāṃ dadarśa ha
>
> He observed the women—wailing like anguished ospreys.
>
> XI.11.5

There are thousands of them, their arms raised upward as they shriek: a traditional gesture of feminine grief.[38] These are the mothers, wives, sisters, and daughters.

The field is covered with not only bodies of the defunct—human and animal—but also with jackals, vultures, and predatory ravenous demons (XI.16.5–8). Some of the women attempt to re-unite the various parts of a body that had been hacked apart in battle (XI.16.50). Many of the bodies have been partially consumed by scavengers and are unrecognizable. Some of the women sing laments for the ruined and unrecognizable corpses.

In this *parvan*, the distraught widows of the fallen tour the battlefield at Kurukṣetra, identifying their slain kin and lamenting. This, for a hero, marks the incipience of their fame: for the women praise and celebrate the prowess of husbands, sons, and fathers, simultaneously as they mourn. In a sense, it is the women who are functionally the proto-poets, the first ones to sing of the greatness and the exploits of the deceased: it is women who are the first to apportion the *kīrti* 'fame' that a hero receives at the close of an embattled, valorous life. For a hero there is no fame without death in combat, and the women are in the initial position to express verbally the substance of that *kīrti*: in singing of their grief and of their simultaneous anger.[39] They are the foremost vocal witnesses.

The first important formal lament that an audience hears comes during the second week of battle, when Subhadrā sings of her sorrow for Abhimanyu, her young son who had been tragically felled (VII.55.2–31). He was the most juvenile of the warriors to take to the field and the pity is thus greater.

She begins in the formulaic manner, asking the usual rhetorical questions:

38. See Alexiou 1974 and Holst-Warhaft 1992. Such gestures are visible on Greek red-figure vases.

39. See McGrath 2004: 10. Hypothetically, this moment invokes the origin of epic.

hā putra mama mandāyāḥ kathaṃ saṃyugam etya ha
nidhanaṃ prāptavāṃs tāta pitṛtulyaparākramaḥ

O son of my unhappiness, how, having gone to battle
have you obtained ruin: son, whose valor was equal to your father's?

VII.55.2

Note that a wife refers to the son as *tāta*, a term usually uttered between men. Then she makes the usual comparison, contrasting the bloody destruction of the body with its former luxurious life.

katham indīvaraśyāmaṃ sudaṃṣṭraṃ cārulocanam
mukhaṃ te dṛśyate vatsa guṇṭhitaṃ raṇareṇunā

How, my darling, possessing lovely eyes and beautiful teeth,
your face—a dark blue lotus—is seen covered with the dust of battle?

VII.55.3

These interrogatives, matching former beauty and opulence with the filth and decay of annihilation, continue throughout the lament. She describes and praises the particular aspects of his body—arms, chest, neck—wrecked by the carnage of war. He, who once lay upon wonderful couches, now lies broken upon the rough earth; one who was formerly surrounded by lovely women and singing poets, is now encompassed by scavenging birds and jackals.[40]

yo'nvāsyata purā vīro varastrībhir mahābhujaḥ
katham anvāsyate so'dya śivābhiḥ patito mṛdhe

A strong-armed warrior who formerly was attended by chosen women:
how—fallen on the earth—is he now attended by jackals?

VII.55.7

Then—as is typical of this genre of speech—grief becomes fused with anger and fury, and Subhadrā begins to curse her husband's companions who failed to protect him: *dhigbalam dhigvīryam* 'damn strength, damn heroism', especially as it applies to Bhīma or Arjuna (VII.55.12,ff.). 'Now I see the earth void', she cries (*adya paśyāmi pṛthivīm śūnyām*). 'A nephew of Kṛṣṇa, a son of Arjuna, how shall I look at you, a hero made chariotless,' she asks.

She begins to contrast the *gatir* 'end' of others with that of her husband. Again, the rhetorical repetitions and interrogatives supply

40. In Harivaṃśa LXXVII.6, the lamenting women go so far as to cry, *ko naḥ pāṃsuparītāṅgyo ratisaṃsargalālasāḥ / latā iva viceṣṭantyaḥ śayanīyāni neṣyati* 'who will lead us—shaking like creepers, limbs possessed by dust, longing for sex and pleasure—to beds?'

her song with great charge and tension. She repeats many imperatives, requesting and imploring that he seek such an 'end' which would formerly have been available to him.

Draupadī, her co-wife, joins in the lament, along with Subhadrā's daughter-in-law, Uttarā (VII.55.32). The mother, the co-mother, and then the wife: this is the gradation in their expression of formulated sorrow.[41] All of them faint and collapse upon the ground, unconscious. Kṛṣṇa merely consoles her, saying that Abhimanyu had obtained the fame due to a *kṣatriya* and the best *gatir* for *kṣatriyas* (VII.55.37). He and Arjuna then retire, their grief not mixing appropriately with the more emotional and social grief of the women.

In the course of the Aśvamedha *parvan*, at one point, just before Uttarā gives birth to Parikṣit—the future king of the Bhāratas and nephew of Kṛṣṇa—she and Kuntī and Draupadī, along with the *kuruyoṣitas* 'the Kuru wives', assemble to re-lament ceremoniously the death of Abhimanyu. Uttarā, *kurarīva nanāda* 'screamed like an osprey' (XIV.60.24), and Draupadī and then Kuntī sing brief laments extolling Abhimanyu and praising him. It is an unusual practice, to lament for a deceased father immediately prior to the birth of his son, and seems almost apotropaic. One wonders if this was customary practice?

When in the city of Hāstinapura, the news of Droṇa's demise reaches the old king and the women of the court, there is great lamentation: 'a great sound of pain' (*ārtanado mahān*) rises, and,

> sa śabdaḥ pṛthivīṃ sarvāṃ pūrayāmāsa sarvaśaḥ
>
> That sound filled the earth on all sides.
>
> VIII.3.2

Then, in accord with the role of women as mourners,

> śokārṇave mahāghore nimagnā bharatastriyaḥ
>
> The Bhārata women were sunk in a terrific sea of grief.
>
> VIII.3.3

Many of them, including Gāndhārī, fall senseless upon the earth, overwhelmed by their passion.

Later, after the battle at Kurukṣetra is over, when the Kaurava women hear of Duryodhana's defeat, as one they begin to lament.

41. In Scroll XXIV of the Iliad, the formal lamentations for Hektor are successively performed by Hekuba, then Andromache, and then by Helen: the mother, wife, and sister-in-law.

tatas tā yoṣito rājan krandantyo vai muhurmuhuḥ
kurarya iva śabdena nādayantyo mahītalam
ājaghnuḥ karajaiś cāpi pāṇibhiś ca śirāṃsy uta
luluvuś ca tadā keśān krośantyas tatra tatra ha
hāhākāra vinādinyo vinighnantya urāṃsi ca
krośantyas tatra ruruduḥ krandamānā viśāṃ pate

Then those women, O king, crying repeatedly
like ospreys, making the earth resonant with the sound:
and with fingernails and hands they struck their heads,
and crying, they disheveled their hair indiscriminately,
crying ha, ha, and striking their breasts;
crying, they wept, lamenting piteously, O lord of people.

IX.28.65–67

This is the formulaic model for women as they lament their deceased menfolk: husbands, brothers, fathers, and uncles. Such behavior is ritual and is something that men do not typically perform: rather, this is an activity accomplished by women solely for men.[42]

Likewise, when Arjuna has defeated the *gandharvas* in Book Three,

vinadantyaḥ striyaḥ sarvā niṣpetur nagarād bahiḥ
prakīrṇakeśyo vyathitāḥ kuraryeva duḥkhitāḥ

All the women fell out from the city, crying,
hair in disarray, agitated like distressed ospreys.

III.170.55–56

They fall upon the earth and weep for their fallen sons, fathers, and brothers, wailing for their deceased husbands, striking their breasts as they discard clothing and jewelry.

Repeatedly throughout the Āśramavāsika *parvan*, which occurs sixteen years after the great battle, the grief of the women is a repeated refrain: their *tīvraṃ duḥkham* 'bitter sorrow' and their *śoka* 'grief' for slain husbands, brothers, and sons is unbearable. Such is the monodic tone with which the epic approaches closure. It is these final and formal laments which contain the refined truth of a hero's life: this is the fame of a warrior and the expression of such possesses the force of dharma and sustains the moral code of *kṣatriya* achievement. Lamentation is an intrinsic proclamation of kinship and the values of heroic life.

As a coda to the above image of this model where women in the

42. After the death of Kṛṣṇa and his brother and their male kin, the women of his household lament in this same fashion (XVI.8.16ff.). Then four of his wives ascend the pyre to accompany him in death (XVI.8.24).

Mahābhārata act as repositories of *kṣatriya* dharma and behave as the primary proclaimers of its force, there occurs a scene when Ulūpī, the snake woman with whom Arjuna once had a child, appears and encourages Babhruvāhana to fight with Arjuna—his father—during the peregrination of the sacrificial horse. The model receives an ironic twist, for Babhruvāhana is the son of Citrāṅgadā: that is, another co-wife of Arjuna, like Ulūpī.

Babhruvāhana had initially sought peace with Arjuna, not wishing to enter into violent conflict, although neither had realized their actual kinship status. Ulūpī—being *kṣatradharmaviśāradā* 'skilled in *kṣatriya* dharma'—instructs her 'son' to fight:

> kuruṣva vacanaṃ putra dharmas te bhavitā paraḥ
>
> Do as I say, son, your dharma will be great!
>
> XIV.78.11

'Fight him' (*yudhyasvainam*), she adds.

Arjuna is soon struck down unconscious, and the mother of Babhruvāhana, Citrāṅgadā, comes out to the field and berates Ulūpī for allowing her 'husband' (*bhartāram*) to be killed (XIV.79.3). She accuses her co-wife of not being a *pativratā* 'devoted wife', 'having caused a husband to be slain by a son' (*ghātayitvā bhartāraṃ putreṇa*). She then says,

> nāhaṃ śocāmi tanayaṃ nihataṃ pannagātmaje
> patim eva tu śocāmi yasyātithyam idaṃ kṛtam
>
> O daughter of a snake, I do not grieve for a son slain,
> but I do grieve for a husband, for whom this reception was performed.
>
> XIV.79.7

Thus two co-wives are arguing about the correct form of *kṣatriya* conduct: the problem being whether a son or a father takes priority. There is no rivalry between the women, only this question of the priority of their menfolk. This is a small scene, but nicely encapsulates a tone that is entirely feminine, poignant, and very real.

Male heroes maintain the world of *kṣatriyas* via a potential threat of bloodshed.[43] For women heroes, it is their apprehension of what con-

43. Battle frequently receives metaphors which are drawn from sacrificial rites; hence the phrase, 'the sacrifice of weapons' (*śastrayajña*; V.57.12), which blurs the brahmin-*kṣatriya* divide.

stitutes correct dharma—as applicable to a situation—and their verbal pronouncement upon that view, which is where they are prominent within a clan.[44] They are the ones to remind the family as to the values which lead to the coherence of the clan in time.

Draupadī, as we have observed, is in no way slack in her analysis and pursuit of vendetta, that system of social balance which lies at the basis of kingship during the Bronze Age and which precedes the institution of litigation. After the death of a hero, his womenfolk must formally and publicly mourn for him, and in doing so they evaluate and praise the martial accomplishment of his life: hence the foundation of what becomes fame, *kīrti*.[45]

Perhaps the seeming paradox—for us as readers today—between *daivam* and *karma* was not the case in antiquity. Then, *daivam* referred to a force that was immanent in the cosmos, whereas *karma* simply offered a possibility for transcendence, and a means toward an achievement of *kīrti*. For *kṣatriyas* there is no actual opposition between the two concepts, such being a modern contradiction: the apparent inconsistency lies between two ontologically different registers, which do not in fact negate each other. The mundane activities of *dharma* and its practical reasons are not necessarily canceled and overruled by this other, supernal and divine force of *daivam*.

In words, it is the women heroes who mediate between these two domains, admonishing the men. A *kṣatriya*'s standing among his kin, and among his enemies, is as we have seen above, entirely organized by how his womenfolk—by speech—support and encourage his position. It only remains for him to act with efficient violence as a hero, and with moral rectitude as a king.

One wonders how the poets of Bronze Age antiquity presented these forceful speeches of women, and what degree of femininity they impersonated in these differing, varying, and often critical voices. Perhaps certain poets were more adroit and proficient than others in their performance of women speakers, and embellished their singing with drama rather than simply descanting a formal recitative; for these speeches where women proclaim what is right are almost a genre in themselves.

44. One should recall that Vāc, the Vedic goddess of speech, is feminine and often identified with Sarasvatī. RV X.125.5 states: *ahám evá svayám idáṃ vadāmi / júṣṭaṃ devébhir utá m´ānuṣebhiḥ* 'So I myself say that [which is] worshipped by humans and deities.'

45. Thus it is that, *etāvān eva puruṣo yaj jāyātmā prajeti ha* 'a man is according to his wife and offspring' (Manu, IX.45).

VI

EPILOGUE

THE BURDEN OF THIS STUDY has been directed towards surveying the character that women evince in maintaining continuities of *kṣatriya* culture and communitas and how the currency of women in Mahābhārata facilitates male *kṣatriya* action.[1] Many of the passages examined display cultural forms that are appropriate for all twice-born castes, the *āryavṛtta* 'Aryan way'; yet the focus of this work has been aimed at women of the second *varṇa*, whom Hopkins titled 'the Ruling Caste', as depicted in the syncretic world of epic poetry.[2] One should recall at this point that women in the Mahābhārata are heroes and are not human, even if they often appear so: they are often supernatural in one way or another.

It is truly fascinating that the epic poets were so fluent and adept at interpreting the varieties of feminine voice, and so capably subtle in representing such verbal and emotional innuendo.[3] The great range of feminine expression that we have examined in this study surely reflects a gifted inventiveness on the part of the male poets, and despite the fact that the society portrayed in the poem is principally heroic, these poets were masterly in representing and dramatizing the nuance and qualities of non-heroic feminine speech. One could make the claim that parts of the epic must have often been like a theater of travesty, in the literal sense of the word.[4]

1. Women in epic Mahābhārata can be said to possess a fiduciary quality; their physical, emotional, and moral integrity is vital for the correct functioning of warrior society, and their removal—actually or mentally—is the source of great disorder for that society. If there is one general message which epic Mahābhārata communicates it concerns the necessity of judgment which correct *kṣatriya* life requires, and simultaneously, the futility of judgment; implying that action is the locus of all true value for a *vīra* or *śūra*, 'warrior' or 'hero'. As we have observed throughout this study, such action is originally driven by behavior which circulates about the place of women—one woman in particular—and the struggle either to elicit or to dominate their desire.

2. Hopkins,1888.

3. See Pantel 1992: 1–8.

4. As a general and final note on epic poetics, for an audience, the epic possesses two qualities of sensibility: that of sound and that of sight. Audially, the performance of the poem

As we have seen, women in epic Mahābhārata are crucial and central figures in Bronze Age clan life and are vital agents in the formation and maintenance of kinship structures, both hierarchical and heterarchical: within the family and between related kin groups.[5] They, as formal and instructive SPEAKERS, sustain a guardianship of *kṣatriya* dharma: this is manifest at key moments in the poem's progress where the values which inhere to human life are put in question, weighed, and transmitted. The mother-in-law and the wife play especially critical roles in these systems of family history, integrating and stabilizing their immediate society and urging the heroes to pursue certain policies. Those policies, although they concern the operations of dharma, actually point to and hinge upon processes of physical conflict that end in death.[6]

One must qualify these claims by stating that there is no single woman in the poem who is as complex in character and as deeply implicated in the narrative as Draupadī. The spectrum of her emotions ranges from scenes of intimate frivolity and moments of coy and seductive modesty to speeches that advocate extraordinary and unmitigated bloodshed. Draupadī's unique person lies at the core of epic Mahābhārata. Her name, as it is a patronym, is unusually male.

Born out of a sacred fire, her lack of human generation marks Draupadī as someone profoundly unnatural, and yet her life is thoroughly human in its suffering and sensibility for affection. Her understanding of the function and operation of kingship is paramount, and yet Draupadī demonstrates both a remarkable admiration and simultaneous criticism for her eldest husband, Yudhiṣṭhira. With

has a repetitive, staccatic form, almost like modern *techno* music. As a medium of intense and constant visualization, the poem projects a series of varying images and pictures. In terms of poetic inspiration, the distinction between what the poets hear and what the poets see—I would submit—denotes the difference between the archaic and the classical world. For a poet like Saṃjaya, who "sees" the substance of his song, the epic is a mimesis of this vision. For a poet like Vaiśaṃpāyana, who has learned the epic from a previous poet, there exists only the repetition; mimesis in his case lacks the full translation between the senses, for it is language and not experience that is being rendered. Modern inspiration is of an order similar to the latter form. Sobin 1999: 45, observes that "In every archaic culture, a grammar of images, of pictographs, precedes that of letters: the sign, or *sema*, is first of all pictorial."

5. The term "heterarchy" was coined by Crumley 1995. Concerning the transition from Bronze to Iron Age, Kristiansen and Larsson 2005: 366, comment on how there was a concomitant move "to distinguish between gods and heroes, the heroic generation belonging to the Bronze Age and the time before." Finkelberg 2005: 8ff., offers a depiction of how the cognate Greek epic tradition created "a foundational myth [of a heroic age] that promulgated the idea of a common past".

6. "Young women ... show higher mortality than men because of the risks of giving birth, while adult men demonstrate highly increased mortality compared to women, most probably because of warfare." Kristiansen and Larsson 2005: 247.

Bhīma, the poets often portray her as intimate: he is the one who cries out at her degradation and who seeks personal revenge, and it is to him that she turns when whimsical. Arjuna is said to be her great love, yet the poets do not dwell upon this passion, which remains veiled. He is certainly the most virile of her menfolk.

Her ability with speech is supreme and unmatched. Not only is she competent, learned, and calculating, but she possesses great rhetorical skills of address and manages to gauge her audiences precisely. Draupadī can be said to be triform in this fluency with language: her speeches with Yudhiṣṭhira manifest an enormous comprehension of law and in this she is completely the *dharmapatnī*; her private exchanges with Bhīma reveal her as a *pativratā*, involved and dependent; whilst her embittered words of rage and lust for vendetta suit her perfectly as a *vīrapatnī*, a true *kṣatriya* wife, and—so the poets say—one most adoring of Arjuna.[7]

Despite not being born from a mother and not having a genetic father, Draupadī more than fully informs the paradigm of what it means to be feminine in this poem. Her highly nuanced person supplies a most distinct particular from which general conclusions can be inferred.[8] If anything, grief is the one quality or sign which marks women in epic Mahābhārata, and Draupadī is exceptional in this respect.

Within the text of Mahābhārata, the distinction between the male and feminine approaches to *vīrya* are overt. We see how a woman as unique as Draupadī is verbally and emotionally charged with passions for aggression and fame as male war heroes are. Women do not perform acts of destruction, however—that is the difference—they only incite them.[9] In the economy of poetics for male heroes, life is exchanged for death and 'fame' (*kīrti*), whereas for the women in the epic there exists no such transaction: the sign of femininity is much more fluid and concerns language and affiliation. Let us briefly review how certain men in the epic speak about women.

7. Alternatively, it can be argued that Draupadī verbally provides for her three senior husbands in a manner that spans the trivalent Indo-European functions as schematized by Dumézil 1968: I. 118–124; and 1966: 225 where he discusses the *aśvamedha*. There, the queen, in the place of *śrī*, anoints the body of the victim, which has been divided into three parts, to represent *tejas*, *indriya*, and *paśu*.

8. In terms of her marital worth, Draupadī exceeds that of any other woman, insofar as she equates with five men.

9. Scharfe: 1989: 175, comments that for heroes, "combat, the foremost activity of men ... was seen in analogy to a ritual offering." That is, the metaphors of death and combat are often taken from the 'sacrifice' (*yajña*). There is no complementary use of such metaphors as they apply to the feminine world.

In the first place, Bhīma, in the Āraṇyaka *parvan*, says that *balam* 'physical force or strength' is inappropriate in women (III.34.78). As we have seen, feminine potence lies beyond coercion, and Yudhiṣṭhira can say to his brother, *mā ... striyaṃ vadhīḥ* 'do not kill a woman!' (I.143.2). Women in heroic culture are outside of that scheme of physical vehemence, and even Draupadī, who is arguably the most fierce woman in the epic, never actually performs an aggressive act; Ambā must transform into a man in order to pursue her idea of vindication.

Women are, according to Mahābhārata cosmology, typically *kṣetra* 'the field', and men, *kṣetrajña* 'knowers of the field'.

> saṃsāratantravāhinyas tatra budhyeta yoṣitaḥ
> prakṛtyā kṣetrabhūtās tā narāḥ kṣetrajñalakṣaṇāḥ
> rajasy antarhitā mūrtir indriyāṇāṃ sanātanī
>
> Women should be understood as causing the characteristics of the world.
> They are the nature, being the field: men are the form of the field.
> They are the eternal embodiment of the senses, hidden in passion.
>
> XII.206.7–8

One can construe this as meaning that women obtain to a state or to being as such; whereas for men, knowing is more their condition of worldly presence.[10] Men are thus removed from 'being' by virtue of their particular knowledge: an understanding of fighting perhaps, which is the primary mark of *kṣatriyas*.[11] The experience and practice of brutality makes men more objective in their apprehension of the world, they know how to act, whereas women, as *kṣetra*, are able to remain more subjective, ontologically speaking, and thus more adept at the speaking of emotion.

When a woman in the epic says, *bhartā me daivataṃ param* 'my husband is the highest deity' (III.198.29), this is not so much an expression of subordination by the woman, but a statement that the worldly and mundane is immediate—that is, the spouse—and prior to any abstract notion as to behavior. Women's earthly affiliations reside primarily in her scale of proximate human relations, the family and the clan; which is not always the case with *kṣatriya* men, where martial endeavor, and its strategic and tactical praxis, inform their life.

10. See Ortner 1974 on this a-symmetry.

11. In his commentary to the Vulgate Mahābhārata, Nīlakaṇṭha, at V.28.3, glosses the phrase *ādyaṃ liṅgam* 'the primary sign' for caste as, *brāhmaṇasya svādhyāya ... kṣatriyasya śaurya* 'recitation of the brahmin ... heroism of the *kṣatriya*.' Brahmins transcend speech through ritual, *kṣatriyas* transcend the body via death and its corollary, the experience of physical pain.

Secondly, Bhīṣma, during his long didactic speech to the *dharmarāja* Yudhiṣṭhira, makes the curious statement that:

> devatānāṃ samāvāyam ekasthaṃ pitaraṃ viduḥ
> martyānāṃ devatānāṃ ca snehād abhyeti mātaram
>
> One understands the father as an assembly of deities combined as one;
> and because of love, one approaches the mother as the divine and mortal.
>
> XII.258.40

There is thus something inherently human about the feminine, affection here being the sign of the feminine, and something potentially unearthly about the male: according to Bhīṣma's equation. This is due to emotion, *sneha*, the 'stickiness' of human feelings, which here are allied more with women; perhaps because force and the *kṣatriya* practice of killing remove men from such affective spheres of experience, or at least separates men from women, in terms of sentiment.

Earlier, lying on his couch of arrows, Bhīṣma had told a story to Yudhiṣṭhira in which the significance of a wife was praised. He said,

> bhāryā hi paramo nāthaḥ puruṣasyeha paṭhyate ...
> nāsti bhāryā samo bandhur nāsti bhāryā samā gatiḥ
>
> For it is written that a wife is the highest refuge of a man on earth ...
> There is no kin like a wife. There is no way like a wife.
>
> XII.142.8 and 10

Later in his declamation, Bhīṣma describes the importance of the maternal affection for a son. This is a long aria, in praise of maternity. He begins,

> asya me jananī hetuḥ pāvakasya yathāraṇiḥ
> mātā dehāraṇiḥ puṃsāṃ ...
>
> The mother is the cause of this birth of mine, as the fire-stick is of fire:
> the mother is the fire-stick of the body of men ...
>
> XII.258.24

He continues to say, *rakṣaty eva sutaṃ mātā* 'so the mother protects the son', and that,

> tadā sa vṛddho bhavati yadā bhavati duḥkhitaḥ
> tadā śūnyaṃ jagat tasya yadā mātrā viyujyate ...
> nāsti mātṛsamā chāyā nāsti mātṛsamā gatiḥ
> nāsti mātṛsamā trāṇaṃ nāsti mātṛsamā prapā

> So he becomes old, as he becomes sad;
> so his world becomes void, as he is separated from his mother ...
> There is no refuge like the mother. There is no way like the mother.
> There is no defence like the mother. There is no reservoir like the mother.
>
> XII.258.28–29

Bhīṣma goes on to describe all the qualities of maternity as it concerns sons:

> mātā jānāti yad gotraṃ mātā jānāti yasya saḥ
>
> A mother knows what the clan is; a mother knows of whom he is.
>
> XII.258.33

For the moribund Bhīṣma, the arch-hero of the poem, the mother is this fount of all significance and worth in human and especially social life. One cannot imagine an Achilles or Agamemnon saying this. Feminine *vīrya*, as it is portrayed in epic poetry, circulates about the warrior activities of men and like a tracery of kinship and of speech, drives those men.

Thirdly, Vidura, one night, as he sings of popular wisdom and dharma to his restless king, says of feminine desire: *striyaḥ kāmitakāminyaḥ* 'women desire the desired' (V.33.51). Women, as mothers, are one of the five fires, Vidura continues, which require to be worshipped; the other four being father, self, the guru, and the ritual household fire itself (V.33.62). He says that these five fires are like the fives senses. In the previous *adhyāya*, the five senses are listed, and in the second place, where mothers had just been cited, is the sense of hearing; the father being in the first place, which is sight (V.32.24). Men and seeing, women and hearing: this is the taxonomy.

Then, Vidura goes on to say that there are another five items to be honored in order to acquire *yaśas* 'glory'. Here, in the second place, after the deities, the 'ancestors' (*pitṝn*) are listed (V.33.63). By metonymy then, women—as mothers—are connected with the past kin, whereas the men—or fathers—are connected with the heavens, where the deities ostensibly reside; presumably this includes feminine deities.[12] Again, as above, one observes that women—in epic society—possess a principal affiliation with humankind rather than with any abstraction or ideal.

12. There is thus an expiation required if a man marries a woman who has been previously married, that is, a man who is *didhiṣur* (XII.35.4). The expiation is required to annul the previous allegiances to her first husband's kin and ancestors.

He closes his words by saying that, *prabhavo na adhigantavyaḥ strīṇām* 'the origin of women is not to be discovered' (V.35.62). Presumably, he means that the etiology of the feminine psyche is something not available to men's understanding.[13] It is a strange statement to make, to admit that femininity is beyond male comprehension and familiarity; for the deities could also be described as possessing a similar ineffable provenance.

In the solitude of the forest one night, Yudhiṣṭhira declares,

> yā bhartari śuśrūṣā tayā svargam upāśnute
>
> Since [she is] obedient to a husband—a woman obtains heaven.
>
> III.196.20

Yet such a statement has a rhetorical or ideological force, because, as we have seen, women are fully autonomous agents, and in many cases it is the women who instruct men on how to conduct themselves. Nominally, men would appear to be the controlling figures within family systems, and yet practically, for *kṣatriyas* at least, women behave as individuals of strong and active volition and guidance. Draupadī in particular is superlative in this respect of *vīrya*, but there are also women like Kuntī or Gāndhārī.[14]

Finally, Yudhiṣṭhira—in the altercatio with his father, Dharma—remarks that 'a wife is a friend in the house' (*bhāryā mitraṃ gṛhe*; III.297.45). For *kṣatriyas*, *mitra* is a highly charged term and denotes a quality which is inviolate: friendship, like speech, is a component of life—for a *kṣatriya*—that is neither to be questioned nor doubted, it is irrefragable.[15] We noted above how, when Kuntī spoke to her sons as they returned from the *svayaṃvara*, her speech was naturally inviolate, Kuntī being preeminent among women.

Bhīṣma had made the remark during the Sabhā *parvan* dicing scene, *striyaś ca bhartur vaśatāṃ samīkṣa* 'having observed women as dependent on a husband' (II.60.40). Yet we now know that such a statement needs qualification if it is to have any meaning but the superficial, for the dependency is actually a mutual equation of asymmetry and is absolutely reciprocal. As we have noted, what men say about women in the epic is on many occasions different from how they actually behave

13. The "dark continent" that is so external to the discourse of human language?

14. At this point one should again recall that epic portrays a synthetic world of heroic culture and does *not* reveal a historical social system that is domestic and worldly. These men and women are creatures of imagination only.

15. In opposition to this, it is claimed that, *strīpumāṃsor vivādaṃ ... varjya* 'a dispute between a man and woman is to be avoided' (V.35.36).

with women: there is the performative and there is the substantive or actual, and these are distinct.

Bhīṣma is speaking at a point where the kinship structure within which he has lived his life—that of a patrilineal system—has given way to another kind of descent. Bhīṣma is the last to be in a direct line of inheritance and it is only when Arjuna sires a son, Abhimanyu, upon his co-wife, Subhadrā, that a patrilineal system returns once again to that branch of the family. The men whom *kṣatriya* women are actually dependent upon at this point have shifted from the husband to another man, during this period when the matriline takes precedence.[16] From a point of view of kinship, one can aver that Mahābhārata describes the triumph of a system of matriline over a system of patriline: this is the core field of *vīrya*, as it is given in the abstract.

1. Landscape and Rivers

Landscape in the Mahābhārata, when it is described, is often a situation where life in an *āśrama* is being depicted as blithe and harmonious, without tension or conflict.[17] Birds, trees, animals, and humans are lovingly portrayed by the poets as ingenuous, and although not pastoral, in a western sense, the sense of idyll and balance and of natural equilibrium is a key tone.[18] All this is in distinction to Kurukṣetra, the great warfield, which first appears in Book Six and dominates the rest of the poem.[19]

Such bucolic places possess a moral excellence which affects their inhabitants, elevating their dharmic propriety.[20] At the risk of sounding essentialist, there is something decidedly feminine about such regions,

16. It is perhaps for this reason that the Gāndhāreyas are scarcely mentioned in the poem, although the Kaunteyas are frequently referred to; the former side of the family go nearly always by the patronym, the Dhārtarāṣṭras. The Pāṇḍavas are named by both patronym and metronym. Dhṛtarāṣṭra addresses his son as *gāndhāre* at V.83.10, but this usage of the metronym is most unusual.

17. Feldhaus 1995: 110, makes the distinction between *jāṅgala*, "semiarid land, including the pine forests, savannas, scrub jungle, and dry deciduous forests typical of the western parts of north India"; *araṇya*, "the wilderness or wasteland, alien and sinister, far from human settlements, the realm of thorn bushes, wild animals, and robbers"; and *vana*, "the forest or woods closer to the village, comfortable rather than threatening, and useful as a source of wood."

18. 'Nature' here, is of course, a literary trope, and unreal or 'un-natural; it functions merely as a sign, much as eighteenth-century shepherdesses did in certain kinds of European literature. Let us say that nature is being honored in these cases.

19. Notably, one of the most prominent metaphors used to describe male heroes in the epic is supplied by images of a tree in various formations of fertility or collapse. See McGrath 2004: 26ff.

20. At RV X.146, *araṇyānī* is actually personified as a feminine deity.

for they lack the *daṇḍa* which is so typical of male *kṣatriya* culture. In fact it is often the entry of a male which leads to the spoliation of such pristine settings, and in opposition to these vernal scenes stands Kurukṣetra, a topos that is entirely male. Let us examine the axis of such counterpoint.

When Duḥṣanta enters the forest and approaches the *āśrama* of Śakuntalā the region is delicately described: its trees and topography and fauna are all given in enchanting detail. The 'forest' (*vana*) is portrayed as,

> bilvārkakhadirākīrṇaṃ kapitthadhavasaṃkulam
> viṣamaṃ parvataprasthair aśmabhiś ca samāvṛtam
> nirjalaṃ nirmanuṣyaṃ ca bahuyojanamāyatam
> mṛgasaṃghair vṛtaṃ ghorair anyaiś cāpi vanecaraiḥ
>
> Crammed with *khadira* and *arka* and *bilva* trees, full of *kapittha*s and *dhava*s,
> rugged with plains and surrounded by rocks,
> without water or humanity, extending for many miles;
> filled with crowds of game and other wild forest creatures.
>
> I.63.12–13

Such places are uncivil and outlaw, and they are thoroughly natural and bountiful and without trace of human regulation or artifice.[21] It is as if these locations are environments of an especial order, and a retrojection in time occurs and the *kṛta yuga* is re-entered.[22] There, dharma is fourfold and complete, and there is neither decrepitude nor fear, and death itself is delayed or postponed. Beauty and serenity are predominant, as well as the moral excellence of the human beings in such a situation.[23]

21. Perhaps such regions are also to be inhabited by young Indo-European warriors—somewhat like a *vrātya* band—before they are ritually inducted back into adult and civil society. See Vidal-Naquet 1981: Pt. II; Parkhill 1994.

22. The opposite would be, *bahuprajā hrasvadehāḥ śīlācāravivarjitāḥ / mukhebhagāḥ striyo rājan bhaviṣyanti yugakṣaye* 'At the collapse of the eon, O king, women shall become destitute of good conduct, possess short bodies, have many offspring, and allow their mouths to be used as vulvas' (III.186.35). Women will also have 'diseased hair' (*keśaśūlāḥ*), and 'women become pregnant at seven or eight years old' (*saptavarṣāṣṭavarṣāś ca striyo garbhadharā*; III.186.52). 'Wives' (*nāryas*) at this time are 'perverse' (*viparītās*), 'having deceived' (*vañcayitvā*) their husbands; *vyuccaranty api duḥśīlā dāsaiḥ paśubhir eva ca* 'irritably, they also commit adultery with slaves and beasts' (III.186.55).

23. At II.19.4, the audience heard of a similar mountainous region, 'concealed, as it were, by forests—beloved of lovers—of *lodhra* trees' (*nigūḍheva lodhrāṇāṃ vanaiḥ kāmijanapriyaiḥ*). "The tree ... has yellow flowers, and the red powder scattered during the Holī festival is prepared from its bark" (Monier-Williams).

As Duḥṣanta enters further into this exquisitely pastoral terrain the poets lavish many *ślokas* upon the beauty and loveliness of the place: a location in which Śakuntalā appears as if its primary embellishment. The woods are,

> divaspṛśo'tha saṃghuṣṭāḥ pakṣibhir madhurasvaraiḥ
> virejuḥ pādapās tatra vicitrakusumāmbarāḥ
> teṣāṃ tatra pravāleṣu puṣpabhārāvanāmiṣu
> ruvanti rāvaṃ vihagāḥ ṣaṭpadaiḥ sahitā mṛdu
>
> Touching heaven, resonant with sweet-voiced birds,
> the trees shone there dressed with blossom:
> bent with burdens of flower among those new leaves,
> birds and insects were softly humming songs.
>
> I.64.9–10

As Duḥṣanta approaches the hermitage there are elephants and tigers and mighty snakes, all in a state of loving innocence and accompanied by a sound of *mantras* being chanted. The *āśrama* is *brahmalokapratīkāśam* 'a reflection of the world of Brahmā'. Apart from being naturally perfect it is also a zone of ritual perfection, where ascetic brahmins conduct lengthy and complex sacrifices (I.64.30–41). Thus the scene is set for the love affair between a king and Śakuntalā, and the birth of their son Bharat.

Similarly, as Yudhiṣṭhira says to his brother, Bhīma, as they approach Mount Śveta, *amānuṣagatiṃ prāptāḥ saṃsiddhāḥ smaḥ* 'we are become perfected, having obtained superhuman state'. It is the 'superhuman' state which these idyllic places possess that affects those who visit them with something akin to the condition of a previous and more perfect era. These places are uncivilized and untarnished by human time, and so able to perfect those—who in a right manner—make the effort either to enter or to inhabit them. They are situations of natural and unspoiled earthly power, and they have influence upon those who are ethically, emotionally, physically, and perhaps ritually, correct.

> kṛtvaiva kekāmadhuraṃ saṃgītaṃadhurasvaram
> citrān kalāpān vistīrya savilāsān madālasān
> mayūrān dadṛśuś citrān nṛtyato vanalāsakān
>
> They saw beautiful peacocks dancing, playing in the woods,
> lovely bands: having extended their plumes, sportive, languid,
> having made sweet cries, sounds that were sweet with song.
>
> III.155.54

The depiction of the beauties of Mount Śveta at III.155.27ff., for instance, are so delicately described as to form an intermission or hiatus within the impetus of the poem that functions as a lyrical interlude.[24] There is a fecundity and natural fertility about such spots which exist in a state of marvelous poise, in steady contrast to the male destructiveness of Kurukṣetra which is the nucleus or navel of the poem. I would propose—simply by virtue of this counterpoint—that these sites and this kind of loving description of exceptional topography partake of feminine qualities, as opposed to the masculine and bloodthirsty situation of Kurukṣetra. This is not to make the distinction that the feminine is 'nature' and that the male is 'culture': the equation is between *śama*, and *daṇḍa*, 'tranquillity' and 'hostility', which sometimes parallels the trajectory that exists between men and women in this Bronze Age world.

Thus an audience hears that once, before any of the horrific conflict of the poem began, Arjuna and Kṛṣṇa along with their women—wives and co-wives—set off for the forest to sport 'in the water' at a *vihāradeśa* 'playground'. There, delightful foods were arranged and music from flutes and drums and *vīṇās* was heard; the trees and the water were all beautiful and entrancing. The two men in the company of the women *cikrīḍuḥ* 'played'. Expensive presents were distributed among the ladies.

> kāścit prahṛṣṭā nanṛtuś cukruśuś ca tathāparāḥ
> jahasuś cāpārā nāryaḥ papuś cānyā varāsavam
> ruruduś cāpārās tatra prajaghnuś ca parasparam
> mantrayāmāsur anyāś ca rahasyāni parasparam
>
> Some joyous women danced and others cried out,
> others laughed, and some drank rum;
> here and there others wept and some slapped each other,
> others spoke in mutual privacy.
>
> I.214.23

It is a charming, sensitive and mildly amorous moment in the poem, where two heroes are at rest in the woods as their women disport and amuse themselves. An easiness and gentility is at work whose predominant tone is feminine and rococo, within a purely sylvan environment. It is a scene, almost a tableau, which immediately precedes an incident of extraordinary conflagration, when the forest of Khāṇḍava is consumed along with all its life in a fiery holocaust. This is an instant of destruction that Kurukṣetra later amplifies absolutely, for nothing survives either obliteration (I.217–19).

In these benign and genial environments, the sight of a woman in

24. See I.63.12, where the *āśrama* of Śakuntalā's father is portrayed; or, II.146.1ff., the description of Gandhmādana. Both places partake of this lyrical genre.

such lovely rural circumstances is sometimes the cause of a spontaneous emission of a man's semen, an event that has no feminine symmetry. Feminine sexuality is so potently charged in these edenic places that the mere glancing sight of a woman has such instant and passionate consequence.[25] Again, the negative reflection of such an image is Kurukṣetra, the site of death rather than generation.

To further this idea of opposition with the motif of natural landscape in the Mahābhārata, there occurs one particular metaphor which stands out from the text more than others: this is the metaphor of the *nadī*, the 'river'. It is an image constantly reiterated throughout the course of the epic.[26]

> śūrāṇāṃ ca nadīnāṃ ca prabhavā durvidāḥ ...
>
> The source of rivers and of heroes is difficult to know ...[27]
>
> I.127.11

Rivers and the great *kṣatriyas* are thus compounded, in both opposition and complement. This is a complex metaphor that recurs during times of physical conflict where armies are engaged with each other, and it is a metaphor which is freighted with many further internal metaphors and metonyms, which carry the similitude further.

There is the river, typically a river of blood, that flows towards Yama, death and the underworld, taking within its course the dead *kṣatriyas* who have perished in battle. The metaphor of the river is full of lesser images of islands, rocks, creatures, torn trees, et cetera, which refer to the dead elephants and horses, the deceased warriors, the broken chariots, and other disjecta of martial destruction.[28]

25. As when, *sahasā ... vikāraḥ samapadyata / tena susrāva reto'sya* 'suddenly an agitation occurred, by which his semen issued' (I.120.11).

26. Feldhaus 1995, has written at length about the connections between rivers and femininity in contemporary Maharashtra; see Ch. 2 especially. Harlan 2003: 98, observes: "It is widely accepted in India [today] that an ascetic's self-sacrifice in a sacred river delivers him from rebirth and gives him salvation. Self-sacrifice by *satis* and heroes also conveys liberation."

27. Many Indians today would argue that the greatest of the heroes in the poem—although his heroic action is limited—is Bhīṣma. His mother is the most fecund of all rivers, Gaṅgā, and she is perhaps the most *feminine* of mothers, therefore. It is remarkable that Bhīṣma himself becomes infertile, due to his vow of celibacy. Nevertheless, as we have seen, he is the one figure in the clan to organize the marital affairs of most of the younger men on the side of Pāṇḍu.

28. There is a unique reference to the *nadī* in Harivaṃśa LV.28–39, where the metaphor is that of a woman; the various elements of the metaphor concern parts of her body: hair, forehead, face, eyes, smiles, hips, breasts, navel, feet, clothing, and cosmetics. In this case the river is the Yamunā.

sa vīraḥ satyavān prājño dharmanityaḥ sudāruṇaḥ
yugāntakāle yanteva raudrāṃ prāskandayan nadīm
śoṇitodāṃ rathāvartāṃ hastyaśvakṛtarodhasam
kavacoḍupasaṃyuktāṃ māṃsapaṅkasamākulāṃ

That warrior, truthful, wise, always dharmic, compassionate,
caused a river to flow, awful, as a guide at the end of an eon.
Blood, its water; chariots, its whirlpools; its banks made of horses
and elephants,
crammed with mud and flesh, its rafts were joined breastplates ...

VII.13.8 and 10

Throughout the battle books, the formulae of this complicated image return again and again, always with slight poetic variation; destruction is made abstract and fluvial, a great fluid force that runs away with all that has been ruined and broken by armed conflict. This is the one image that stands directly opposed—conceptually—to the idyllic and pure form of landscape given above.[29]

To amplify this metaphor, during his long recumbent lecture Bhīṣma tells Yudhiṣṭhira that, 'the sea is the husband of rivers' (*āgaraḥ saritāṃ bhartā*; XII.59.122). That is, by implication, rivers function as a wife in the metaphor. In the same Book, Arjuna had told Yudhiṣṭhira—fusing the idea of dharma and river—that,

dhanād hi dharmaḥ sravati śailād girir nadī yathā

Dharma flows from wealth as a mountain river from a mountain.[30]

XII.8.23

It is significant, however, that the 'river', the *nadī*, which figures so vividly and constantly throughout the poem—especially during the battle books, where it operates as a metaphor of death—should here be used as a metaphor of the dharma that derives from or is generated by property. In this case and sense, dharma can be glossed as 'value', and it is something that runs directly as a river.[31]

29. On one occasion in the poem, *ātmā* 'spirit or self' receives this qualification as a *nadī*: with *puṇya* 'merit' and *satya* 'truth', and other aspects of non-material and ethical life being qualified as the crossings, the water, the banks, and so on. This is a unique instance of the metaphor, however (V.40.19ff.). There also exists the cultural association of 'the waters' (*āpas*), that primary force in the cosmos which was released by Indra's victory over Vṛtra, given in RV I.32.

30. This discussion, where Arjuna describes the importance of wealth for kingship, conflates the terms *artha* and *dhana*, both of which denote 'property', whether moveable or not and whether taxable or not; *vitta* being another term with a similar application and ambiguity. Whether this is exchange value or intrinsic value that is implied here is a moot point.

31. To enforce this reading a little further, heroes in battle are often described using the metaphor of being unapproachable 'mountains', as at VIII.43.38.

Rivers as similes and metaphors thus course throughout the poem, bearing several complex messages. The idea of the *nadī* is something that I would propose is, in its typical sense, potentially feminine; for rivers are, of course, almost always of feminine divinity and nature, their archetype being the Gaṅgā.[32] Yet here, however, femininity is shown as being deathly and not ideal.

As an encapsulation of this message, during his long deathbed narration to King Yudhiṣṭhira, Bhīṣma makes the comment that,

> yathā patyāśrayo dharmaḥ strīṇāṃ loke yudhiṣṭhira
> sa devaḥ sā gatir nānyā kṣatriyasya tathā dvijāḥ
>
> As the dharma of women, Yudhiṣṭhira, depends on the husband,
> he is a deity, there is no other way: just so the dharma of the *kṣatriya* depends on the brahmin.
>
> XIII.9.19

Such a statement indicates the potence intrinsic to women in this late Bronze Age culture, and their strength and command, for in this equation the feminine is in the place of the *kṣatriya*. For brahmins were the ones to possess authority whilst the *kṣatriyas* were the ones to possess power.[33] Women are seen to possess an influence which is sometimes charged with a certain negative force that is most well demonstrated by Draupadī's often volatile temperament.

Thus, from the point of view of literary tropes, the epic audience receives messages that I would propose visually enforce this dual aspect of the feminine: the tranquil and the destructive, the beneficent and the cruel. This is the deity that in myth possesses a binary function as either Ṣrī or a Kālī, Sītā or Durgā.[34]

As an appendix to this usage of riverine imagery, there also existed the *tīrthas* 'crossings' or 'fords', places that were situated upon the banks of rivers where it was not only possible to ford the stream but to also metaphorically 'cross over' to another world or life. The *nadī* in this case acts as a margin, an ultimate periphery, beyond which there exists a certain 'release' or *mokṣa*. For male *kṣatriyas*, battle—as a river—supplied this transcendent state.

In later historical times—during the more classical period—pilgrimage to sacred rivers with the purpose of bathing at appropriately

32. 'Queen of seas' (*samudramahiṣī,*; III.185.18). See XIII.27.25ff. for a good description of the divine beneficence of the Gaṅgā.

33. Dumont 1966 discusses this equation extensively.

34. Kinsley 1986 offers an excellent catalogue of the binary nature of the goddess in her many aspects and forms.

sanctified *tīrthas* to some extent displaced the central and dominating function of the sacrifice in ritual life. Such *tīrthayātras* 'pilgrimages' were less brahminically oriented and controlled and were open to the participation of women. These specifically fluvial landscapes were considered as benign and supernaturally charged, and stood in counterpart to brutal death and, by extension, to all that occurred at Kurukṣetra.

2. Sexuality

In the Aśvamedha *parvan* a brahmin's wife speaks of her marital dharma. This is not exactly a *kṣatriya* disposition, but the import is applicable to all women. She says,

> satyaṃ ratiś ca dharmaś ca svargaś ca guṇanirjitaḥ
> strīṇāṃ patisamādhīnaṃ kāṅkṣitaṃ ca dvijottama
> ṛtur mātuḥ pitur bījaṃ daivataṃ paramaṃ patiḥ
> bhartuḥ prasādāt strīṇāṃ vai ratiḥ putraphalaṃ tathā
>
> Truth and delight and dharma and heaven are won by the qualities
> of women; and, O best twice-born, the desired union with a husband.
> The mense of a mother, the seed of a father—the husband is
> the highest divinity—truly, because of the grace of a husband
> the fruit of a son is the delight of women!
>
> XIV.93.24–25

This is the standard paradigm of conjugal dharma, along with a hypothetical physiology concerning conception, where feminine blood from the uterus is an active ingredient in procreation by its admixture with male semen.[35] Let us consider the question of feminine sexuality in general, as it is manifest throughout this epic.

Vidura, in a passage already cited, says that of the seven *doṣāḥ* 'wrongs' for men, women are in the first place. Here, he is speaking of addiction, 'vice or passion' (*vyasana*; V.33.63–64).[36] The others are dice, hunting, drinking, bitter speech, cruel punishment, and despoilment of property.[37] On the other hand, an audience never hears of women being

35. 'The semen' (*retas*) 'enters her mense' (*sa vai tasyā rajāpadyate*; I.85.10), which led to the conception of the *garbha* 'foetus'. 'The vital air draws out the uterus and foetus, semen is mixed with sap and blossom in season' (*vāyuḥ samutkarṣati garbhayonim ṛtau retaḥ puṣparasānupṛktam*; I.85.14). This idea of menstrual blood and semen fusing to create an embryo is fully described in the Carakasaṃhitā IV.3.

36. Thus the 'killer of an embryo' (*bhrūṇahā*), although Vidura decries him, is not on this list. Such a person—not necessarily a man—does not deserve 'guest water' (V.38.4).

37. In Manu VII.47, women are in the fifth place in a similar series: those women were intended as barbarian.

excessively addicted to the company or pleasure of men.[38] However, Vidura also speaks of the 'fresh butter of joy' (*harṣasya navanītāni*) as being eightfold, and therein lists *saṃnipātaś ca maithune*, 'sexual intercourse' (V.33.79). Yet prior to this—in his series—he cites the society of friends, attainment of wealth, and embracing with a son. It is noteworthy that sexual delight is of a lesser valence in this set.[39]

Perhaps this libidinal capacity of women is profoundly connected with the myth that women enjoy more sexual gratification than men.[40] The narrative of king Bhaṅgāśvana in the Anuśāsana *parvan* is a typical example of such a view, where the king is transformed by Indra—upon bathing in a lake—and becomes a woman. He, as a woman, avers that, *striyāḥ puruṣasaṃyoge prītir abhyadhikā sadā* 'the satisfaction of a woman in sexual union with a man is always superior' (XIII.12.47).

In the narrative of Aṣṭāvakra in the same book, Bhīṣma describes a woman who speaks of the pleasures of sexual congress, and how women, therefore, *na jānanti* 'do not know' father, clan, mother, brothers, husband, sons, and the husband's brothers (XIII.20.66). Even the deities, she says, Agni and Varuṇa included, cannot comprehend *priyāḥ strīṇām* 'the pleasure of women': *kāmo ratiśīlā hi yoṣitaḥ* 'for love is the conduct of woman's passion' (XIII.20.64).

> sthavīrāṇām api strīṇāṃ bādhate maithunajvaraḥ
>
> Sexual passion binds even strong women.
>
> XIII.22.5

It is remarkable that during this brief speech of four *ślokas* by the *strī* 'the woman', she employs three terms to denote femininity: *strī*, *yoṣit*, and *nārī*. She closes her remarks with the comment that such pursuits by women are destructive of clan—playing on the homophony of *kula* and *kūla*, 'clan' and 'bank'—'like the best of rivers destroy their banks' (*ghnanti kūlānīva saridvarāḥ*; XIII.20.67). Feminine sexuality destroys boundaries.

It is this imagined sexual voracity of women which is *anatikramaṇīyā* 'not to be surpassed', and the extraordinary pleasures therein which are inaccessible to men—or the male imagination in this poetry—which perhaps qualifies them as potentially stronger and therefore threatening when their negative mood or aspect is engaged.[41] According

38. Apart from that one occasion when Karṇa was insulting Śalya in Book Eight.

39. Vidura is quick to say that *saṃdhim paradārābhir* 'congress with another's wife' is not acceptable (V.33.89).

40. This is what I would describe as a male myth. Women do not make this claim.

41. Harlan 2003: 74 reports the contemporary pejorative and alternate view from Rajasthan,

to Aṣṭāvakra, it is because of this intimidating—for men—sexuality that, *na strī svātantryam arhati* 'women do not deserve independence' (XIII.21.12). Yet, on the other hand, women in the epic do not speak of male sexuality with such projected anxiety.

The narrative of Pañcacūḍa, also in Book Thirteen, reiterates much of this view of feminine sexuality that Aṣṭāvakra has described:

> dṛṣṭvaiva puruṣaṃ hṛdyaṃ yoniḥ praklidyate striyaḥ
>
> For having seen a charming man, the vagina of a woman becomes moist.
>
> XIII.38.26

Yet Pañcacūḍa in the same breath can say:

> prājñasya puruṣasyeha yathā vacas tathā striyaḥ
>
> As of a wise man, so too is the speech of women.
>
> XIII.38.24

The gnomic or enigmatic quality that obtains here concerning the language of the feminine necessitates an act of interpretation if the message is to be correctly understood, for there exists the possibility of more than one meaning to such communication, where nuance and innuendo operate. As we have seen throughout the epic, the expression of dharma in its pronouncement is always various in signification and requires interpretation and commentary. There is a polyvalence of meaning at play, a necessary ambivalence before any message is received, concerning both wisdom and feminine use of language. This polyvalence appears to be aligned with how feminine sexuality is conceived within the epic, somehow it is beyond male patterns of dominance, being inherently elusive.

Bhīṣma, the ancient celibate, in response to Yudhiṣṭhira's further enquiry on the subject of the feminine, says:

> agnir iha pramadā dīpto māyāś ca mayajā vibho
> kṣuradhārā viṣaṃ sarpo mṛtyur ity ekataḥ striyaḥ
>
> Here—fire is a wanton woman, blazing illusion, illusive, O king,
> bearing a razor, poison, a snake, death: altogether—are women!
>
> XIII.40.4

---

where "insult songs (*galiyan*) that women sing during wedding festivities ... proclaim, among other things, the sexual ineptitude of grooms and their male relations as well as the sexual voraciousness of their female relations, especially mothers."

The feminine is obviously dangerous, inherently out of reach for male constraint and thus potentially destabilizing of male order. Bhīṣma goes on to describe women—in another one of his didactic narratives—as being of 'vehement and blunt courage' (*tīkṣṇās tīkṣṇaparākramāḥ*; XIII.43.22). He adds that they are only happy 'in sexual intercourse with men' (*maithune saṃgame nṛbhiḥ*).

To extend this model of danger into the realms of satire, in nice contrast to the example of femininity where women are speakers of truth and on occasion perform formulaic expressions of grief, there are, in Karṇa's eyes at least, the Madraka women. In an attempt to insult Śalya, his Madrasi charioteer, Karṇa decries the lack of dharma among the women of Madras, where there exists a complete lack of feminine sensibility for politesse and decorum.

> puṃbhir vimiśrā nāryaś ca jñātā ajñātāḥ svayecchayā
> pītvā sīdhuṃ sagomāṃsaṃ nardanti ca hasanti ca ...
> vāsāṃsy utsṛjya nṛtyanti striyo yā madyamohitāḥ
>
> The women mingle with men, known and unknown, according to wish,
> having drunk rum with beef, they laugh and they shriek ...
> Women, who drunk on spirits, having cast off their clothes, dance.
>
> VIII.27.76–77 and 85

Such women are *mithune'saṃyatās* 'unbridled in copulation', and 'their actions are without control' (*yathākāmacarās*) and they urinate like camels or asses (VIII.27.86).

Karṇa, some *adhyāyas* later, describes in a similar fashion the dissolute ways of the women of Vāhlīka, stressing their promiscuous and undiscriminating sexuality, their frequent inebriation, their lubricious dancing and voracious meat-eating (VIII.30.16–33).

> ... drakṣyāmi sthūlaśaṅkhāḥ śubhāḥ striyaḥ
> manaḥśilojjvalāpāṅgā gauryastrikakudāñjanāḥ
> kevalājinasaṃvītāḥ kūrdantyaḥ priyadarśanāḥ
>
> ... I see beautiful women, possessing large vulvas,
> the corners of their eyes blazing with red arsenic, peaked with yellow ointment,
> beautiful, leaping, covered in skins.
>
> VIII.30.21–22

This is not to say that such characteristics of drunkenness and sexual promiscuity are entirely feminine and never demonstrated by male heroes. It is to say that the hypothetical purity of the feminine has more at stake, perhaps because it so charged with the ideal of women being more accustomed to the nature of dharma. When this propriety falls away the image is one that is especially threatening and horrible for men: these would not be the loyal women capable of singing about the fame of their deceased menfolk.

In this society, constraint is the mark of decency and dharmic equilibrium, and for women—who are more attuned and aware of good order, as we have observed above—to depart from that state of decorum is particularly vile. Such behavior is not so distasteful when exhibited by men, because ferocity and the creation of disorder is very much a specific object of *kṣatriya* conduct. Once again, we observe an active asymmetry between the male and feminine—they are not equal— and the standards and codes do not mirror each other but finely complement each other.

Concerning prostitution and women who can be termed as 'loose', in terms of myth, of all the deities, it is only Śiva who appears, *strībhiś cānu sahasraśaḥ* 'followed by a thousand women' (III.40.5).[42] No other male deity makes such an entry into the poem. The activities of Śiva are thus accessible to women, which is not always the case with men, and these women who accompany the deity are devotees of a sort. Śiva, being a figure of boundaries and extremes, of overt sexuality and sexual ambiguity—as with Arjuna at the court of Virāṭa—is naturally more available to the feminine.

In the Virāṭa *antaḥpura*, when Arjuna disguises himself as a eunuch and feminizes himself among the courtesans and wives, he describes his activities by saying, *gāyāmi nṛtyāmy atha vādayāmi* 'I sing, I dance, I play music' (IV.10.8). Yet, we have repeatedly observed how for married women there remain many other areas of extraordinary influence and power: dancing and singing are marginal, in fact, to what women accomplish within their establishments. In the *zenana*, there is a strict ranking of household and sexual status at work, and intimacy is definitely not the feminine's sole interest in life.

In the Mahābhārata the question of prostitution—women who transgress the boundaries of household or marital sexuality—scarcely arises except by implication.[43] The term for 'whoring' or 'fornication' is

42. At III.163.39 Śiva is also, *saha strībhir*.

43. 'Unchaste woman' (*bandhakī*). 'As a polluted woman is not led into the house of a brahmin' (*na ... nīyate ... strī śrotriyasyeva gṛhe praduṣṭā*; II.57.15). 'There are whores in the land of gamblers' (*bhavanti deśe bandhakyaḥ kitavānām*; II.61.1). 'That man does not live whom the whores praise' (*yaṃ praśaṃsanti banhdakyo na sa jīvati mānavaḥ*; V.38.42).

grāmya: something which was originally done in a village.[44] Given the social status and rank of most of the figures in the poem, this aspect of overt and specific sexuality tends to fall under the domain of the co-wife or lover, only now and then is there mention of the *veśyā* 'courtesan'.[45]

In the tale of Ṛśyaśṛṅga, he—a young man—has never encountered a woman before, and is unaware of sexual difference. He describes a passing courtesan to his father as, *na vai hrasvo na atidīrgho manasvī* 'neither short nor tall, of good spirits' (III.112.1). He continues to portray the ornaments, hair, and limbs of this man to his father, emphasizing her charms: the breasts being *dvau piṇḍau* 'two round lumps'. The sight of all these enchantments causes 'great affection and delight' (*prītiḥ parā ... ratiś ca*) to arise within the young man's heart. He describes a first kiss to the father:

> vaktreṇa vaktraṃ praṇidhāya śabdaṃ
> cakāra tan me'janayat praharṣam
>
> He touched the mouth with the mouth: it made a sound
> that caused me joy!
>
> III.112.12

She-he, being intoxicated, then 'seduced the son of the *ṛṣi*' (*pralobhayāmāsa sutaṃ maharṣeḥ*; III.111.16).

The father merely tells the son that such personages are *rakṣāṃsi* 'demons'—given in the neuter—that are cruel, wicked and to be avoided. Naturally, the youth escapes his father's strictures and succeeds in finding the *veśyā*, who takes him aboard her pleasure vessel and keeps him in the *antaḥpura*. Instantly, the skies rain: the lack of rains being the cause for the elaborate seduction, for Ṛśyaśṛṅga had been so innocent and pure that—in a situation of drought—it had been prophesied that only the awakening of his sexuality would cause rainfall to occur (III.113.10).

There is also the *gaṇikā* 'whore', as when in Book Four King Virāṭa commands that the roads to the town be adorned and that the important personages of the court go out to meet his son, Uttara, who is returning from victorious battle.[46] He orders that 'adorned whores' (*gaṇikāś ca svalaṃkṛtāḥ*) be part of the welcome. Dhṛtarāṣṭra makes

44. As at II.61.20.

45. Monier-Williams glosses this term *veśyā*, as 'intranda', to be entered; one who inhabits a brothel.

46. There are also *puṃścalī* 'women who run after men', harlots, as at V.37.28. Vidura tells his king that these are to be 'shunned' (*varjanīyāḥ*), as too should *vidhavā bālaputrā* 'widows with infant sons'. Old man Vidura, however, also thinks that men who practice frequent bathing will attract 'the choicest women' (*pravāraś ca nāryaḥ*; V.37.29).

a similar command when Kṛṣṇa is about to enter his city: he offers enormous gifts of wealth and instructs that his sons and grandsons go out to meet the guest, along with thousands of 'adorned and lovely royal courtesans' (*svalaṃkṛtāś ca kalyāṇyaḥ ... vāramukhyā*; V.84.15). Both of these instances indicate a certain high standing for an undefined class of loose women.

Before his fifth throw in the dicing game, Yudhiṣṭhira stakes a hundred thousand *dāsī* 'women servants'. These are depicted as:

> ... taruṇyo ... prabhadrikāḥ
> kambukeyūradhāriṇyo niṣkakaṇṭhyaḥ svalaṃkṛtāḥ
> mahārhamālyābharaṇāḥ suvastrāś candanokṣitāḥ
> maṇīnhema ca bibhratyaḥ sarvā vai sūkṣmavāsasaḥ
> ... carantīmāḥ kuśalā nṛtyasāmasu
>
> ... tender ... beautiful,
> wearing upper-arm bracelets of shell, decorated with necklaces of gold pieces,
> bearing costly garlands, possessing lovely garments smeared with sandal;
> all wearing fine clothes with gold and jewels,
> they are proceeding skilled in song and dance.
>
> II.54.12–14

Such portrayals of this kind of femininity are rare in the poem, as too is the uncommon mention of the 'eunuch or transvestite', men who have adopted a feminine way of life and who have incorporated feminine qualities as part of their daily bearing and psyche—much as Arjuna behaves in the *zenana*.[47]

There is no mention of feminine homoeroticism in the Mahābhārata, nor of sodomy.[48]

As an intriguing adjunct to the above there exists the account of Kaikeyī in the micro-epic of the Rāmāyaṇa, in Book Three. There, a thoroughly

47. Duḥśāsana insults the Pāṇḍavas with this term at II.68.10. He also refers to the five brothers collectively as 'fruitless seed of sesamum' (*yathāphalāḥ ṣaṇḍhatilā*; II.68.13). Another term for 'eunuch' is *ṣaṇḍha*, which also means, "the vulva of a woman who has no menstrual periods and no breasts ... the neuter gender" (Monier-Williams). Duḥśāsana also calls Bhīma a 'cow' (*gaur*; II.68.19). All these terms of abuse are freighted with a latent sexual posture, the qualities of feminine sexuality for a hero being somewhat troublesome and to be avoided except in denigration.

48. Under the category of possible adulteries, Manu cites the intercourse of girls and girls, and women and girls: *kanyaiva kanyāṃ yā kuryāt* and *yā tu kanyāṃ prakuryāt strī* (VIII.369–370).

feminine compulsion is portrayed, which male desire cannot resist: this is elicited via beauty and the use of ornament and personal charm.

Kaikeyī, one of a pair of co-wives to Daśaratha, had approached her husband, *sarvābharaṇabhūṣitā* 'adorned with all her jewelry'; *śucismitā* 'smiling brightly'; *hasantīva* 'as it were—laughing'; *bibhratī rūpam uttamam* 'bearing great beauty' (III.261.19–20). 'Having perceived her own power' (*ātmano balam ājñāya*), she puts Daśaratha into a position where—as a royal *kṣatriya*—he must sustain the validity of his word, a promise that she has drawn from him.

There is no woman in the narrative of Mahābhārata who is quite as conniving with her sexuality as this wife. Kaikeyī fully exploits her femininity vis-à-vis men's desire, and her vicious calculation in fact causes her husband later to die of grief. Women in Mahābhārata are generally not portrayed in so thoroughly negative a fashion, nor in a light which purely emphasizes cosmetic appearance and sexual charm.

To conclude this section, let us examine the use of one word. *Yoni*, which means—on a level of metaphor—'source,' technically refers to the 'vagina, uterus, receptacle', and it is a term often used throughout the poem to indicate purity or profound origination, the font of initial strength. Kṛṣṇa is described as *devayonitas* 'womb of the deities', and this is because he is *vasutva* 'the source of riches' (V.68.3). Like a womb, *atattvaṃ kurute tattvam* 'he makes unreality real', he is the genetrix itself (V.68.14).[49] In many cultures, genitalia supply terms for abuse, but not here: in fact, the situation is the opposite.

3. *Women Heroes Today*

Women in epic Mahābhārata resound in contemporary and sometimes pre-modern Indian society as icons of culture and as models for social action, as the old epic continues to engender cultural forms today. "The importance of this great epic, also called the Pañcama Veda ... in the collective psyche of the Indian people is well established, and has sustained their beliefs and governed their conduct to this day."[50] Draupadī

49. He is also 'the sea of words' (*vācaḥ samudram*): a very nominal sense of that sourceful reality (V.69.5).

50. Shah 1995: 2. Mankekar 1999: 251, quotes the Tamil writer Subramania Bharati who "wrote a poem on Draupadi entitled 'Panchali's Vow', in which he compared her disrobing to colonial domination." She adds, "Gandhi and his contemporaries focussed on Draupadi's agency to encourage Hindu *women* to participate in the freedom struggle." Viewers "appropriate Draupadi's disrobing, the moment when she is at her most vulnerable, to reflect on and critique their own positions in family, community, and nation" (ibid., 254).

as a figure of charged femininity continues to reverberate nowadays across much of India. Let us look at four examples of such present-day resonance; for by regarding these modern instances a certain heuristic utility can be evoked, to cast light upon how the medium of epic poetry might have once flourished.

Firstly, the question of polyandry continues to fascinate audiences and Draupadī still receives attention in the contemporary South Asian press. In the *Times Of India* recently an article appeared which claimed: "Incidentally, the Toda believe that they are descendants of the Pandavas and, hence, practice polyandry. But the threat of extinction has made them monogamous." The whole of page six of this issue of the paper was devoted to the question of polyandry, the headline being "Modern Draupadis." Cinema, demography, the issue of dowries: these supplied just a few of the article's subtitles.[51]

"It is sheer economics that is behind these 'modern Draupadis,'" writes Kuldeep Singh Deep, citing the example of "Gandukula village [in the Punjab] where seven brothers share two wives between them."[52] The caption for this article stated:

> And you thought polyandry died with the Mahabharata ... As land-holdings shrink and an adverse sex ratio makes women scarce, wife-buying and sharing are no longer frowned upon in Punjab's Malwa region ... Small landholdings—only 3.5 acres on average—have resulted in the revival of polyandry ... In this scenario, they [the brothers] can either forcibly marry a distant relative or buy a wife. In both cases, the brothers can manage only one woman among themselves, resulting in wife-sharing.[53]

51. *Times Of India*, Ahmedabad, August, 7th, 2005, p.6. The practice of unmarried brothers sharing the wife of married brother—sexually—is not uncommon in north India today.

52. Ibid.

53. "The Todas are a tiny community that lives in the Nilagiri mountains in southern India and claim descent from the Pandavas. Among them fraternal polyandry was a common practice until recently, though with modern civilization making inroads into their munds, their villages, this has become rare now. Apart from their marriage customs, their sexual mores too are strikingly different from mainstream India's as well as from those of all nearby communities, including other tribal communities.... A husband to the woman does not marry her separately only one of them [of the brothers] does so, usually the eldest one, but she becomes equally the wife of all of them. And if a brother is born after the woman's marriage, she becomes even this child's wife.... Since the woman lives with all the brothers simultaneously, there is no way of deciding who the father of any particular child is. What the Todas do is to conduct a ceremony called pursutpimi. The ceremony is usually performed in the eighth month of pregnancy and consists of presenting a bow and an arrow to the woman. The husband who performs the pursutpimi becomes the official father of the child. The child will, all his life, be known as this man's child. All the children born to the woman will be considered his until another husband performs the bow ceremony.... Such is the importance of the ceremony that even if an unmarried girl conceives, the ceremony has to

The informant in this article, Kuldeep Singh Deep, "a social activist, playwright and teacher at the secondary school in Boha ... stages street plays to spread awareness." He was reported as saying, "women are reduced to tears when they watch the play but tears won't help. They have to find a voice so that Draupadi remains not just a character in an epic."

In the district of Kacch an acquaintance once told me that, "Bhīṣma is a symbol of helplessness, for being the greatest and most powerful of the heroes he was still unable to protect Draupadī when she was being undressed. Human beings in general are this helpless and Draupadī is also a symbol of how completely helpless modern women are in India today, for she is the most abused of women."[54]

Secondly, concerning the performance today of the *svayaṃvara* rite, a Gujarat Tourist Board broadsheet issued during the summer of 2005, made the statement about a festival held each year at the town of Tarṇetar where:

> The special feature of the fair is matchmaking between the youth of the Kolis, Bharwads and Rabaris. It is believed that the svayamvar of the Panchal Princess Draupadi was held here wherein Arjuna won her hand. Even today, the tradition of svayamvar continues and the tribal girls attending the fair have a right to choose their husbands from the assembled youth. The youth come attired in exquisite clothes and jewelry with ornate umbrellas, which signifies that they are ready for a matrimonial alliance.[55]

This is a rare instance of a marriage form that does not exist elsewhere in the modern India.[56] It is the only attested instance of *svayaṃvara* proceedings that I have ever encountered. Most marriages

---

be performed [and] it is usually done by a man who is eligible to marry her, most commonly by her maternal uncle's son since he is her first and natural choice as husband. If a husband dies after performing the bow ceremony and no other husband performs it afterwards, then all the children born in future to the woman will be considered his, even long after the man is dead." Posted on mahabharata_study@yahoogroups.com, February 22, 2006, by Satyachaitanya. On this list-site there were similar reports of polyandry in Himachal Pradesh, in regions where there are temples dedicated to the Pāṇḍavas: February, 28.

54. Dr. Pulin Vasa, MD.

55. Gujarat Tourist Board pamphlet, nd.

56. Except perhaps among *kṣatriya* Nayar women of Kerala, who sometimes selected their mates: see Jeffrey 1992. Until recently, matriliny was typical and polyandry "almost certainly existed, though it is hotly denied" (36). He also writes (24), "the need for soldiers made life uncertain for young men from military castes. To ensure constant management of family properties, inheritance began to be traced through the children of a family's women ... [H]er brothers, when they returned from the wars, were the recognised male guardians." With the institution of a twentieth-century peace came a gradual end to this system.

in the subcontinent, traditional and otherwise, are arranged by parents and the young couple are merely introduced in the period prior to the ceremony. In some cases bride and groom do not even see each other until after the ritual is completed. The Rabari clan in Kacch maintain many such connections to the Pāṇḍavas in their charter myths and ritual practices.

Thirdly, looking at local dramatic traditions, in his study of traditional Draupadī cults in south India, Hiltebeitel writes,

> Yet the song is not just about the epic Draupadī. The goddess who tours the village on her "chariot" and whose epic story is enacted on stage will have her fixed and locally presiding stone icon in her village temple, where her priest, or *pūcāri*, honors her with songs that are similar to the dramatists' song in one signal respect: both invoke her as "the lady who resides in Gingee." At all such singings, the claim is thus renewed that Draupadī is not only the chief heroine of the *Mahābhārata*, but a goddess, connected with the rural market town of Gingee.[57]

Hiltebeitel writes concerning Draupadī's marital situation: "her relation to the five Pāṇḍavas casts her as their 'Supreme Śakti'—all-powerful goddess—rather than their wife."[58]

This conflation of heroine and deity, of Sanskrit epic and local drama, of ritual, poetry, and myth, is not uncommon in contemporary twenty-first-century India. The Indo-European epic has filtered down through song and local theater and visual iconography for millennia, and the figures of the poem are important cultural motifs that continue to sustain modern-day Hinduism. In fact such figures are common in cinema and on television.[59]

Harlan, in her study of contemporary women's hero narratives in Rajastan, writes:

> Women typically regard death not as a testimony from the past that supports a claim to status now, but as a beginning of the hero's availability to the family in succeeding generations, including and

57. Hiltebeitel 1988: 3.

58. Ibid., 6.

59. Sax 2002: 121, offers an interesting variant on contemporary Mahābhārata performance, where "competitive bardic recitation ... by Rajput men in the local dialect [in which] one bard challenges another to recall some part of the story; if the man so challenged is unable to recall the detail, he is considered defeated ... Less often, one bard will 'put down' another by interrupting his recitation with a correction, but this is rare because bardic competition is governed by a code of politeness."

especially the present generation, to which the hero continues to bestow blessings, and by which the hero continues to require propitiation.[60]

Sax, in his description of the *pāṇḍav līlā* in the Himalayas, contrasts the roles—as they are performed—of Draupadī and Kuntī.[61]

> Daughter-in-law and mother-in-law embody both sides of the distinction between the fierce, bloodthirsty goddess and sexually active female, on the one hand, and the benevolent, vegetarian goddess and nurturing, nonsexual mother, on the other.

One notes the simultaneously creative and destructive aspects of the feminine once again at work.

Mankekar, in her examination of how women in India responded to the televised film of the Mahābhārata, relates the account of one of her informants, who had been raped by the father-in-law. Seeing how Draupadī was treated in the *sabhā*—in the film—the informant then spoke of her own experience.

> Surjeet Kaur had appropriated the story of Draupadi to speak of her sexual abuse at the hands of her father-in-law. Like Draupadi, she had been dishonored by an in-law ... And like Draupadi's husbands, who watched passively while she was being disrobed, Surjeet's husband had pretended not to notice what had happened.[62]

The feminine as it is depicted in epic Mahābhārata—in the folklore of the modern Indian press, in village ritual and theater, and on the silver screen—often portrays these epic women as figures of grief and sorrow. For an audience, the mnemonics of the poem constantly play upon this mode, insofar as women are described. Male heroes suffer in terms of death, but feminine anguish is much more vital and social.

I would like to close this study of the feminine in this epic with a brief visual snapshot, similar to what Ananda Coomaraswamy shows in his book on *Early Indian Architecture,* where he gives close-up details of the bas-reliefs of Sāñcī.[63] The man on horseback at Sāñcī is the young Buddha.

There are not many images from civic life given in Mahābhārata,

60. Harlan 2003: 88.

61. Sax 2002: 135.

62. Mankekar 1999: 130. "For even as women accepted Draupadi as a symbol of Indian Womanhood, they used her disrobing to critique their own lives and to theorize gender relations in the worlds they inhabited" (ibid., 225).

63. Coomaraswamy 1992: 6 and 8.

and when they do occur they are especially charming. Firstly, there is an earlier image given in the poem, when king Duḥṣanta had left his capital in order to go hunting and embarked upon his affair with Śakuntalā: what soon became the occasion for the conception of Bharata, who gives his name to this epic and to the rising of the Kurus (I.62.2).

> *prāsādavaraśṛṅgasthāḥ ... dadṛśus taṃ śūram ātmayaśaskaram ...*
> *striyaḥ ... tuṣṭuvuḥ puṣpavṛṣuś ca sasṛjus tasya mūrdhani*
>
> The women—standing in royal palace turrets—looked at that hero who made his own fame ...
> The women sang praises and threw showers of flowers on his head.
>
> I.63.5 and 8

There is another similar prospect when Arjuna arrives for the first time at Dvārakā:

> anvalokeṣu nārīṇāṃ sahasrāṇi śatāni ca
> bhojavṛṣṇyandhakānāṃ ca samavāyo mahān abhūt
>
> There was a great assembly of hundreds and thousands
> of Andhaka, Vṛṣṇi, and Bhoja women looking on ...
>
> I.210.18

As part of the charming image of Kṛṣṇa, traveling towards Hāstinapura as an ambassador of concord, there is given:

> taṃ kiranti mahātmānaṃ vanyaiḥ puṣpaiḥ sugandhibhiḥ
> striyaḥ pathi samāgamya sarvabhūtahite ratam
>
> Women—having assembled on the road—scattered sweet-smelling woodland
> blossoms on that great-souled one intent upon the good of all beings.
>
> V.82.14

The occasion here is the formal entry of Kṛṣṇa, on a chariot with all his guards and riders, to the court of Dhṛtarāṣṭra: he comes as an ambassador of peace. The picture—which comes to mind with facility—is of,

> vedikāpāśritābhiś ca samākrāntāny anekaśaḥ
> pracalantīva bhāreṇa yoṣidbhir bhavāny uta
>
> Palaces, with young married women in great numbers
> crowded on balconies; borne down, trembling, as it were, with the weight ...
>
> V.92.25

It is an image of women looking, of their eagerness and keen light-heartedness; and despite the gravity of their multitude, they are admiring the man who attempts to bring peace and not war.

'May there be peace' is the opening line of his speech, *śamaḥ syāt* (V.93.3).

BIBLIOGRAPHY

ABORI	*Annals of the Bhandarkar Oriental Research Institute*
BICS	*Bulletin of the Institute of Classical Studies*
HOS	*Harvard Oriental Series*
IHQ	*Indian Historical Quarterly*
IIJ	*Indo-Iranian Journal*
JAS	*Journal of Asian Studies*
JAOS	*Journal of the American Oriental Society*
JIES	*Journal of Indo-European Studies*
JRAS	*Journal of the Royal Asiatic Society*
KZ	*Zeitschrift für vergleichende Sprachforschung auf dem Gebiete der indogermanischen Sprachen*
MAS	*Modern Asian Studies*

Alexiou, Margaret (1974), *The Ritual Lament in Greek Tradition*, Cambridge.

Allchin, F. R. (ed.) (1995), *The Archaeology of Early Historic South Asia*, Cambridge.

Allen, N. J. (1996), "The Hero's Five Relations: A Proto Indo-European Story," in: J. Leslie (ed.), *Myth and Myth Making*, London, 5-20.

—— (1999), "Arjuna and the Second Function: a Dumézilian Crux," *JRAS* Third Series, IX.3 (November): 403-418.

—— (2002), "Mahābhārata and Iliad: A Common Origin?" *ABORI* 83: 165-177.

Altekar, V. S. (1956), *Position and Status of Women in Indian Civilization*, Delhi.

Apffel-Marglin, F. (1985) *Wives of the God-King*, New York.

Apte, U. M. (1978), *The Sacrament of Marriage in Hindu Society*, Delhi.

Austin, J. L. (1975), *How to Do Things with Words*, Cambridge, Mass.

Bachofen, Johann Jakob (1948), *Das Mutterrecht: Eine Untersuchung über die Gynaikokratie der alten Welt nach ihrer religiösen und rechtlichen Natur*, in: *Gesammelte Werke*, vols. II and III. Basel.

Bakker, E., and Ahuvia Kahane (eds.) (1997), *Written Voices, Spoken Signs*, Cambridge, Mass.

Bean, Susan S., and Shashi Tharoor (2006), *Epic India. M.F. Husain's Mahabharata Project*, Salem, Mass.

Benveniste, E. (1969), *Le Vocabulaire des Institutions Indo-Européenes*, 2 vols., Paris.
Bhardwaj, Surinder Mohan (1973), *Hindu Places of Pilgrimage in India*, Berkeley.
Bhattacharya, Pradip (2005), Panchakanya. *The Five Heroines of India's Epics*, Calcutta.
Bhawalkar, Vanamala (1999), *Women in the Mahābhārata*, Delhi.
Biardeau, Madeleine (1981), *L'hindouisme. Anthropologie d'une Civilisation*, Paris.
Blok, Josine and Peter Mason (eds.) (1987), *Sexual Asymmetry Studies in Ancient Society*, Amsterdam.
Bose, Sugata (2006), *A Hundred Horizons*, Cambridge, Mass.
Brockington, Mary (ed.) (2002), *Stages and Transitions*, Proceedings of the Second Dubrovnik International Conference on the Sanskrit Epics and Purāṇas, Zagreb.
Brockington, Mary and Peter Schreiner (eds.) (1999), *Composing a Tradition: Concepts, Techniques and Relationships*, Zagreb.
Brown, W. Norman (1972), "Duty as Truth in Ancient India," *Proceedings of The American Philosophical Society*, CXVI: 252-268.
Bryant, Edwin (2001), *The Quest for the Origins of Vedic Culture*, New York.
Buck, Carl Darling (1949), *A Dictionary of Selected Synonyms in the Principal Indo-European Languages*, reprinted. 1988, Chicago and London.
Carakasaṃhitā (1981), ed. Jādavji Trikamji, Delhi.
Carter, A. T. (1974), "A Comparative Analysis of Systems of Kinship and Marriage in South Asia," in: *Proceedings of the Royal Anthropological Institute*, 1973: 29-54.
Chari, V. K. (1990), *Sanskrit Criticism*, Honolulu.
Chatterjee, C. K. (1978), *Studies in the Rites and Rituals of Hindu Marriage In Ancient India*, Calcutta.
Chaudhuri, J. B. (1938), "Position of Mother in Vedic ritual," *IHQ* 14: 822-830.
Connelly, Joan Breton (2006), *Portrait of a Priestess*, Princeton.
Coomaraswamy, Ananda K. (1992), *Essays in Early Indian Architecture*, ed. Michael W. Meister, Delhi.
Crumley, C. M. (1995), "Heterarchy and the Analysis of Complex Societies," in: R. M. Ehrenreich, C. M. Crumley, and J. E. Levy (eds.), *Archaeological Papers of the American Anthropological Society Association* 6, Washington D.C.
Das, Veena (1982), *Structure and Cognition: Aspects of Hindu Caste and Ritual*, New York.
—— (2007), *Life And Words*, Berkeley.

Das, Veena, et al. (eds.) (1999), *Tradition, Pluralism, and Identity: Essays in Honour of T. N. Madan*, New Delhi.
Deshpande, Madhav M. (1995), "The Kṣatriya Code of the Bhagavadgītā," in: *Modern Evaluations of The Mahābhārata, Professor R. K. Sharma Felicitation Volume*, ed. S. P. Narang, Delhi.
Devī-Māhātmya. Durgā-Saptaśati (1975), ed. Śrī Sivadatta Misra Śāstri, Vārāṇasī.
Dhand, Arti. (forthcoming.) *Women as Fire, Woman as Sage*, Albany.
Divakaruni, Chitra Banerjee (2008), *Palace of Illusions*, New York.
Doniger, Wendy (1999), *Splitting the Difference*, Chicago.
—— (2005), *The Woman Who Pretended To Be Who She Was*, New York.
Dumézil, Georges (1966), *La Religion Romaine Archaique Suivi d'un Appendice sur la Religion des Etrusques*, Paris. Trans. Philip Krapp (1966), 2 vols, Baltimore.
—— (1968-73), *Mythe et Epopée*. I, II, and III, Paris. Reprinted in one vol. 1995.
—— (1979), *Mariages Indo-Européens*, Paris.
Dumont, Louis (1966), *Homo Hierarchicus*, Paris. Trans. by Mark Sainsbury, Louis Dumont, and Basia Gulati (1970), Chicago.
—— (1983), *Affinity as Value*, Chicago.
Evans-Pritchard, E. E. (1965), *The Position of Women in Primitive Societies*, London.
Feldhaus, Ann (1995), *Water and Womanhood*, New York.
Feller, Danielle (2004), *The Sanskrit Epics' Representation of Vedic Myths*, Delhi.
Ferrari, Gloria (2002), *Figures of Speech*, Chicago.
Fitzgerald, James L. (2003), "The Many Voices of the *Mahābhārata*," *JAOS* 123.4: 803-818.
—— (2004), *The Book of the Women. The Book of Peace, Part One*, Chicago.
Flueckiger, Joyce Burkhalter (1996), *Gender and Genre in the Folklore of Middle India*, Ithaca.
Foley, Helen (1981), *Reflections of Women in Antiquity*, New York.
Geraldine Forbes (1996), *Women in Modern India*, Cambridge.
Ghadially, R. (ed.) (1988), *Women in Indian Society*, New Delhi.
Godelier, Maurice (1982), *La Production des Grands Hommes*, Paris.
Goldman, Robert P. (1977), *Gods, Priests, and Warriors. The Bhṛgus of the Mahābhārata*. New York.
Gonda, J. (1975), "Reflections on the Ārṣa and Āsura forms of Marriage," in: *Selected Studies IV: History of Indian Religion*, Leiden.
González-Reimann, Luis (2002), *The Mahābhārata and the Yugas*, New York.

Grabowska, Barbara (2007), "Abduction of Subhadrā," in: *Theatrum Mirabiliorum Indiae Orientalis*, ed. Monika Nowakowska and Jacek Wózniak, Warszawa, 107-120.
Graeber, David (2001), *Toward an Anthropological Theory of Value*, New York.
Grassman, H. (1872-75), *Wörterbuch zum Rig-Veda*, Leipzig.
Hara, Minoru (1996, 97), "Śrī: mistress of a king," *Orientalia Suecana* 45-46: 33-61.
—— (1974), "A note on the rākṣasa form of marriage," *JAOS* 94: 296-306.
Harlan, Lindsey (2000), "Heroes Alone and Heroes at Home," in: J. Leslie and Mary McGee (eds.), *Invented Identities*, New Delhi and New York, 231-251.
—— (2003), *The Goddesses' Henchmen. Gender in Indian Hero Worship*, New York.
Helms, Mary W. (1998), *Affines Ancestors and Aristocrats*, Austin.
Hill, Peter (2001), *Fate, Predestination and Human Action in the Mahābhārata*, Delhi.
Hiltebeitel, A. (1976), *The Ritual of Battle*, Ithaca.
—— (1988, 1991), *The Cult of Draupadī*, 2 vols., Chicago.
—— (2000), *Rethinking India's Oral and Classical Epics*, Chicago.
—— (2001), *Rethinking the Mahābhārata: A Reader's Guide to the Education of the Dharma King*, Chicago.
—— (2004), "More Rethinking the Mahābhārata: Towards A Politics Of Bhakti," *IIJ* 47: 203-227.
—— (2005), "On Reading Fitzgerald's Vyāsa," *JAOS* 125.2: 241-261.
Hiltebeitel, A. (ed.) (1989), *Criminal Gods and Demon Devotees*, Albany.
Holst-Warhaft, Gail (1992), *Dangerous Voices: Women's Laments and Greek Literature*, London and New York.
Hopkins, E. Washburn (1888), "The Social and Military Position of the Ruling Caste in Ancient India," *JAOS* 13: 57-372.
—— (1901), *The Great Epic of India*. Repr. Delhi, 1993.
—— (1907), "The Sniff-Kiss in Ancient India," *JAOS* 28: 120-134.
—— (1915), *Epic Mythology*, Strassbourg. Repr. Delhi, 1986.
Hughes, Mary Alice (1992), "Epic Women: East and West," *Journal of the Asiatic Society of Bengal*, 4th Serie, 1-2: 33-96; 3-4: 1-106.
Humphreys, Sarah (1983), *The Family, Women and Death*, London.
Ingalls, Daniell H. H. (1995), "On the *Mahābhārata*," in: *Modern Evaluation of the Mahābhārata*, ed. S. P. Narang, Delhi.
Jamison, Stephanie W. (1991), *The Ravenous Hyenas and the Wounded Sun*, Ithaca.
——— (1994), *Draupadi on the Walls of Troy*, in: *Classical Antiquity* 13.1 (April).

—— (1996), *Sacrificed Wife/Sacrificer's Wife*, New York.
—— (1997), "A Gāndharva Marriage in the Odyssey," in: *Studies in Honour of Jean Puhvel*, Part II. *JIES* monograph 21.
—— (1999), "Penelope and the Pigs: Indic Perspectives on the Odyssey," *Classical Antiquity* 18.2: 227-272.
—— (2002), "Giver or Given? Some Marriages in Kālidāsa," in: *Jewels of Authority*, ed. Laurie Patton, 69-83.
Jeffrey, Robin (1992), *Politics, Women and Well-Being*, London.
Jenkins, I. (1983), "Is there Life after Marriage? A study of the abduction motif in vase paintings of the Athenian wedding ceremony," *BICS* 30: 137-145.
Jhala, Angma Dey (2006), *Zenana Women and their Worldview*, D.Phil. dissertation. Oxford University Archive.
Jhala, Jayasinhji (1991), *Marriage, Hierarchy, and Identity in Ideology and Practice*, Ph.D. dissertation, Harvard University Archives.
Jolly, Julius (1951), *Indian Medicine*. Trans. C. G. Kashikar, Delhi.
Kakar, S. (1988), "Feminine Identity in India," in: R. Ghadially (ed.) (1988), *Women in Indian Society*, New Delhi, 44-68.
Kalyanov, V. I. (1978), "The Image of the Indian Woman in the Mahābhārata," *ABORI* LVIII-LIX: 161-172.
Kane, P. V. (1930-62), *History of Dharmaśāstra*, Poona. Repub., 1973-90.
Kantawala, S. G. (1989), *Marriage and Family in the Mahābhārata*, in: Matilal, *Moral Dilemmas*.
Karve, I. (1943-44), "Kinship Terms and the Family Organisation as Found in the Critical Edition of the Mahābhārata," *Bull. of the Deccan Coll. Research Inst.* 5:61-148.
—— (1969), *Yuganta*, New Delhi.
Keith, Arthur Berriedale (1925), *The Religion and Philosophy of the Vedas and Upanishads*, Cambridge, Mass.
Kinsley, David R. (1986), *Hindu Goddesses*, Berkeley.
Koskikallio, Petteri (ed.) (2005), *Epics, Khilas, and Purāṇas*. Proceedings of the Third Dubrovnik International Conference on the Sanskrit Epics and Purāṇas, Zagreb.
Kumar, Nita (ed.) (1994), *Women as Subjects*, Charlottesville and London.
Kristiansen, Kristian and Thomas. B. Larsson (2005), *The Rise of Bronze Age Society*, Cambridge.
Kutumbiah, P. (1962), *Ancient Indian Medicine*, Bombay.
Kuzmina, E. E. (2001), "The First Migration Wave of Indo-Iranians to the South," *JIES* 29.1: 1-40.
Langdon, S. (ed.) (1997), *New Light on a Dark Age*, Columbia, Missouri.
Larson, Jennifer (1995), *Greek Heroine Cults*, Madison.
Lebra-Chapman, Joyce (1986), *The Rani of Jhansi: A Study of Female Heroism in India*, Honolulu.

Lefkowitz, M. R. (1986), *Women in Greek Myth*. Baltimore.
Leslie, Julia (1989), *The Perfect Wife*, New Delhi.
—— (1991), *Roles and Rituals for Hindu Women*, London.
Leslie, Julia and Mary McGee (2000), *Invented Identities*, New York.
Lévi-Strauss, Claude (1958), *Anthropologie Structurale*, Paris, Plon. Trans. Claire Jacobson and Brooke Grundfest (1963), New York.
Lord, A. B. (1995), *The Singer Resumes the Tale*, Ithaca.
Macdonell, Arthur Anthony and Arthur Berriedale Keith (1912), *Vedic Index of Names and Subjects*, Repr. 1982, Delhi.
Madan, T. K. (ed.) (1982), *Way of Life. Essays in Honour of Louis Dumont*, New Delhi.
Mahābhārata (1959), 19 vols., Poona.
Mahābhāratam, with commentary of Nīlakaṇṭha, edited by Pandit Kinjawadekar (1979), 6 vols., New Delhi.
Mani, Vettam (1993), *A Purāṇic Encyclopaedia*, Delhi.
Mankekar, Purnima (1999), *Screening Culture*, Durham and London.
Manusmṛtiḥ (1983), Kullūka Bhaṭṭa commentary, Delhi.
Marriott, McKim (1998), "The female family core explored ethnosociologically," *Contributions to Indian Sociology* (NS) 32: 280-304.
Matilal, Bimal Krishna (ed.) (1989), *Moral Dilemmas in the Mahābhārata*, Delhi.
Mauss, Marcel (1990), *Essai Sur le Don*, Paris. Trans. W. D. Halls. Norton & Company, New York.
Mayer, Peter (1993), "Inventing Village Tradition," *MAS* 27.2: 357-395.
Mayrhofer, M. (1956-80), *Kurzgefasstes etymologisches Wörterbuch des Altindeschen*. 4 vols., Heidelberg.
Maynes, H. (1921), *History of Dhrangadhra State*, Calcutta.
McGrath, K. (2000), Review of Wendy Doniger, "Splitting the Difference," *American Anthropologist* 102.2: 417ff.
—— (2004), *The Sanskrit Hero: Karṇa in Epic Mahābhārata*, Leiden.
Meyer, J. J. (1930), *Sexual Life in Ancient India*. Repr. Delhi, 1971.
Meyer, Kurt and Pamela Deuel (eds.) (1998), *The Tharu Barka Naach: Mahabharata*, Nepal.
Miller, Barbara Stoler (1991), "Contending Narratives, the Political Life of the Indian Epics," *JAS* 50.4: 783-792.
Minkowski, Christopher Z. (1989), "Janamejaya's *Sattra* and Ritual Structure," *JAOS* 109.3: 401-420.
Minturn, Leigh (1993), *Sita's Daughters*, New York.
Mishra, Vijay (1985), "Towards a Theoretical Critique of Bombay Cinema," *Screen* 26.3-4: 133-146.

Mori, Masaki (1997), *Epic Grandeur. Towards a Comparative Poetics of the Epic*, Albany.
Mossé, Claude (1983), *La Femme dans la Grèce Antique*, Paris.
Nagy, Gregory (1990), *Pindar's Homer*, Baltimore.
—— (1996a), *Poetry as Performance*, Cambridge.
—— (1996b), *Homeric Questions*, Austin.
—— (1997), "The Shield of Achilles: Ends of the *Iliad* and Beginnings of the Polis," in: *New Light on a Dark Age*, ed. S. Langdon, Columbia, Missouri, 194-207.
—— (2004), *Homer's Text and Language*, Urbana and Chicago.
Nowakowska, Monika and Jacek Wózniak (eds.) (2007), *Theatrum Mirabiliorum Indiae Orientalis*. Elipsa, Warszawa.
O'Flaherty, Wendy Doniger (1980), *Women, Androgynes, and Other Mythical Beasts*, Chicago.
Oldenberg, H. (1886, 1892), *The Gṛhya Sūtras*. 2 vols. Repr. 1964, Delhi.
Olivelle, Patrick (1993), *The Āśrama System*, New York and Oxford.
Omcherry, Leela (1967), "Classical Music in the Mahābhārata," *Sangeet Natak* (Journal of the Sangeet Natak Academy) 5 (July-September): 78-88.
Ortner, Sherry B. (1974), "Is Woman to Nature as Man Is to Culture?" in: *Women, Culture, and Society*, ed. Michelle Zimbalist Rosaldo and Louise Lamphere, Palo Alto.
Ostor, Akos, Lina Fruzzetti, and Steve Barnett (eds.) (1982), *Concepts of Person*, Cambridge, Mass.
Pal, Pratapaditya (1986), *Indian Sculpture*, vol. I, Los Angeles.
Pantel, Paula Schmitt (ed.) (1992), *A History of Women*, trans. Arthur Goldhammer, Cambridge, Mass.
Parkhill, Thomas (1994), *The Forest Setting in Hindu Epics*, Lampeter.
Parks, Edward (1990), *Verbal Dueling in Heroic Narrative*, Princeton.
Parpola, Asko and Sirpa Tenhunen (eds.) (1998), *Changing Patterns of Family and Kinship in South Asia*, Studia Orientalia 84, Helsinki.
Parry, J. and M. Bloch (1989), *Money and the Morality of Exchange*, Cambridge.
Patton, Laurie L. (ed.) (2002), *Jewels of Authority: Women and Textual Tradition in Hindu India*, New York.
Pinkham, Mildreth Worth (1941), *Women in the Sacred Scriptures of Hinduism*, New York.
Polyani, K. (1968), *Primitive, Archaic, and Modern Economies*, New York.
—— (1977), *The Livelihood of Man*, New York.
Proudfoot, Ian (1987), *Ahiṃsā and a Mahābhārata Story*, Asian Studies Monographs, n.s. 9, Canberra.

Rabinowitz, Nancy Sorkin and, Lisa Auanger (eds.) (2002), *Among Women*, Austin.
Ramusack, Barbara N. (2004), *The Indian Princes and Their States*, The New Cambridge History of India III.6, Cambridge.
Randhawa, T. S. (1996), *The Last Wanderers*, Ahmedabad.
Renfrew, Colin (2001), "Symbol Before Concept: Material Engagement and the Early Development of Society," in: I. Hodder (ed.), *Archaeological Theory Today*, Cambridge.
Rigveda, ed. Barend A. Van Nooten and Gary B. Holland, 1994, *HOS* 50, Cambridge, Mass.
Rocher, Ludo (1979), "The Sūtras and the Śāstras on the Eight Types of Marriage," in: J. P. Sinha (ed.), *Ludwik Sternbach Felicitation Volume*, vol. 1, Lucknow.
Rukmani, T. S. (ed.) (2005), *The Mahābhārata: What Is Not Here is Nowhere Else*, Delhi.
Santina, Peter Della (1989), "Buddhism and the *Mahābhārata*," in: B. K. Matilal (ed.), *Moral Dilemmas in the Mahābhārata*, Delhi.
Sax, William (2002), *Dancing the Self*, New York.
Sax, William (ed.) (1995), *The Gods at Play*, New York.
Scharfe, Hartmut (1989), *The State in Indian Tradition*, Leiden.
Schmidt, H.-P. (1987), *Some Women's Rites and Rights in the Veda*, Poona.
Seaford, Richard (2004), *Money and the Early Greek Mind*, Cambridge.
Sen, Nabeeta (1966), "Comparative Studies in Oral Epic Poetry," *JAOS* 86.4: 397-409.
Settar, S. and Gunther D. Sontheimer (1982), *Memorial Stones*, Dharwad and New Delhi.
Shalini, Shah (19950, *The Making of Womanhood. Gender Relations in the Mahābhārata*, New Delhi.
Sharma, Arvind (1991), *Essays on the Mahābhārata*, Leiden.
—— (ed.) (2002), *Women in Indian Religions*, New Delhi.
—— (2005), *Goddesses and Women in the Indic Religious Tradition*, Leiden.
Sharma, Kavita (2006), *Queens of the Mahabharata*, New Delhi.
Sharma, R. P. (1995), *Women in Hindu Literature*, New Delhi.
Sidhanta, N. K. (1929), *The Heroic Age of India*, repr. 1975, Delhi.
Singh, K. S. (ed.) (1993), *The Mahābhārata in the Tribal and Folk Traditions of India*, Shimla.
Sissa, Guilia (1987), *Le Corps Virginal*, Paris.
Smith, Mary Carroll (1992), *The Warrior Code of India's Sacred Song*, New York and London.
Smith, J. D. (1991), *The Epic of Pābūjī*, Cambridge.
Sobin, Gustav (1999), *Luminous Debris*, Berkeley.

Sörensen, S. (1904), *An Index to the Names in the Mahābhārata*, Copenhagen, repr. 1978, Delhi.
Sternbach, L. (1943-44), "The Rākṣasa-Vivāha and the Paiśaca-Vivāha," *New Indian Antiquary* 6: 182-185.
—— (1951), "Forms of Marriage in Ancient India and Their Development," *Bhāratīya Vidyā* 12: 62-138.
Sukthankar, Vishnu S. (1937), "The Bhṛgus And The Bhārata," *ABORI* 18.
—— (1944), *Critical Studies in the Mahābhārata*, Bombay.
Sullivan, Bruce (1990), *Kṛṣṇa Dvaipāyana Vyāsa and the Mahābhārata,* Leiden.
Sutherland, Sally (1984), "Sītā and Draupadī," *JAOS* 109.1: 63-79.
Sutton, Nick (1997), "Aśoka and Yudhiṣṭhira: A Historical Setting for the Ideological Tensions of the *Mahābhārata*?" *Religion* 27.4: 333-341.
Tambiah, S. J. (1973),"Dowry and Bridewealth and the Property Rights of Women in South Asia," in: M. Fortes, J. R. Goody, E. R. Leach, and S. J. Tambiah (eds.), *Bridewealth and Dowry,* Cambridge Papers in Social Anthropology No. 7, Cambridge.
—— (1985), *Culture, Thought, and Social Action*, Cambridge, Mass.
Thapar, Romila (1993), *Interpreting Early India*, Delhi.
—— (1996), *Time as a Metaphor of History: Early India*, Delhi.
—— (2000), *Cultural Pasts*, Delhi.
Thieme, Paul (1963), "'Jungfrauengatte.' Sanskrit kaumāraḥ patiḥ-Homer," KZ 78: 161-248.
Thomas, P. (1959), *Kāma Kalpa*, Bombay.
Tiwari, Kalika Prasad (1998), *Family in the Mahabharata*, Jaipur.
Vassilkov, Yaroslav (2002), "Indian Practice of Pilgrimage and the Growth of the Mahābhārata," in: Mary Brockington (ed.) (2002), *Stages and Transitions*, Proceedings of the Second Dubrovnik International Conference on the Sanskrit Epics and Purāṇas, Zagreb.
Vātsāyana (1883), *Kāma Sutra*, Benares.
Vernant, Jean-Pierre (1974), *Mythe et Societé en Grèce ancienne*, Paris.
Vidal-Naquet, Pierre (1981), *Le Chasseur Noir*, Paris.
Viswanathan Peterson, Indira (2003), *Design and Rhetoric in a Sanskrit Court Epic*, New York.
Wadley, S. (1988), "Women and the Hindu Tradition," in: R. Ghadially (ed.), *Women in Indian Society*, New Delhi.
Wadley, Susan and Joyce Flueckiger (eds.) (forthcoming), *Nala and Damayanti*.
Watkins, Calvert (1970), "Studies in Indo-European legal language, institutions, and mythology," in: *Indo-European and the Indo-Europeans*, ed. G. Cardona, H. M. Hoenigswald, and A. Senn, Philadelphia.

—— (1995), *How to Kill a Dragon. Aspects of Indo-European Poetics*, New York.
Weil Simone (1947), *La Pasanteur et la Grāce*, Paris, trans. Emma Crawford and Mariovon der Ruhr (1952), London.
West, M. L. (2007), *Indo-European Poetry and Myth*, Oxford and New York.
Wiser, William Henricks (1936), *The Hindu Jajmani System*, Lucknow.
Witzel, Michael (1987), "On the Origin of the Literary Device of the 'Frame Story' in Old Indian Literature," in: *Festschrift U. Schneider*, ed. Harry Falk, Freiburg.
Woods, Julian F. (2001), *Destiny and Human Initiative in the Mahābhārata*, Albany.
Yamazaki Gen'ichi (2005), *The Structure of Ancient Indian Society*, Tokyo.

INDEX